WHIPPING GIRL

WHIPPING GIRL

A TRANSSEXUAL WOMAN ON SEXISM AND THE SCAPEGOATING OF FEMININITY

JULIA SERANO

SEAL PRESS

Whipping Girl
A Transsexual Woman on Sexism and the Scapegoating of Femininity

Published by Seal Press
A member of the Perseus Books Group
1700 Fourth Street
Berkeley, CA 94710

Library of Congress Cataloging-in-Publication Data

Serano, Julia.
Whipping girl : a transsexual woman on sexism and the scapegoating of
femininity / Julia Serano.
p. cm.
Includes bibliographical references and index.
ISBN-13: 978-1-58005-622-9 (alk. paper)
1. Transsexualism. 2. Transsexuals. 3. Feminism. I. Title.

HQ77.9.S47 2007
306.76'8—dc22
2007003954

10 9 8 7 6 5 4 3 2 1

Cover design by Faceout, Emily Weigel
Interior design by Megan Cooney

for Dani
who (once again) provided me with
invaluable feedback, inspiration, support, and love

and in loving memory of Coby
our jenday conure
who used to sit contentedly on my shoulder
while I would write
she was one of the sweetest,
quirkiest, and best friends
that I have ever had
she is dearly missed
"love you, Coby. love you!"

CONTENTS

PART 2
Trans Women, Femininity, and Feminism

Preface to the Second Edition

TEN YEARS AGO, I was in the throes of writing the book that would eventually become *Whipping Girl: A Transsexual Woman on Sexism and the Scapegoating of Femininity*. At the time, I believed that I had important and relatively novel things to say about a variety of issues that all seemed interconnected to me. My recent transition (from having others view and treat me as male, to being viewed and treated as female) provided me with numerous insights into gender and sexism that I wanted to share with the world. That experience, combined with my background as a biologist, led me to question both sides of the "nature versus nurture" debate as it applies to gender. I was also concerned by the ways in which movements that were vital to my existence—such as feminism and queer (i.e., LGBTIQ+) activism—would sometimes forward theories and policies that served to further marginalize other gender and sexual minorities. And I wanted to examine the many under-discussed issues and obstacles faced by those of us on the transgender spectrum, and the parallels that I saw between media, psychiatric, and academic stereotypes of trans people. Finally, I wanted to challenge how trans women and feminine gender expression—individually, but especially in combination—were routinely demeaned and derided in both the straight mainstream, as well as in feminist and queer settings.

I thought that the book would likely be appreciated within trans communities—especially among those on the trans female/feminine spectrum, for whom I was explicitly advocating—and with at least some non-transgender feminists and queer activists—especially those who identify as feminine or femme. But I had no idea that, in the years that would follow, it would eventually be considered to be an important book within feminism, that it would be used in gender and queer studies, sociology, psychology, and human sexuality courses in colleges across North America, that parts of it would be translated and published in other languages, that it would reach and resonate with many people outside of feminist, queer, and trans circles, or that the book (and some of the ideas contained therein) would often be cited and discussed in mainstream publications.[1]

While the major themes that I forward in *Whipping Girl* remain just as vital and relevant today as they were when I was first writing the book, some of the specific descriptions and details will surely seem increasingly dated as time marches on. So in this preface to the second edition, I want to place the book in historical context, as it most certainly was a reaction to what was happening in society, and within activist and academic circles, during the early-to-mid aughts (or "the zeros," as I prefer to call the first decade of this millennium). While a decade is not a huge amount of time in the grand scheme of things, it certainly feels like a lifetime ago when it comes to public understandings and discussions about transgender people.

It's not hyperbole to say that back in 2001—when I first transitioned and began living as an out trans woman—there was very little public awareness of transgender people. News outlets did not cover any serious trans-related issues or concerns (with very rare exceptions, such as the 2002 murder of Gwen Araujo, discussed in the book). The small amount of mainstream coverage we did receive was usually purposefully sensationalistic and/or ridiculing. There was almost no accommodation of trans identities in public policies and institutions. When I would come out to people in the straight mainstream as "trans," "transgender," or even "transsexual," they often had absolutely no idea what I was talking about.

Outside of trans-specific spaces, the only places where I would find any semblance of trans awareness (whether accurate or otherwise) was in queer and feminist circles. This was the result of proximity more than anything else: Both feminists and trans activists were interested in challenging gender-based oppression in society, although these groups tended to frame the matter in different ways (the former in terms of "patriarchy" and the latter in terms of "the gender binary"). Connections between trans folks and the greater queer community stemmed from shared history (trans people played a significant role early on in gay liberation, and in queer activism of the 1990s), shared concerns (as expressions of homophobia and transphobia are similar in origin and often indistinguishable in practice), and demographics (e.g., according to a 2011 survey, 77 percent of transgender people report their sexual orientation as being something other than heterosexual).[2] More than one person has told me that they felt *Whipping Girl* was disproportionately concerned with feminist and queer perspectives, but the reason for this is quite simple: Back when I was writing the book, these were the only two groups (outside of psychiatric/sexology discourses) routinely talking about transgender people, and the only ones who seemed to have any interest in what we had to say.

The dynamics and focus of these movements was also rather different back then. At the risk of overgeneralizing, one could say that feminism and queer activism during the '90s and '00s were in many ways a reaction to the "unilateral" approaches that dominated these movements during the '70s and '80s. Unilateral approaches (sometimes referred to as "identity politics" or "reverse discourses") tend to be centered on the concerns of one particular marginalized group (e.g., women, homosexuals) who is imagined as being oppressed by an opposing group (e.g., men, heterosexuals). In practice, this framing ignores the many differences within these groups (e.g., women differ greatly in their backgrounds, experiences, and the obstacles they face), and often leads activists to propose one-size-fits-all solutions that ignore many constituents' issues and needs. It also discounts (and sometimes demonizes) people who do not neatly fit within the imagined oppressor/oppressed binary (e.g., transgender and intersex people). In other words, unilateral approaches to activism inevitably erase or exclude many people who have a stake in the movement.

In response to such unilateral approaches, the '90s saw the rise of several movements—third-wave feminism, queer activism, and academic disciplines like poststructural feminism and queer theory—that were intentionally pluralistic, espoused and celebrated difference, and contested all binaries and rigid identities. The transgender movement sprung out of this wave and forwarded similar sentiments—it was a purposefully anti-identity movement that welcomed anyone who defied gender conventions and/or who supported those who did.

That was the activist milieu that I came out into during the early '00s in the San Francisco Bay Area. And at first, the queer/trans community I encountered there seemed incredibly open and accepting of difference. But I eventually came to recognize that while the community did not police individuals' identities, it was not without hierarchies. For instance, while people who explicitly or visually blurred binary gender distinctions were routinely celebrated, transsexuals who unapologetically identified as women or men were often dismissed as "reinforcing" that binary. And while queer and trans expressions of masculinity were routinely celebrated in those spaces, queer and trans expressions of femininity were usually viewed as suspect (unless they were presented as merely playful or ironic). It became increasingly obvious to me that these two hierarchies—especially in combination—put trans women (many of whom also identify as feminine) in a precarious position in those settings.

After watching these community attitudes play out while attending Camp Trans in 2003,[3] I became engrossed in this issue. Up to that point, I had primarily been a slam poet; many of my pieces dealt with either the transphobia I faced since coming out as trans or the sexism I faced since I began navigating my way through the world as a woman. But I now turned my attention to writing personal essays that explored how these two forces combined to impact my life, and the lives of trans women more generally. The first essay I wrote along this line was "Skirt Chasers: Why the Media Depicts the Trans Revolution in Lipstick and Heels," which first appeared in *Bitch* magazine in the fall of 2004, and which appears here as Chapter 2. Then in June 2005, I self-released a chapbook called *On the Outside Looking In: a trans woman's perspective on feminism and the exclusion of trans women from lesbian and women-only spaces,* which included "Skirt Chasers," as well as essays that would later form the basis of "Trans Woman Manifesto" and Chapter 12: "Bending Over Backwards" in this book.[4]

It was in that collection that I first introduced the concept of *trans-misogyny,* which has subsequently become one of the main ideas that *Whipping Girl* has become known for. I believe that I coined the term, although I wouldn't be surprised if it appeared independently elsewhere, as it perfectly encapsulates the interplay of transphobia and misogyny that I was striving to articulate. Over the course of writing *Whipping Girl*, I broadened this scope further, describing most instances of gender-based discrimination as involving some combination of *oppositional sexism* (the delegitimization gender non-conformity) and/or *traditional sexism* (the delegitimization of femaleness and femininity). I was particularly proud of this conceptualization at the time, as it allowed me to unite the long-time concerns of both transgender activists and feminists, while also making it clear how this system might be especially unforgiving with regards to trans women and others on the trans female/feminine spectrum.

Also in 2005, through a bit of right-place-right-time serendipity, Seal Press became aware of and took an interest in my work. I used *On the Outside Looking In* as an example of the type of book I was hoping to write, and on the strength of that, they offered me a book contract. The manuscript deadline was to be in December 2006 (about a year and a half out). Aside from the aforementioned essays, I had a handful of slam poems that fit with the theme of the book and which subsequently became chapters ("Deconstructive Surgery," "Self-Deception," "Submissive Streak," and "Barrette Manifesto"). But the rest of the book was written during that interim year and a half.

One of the biggest hurdles facing trans writers and activists is that most people in our culture believe that there are natural and essential differences between women and men. So I knew that I would need to call these assumptions into question if I wanted readers to understand trans people's circumstances and perspectives. But as I already discussed, a significant portion of the book's potential audience would be informed by feminist and queer theory, which often asserts that gender is merely a social artifact or wholly the product of socialization. And these latter beliefs often undermined transsexuals in those settings, as they rendered it implausible that we could have some kind of self-understanding regarding our own gender that differs from our assigned and socialized gender. Being a biologist, it struck me that both the strict nature and strict nurture sides of this divide stemmed from the misguided assumption that biology occurs in a simple straightforward manner, when in fact biological traits are both unfathomably complex and are influenced by our environment and experiences. I tried to articulate this in *Whipping Girl* via my rudimentary "intrinsic inclinations" model. While many readers told me they appreciated it, others have presumed that I was merely preaching biological determinism or making an overly simplistic "born that way" argument. So in my second book *Excluded: Making Feminist and Queer Movements More Inclusive*, I more thoroughly fleshed out this model and addressed many of the concerns that I have encountered.[5] In subsequent years, I have noticed an increase in nuanced discussions about biology and gender occurring within feminist and queer settings—I'd like to think that the arguments that I've made in both of these books have played some role in nudging these conversations in a more reasonable and interdisciplinary direction.

Another hallmark of '90s and '00s feminist and queer theory was portraying gender as something that we "do" rather than something that we "are." This was perhaps most evident in the prevalent catch-phrases of the time—"all gender is drag" and "all gender is performance"—which were sometimes cited in attempts to dismiss transsexuals and other groups.[6] While gender *can* be something we "do," it is clearly far more complex than just that. And one crucial aspect of gender that was largely absent from this framing of "doing" and "performing" gender was how our genders are *perceived* and *interpreted* (and sometimes misinterpreted!) by others. My interest in this aspect was greatly informed by my own transsexual experience, having faced very different expectations and assumptions, and having my words and actions take on new meanings in the eyes of others, now that I am viewed as a woman rather than a man (as I describe in great detail in this book). It seemed to me that these sorts of assumptions and meanings—which we project onto some people but not others based upon their (real or perceived) gender and/or sexuality—play a central role in all forms of sexism. I tried to make this case throughout *Whipping Girl*, and expanded on many of these ideas in *Excluded*.[7]

It was thinking through these sorts of double standards in how people are perceived and interpreted that led me to forward some of the concepts and language that *Whipping Girl* has become most known for. Up to that point, anti-trans discrimination was generally framed in terms of *transphobia*—a fear of, or aversion to, transgender people. And while that certainly exists, this construct did not seem to account for the many smaller, yet endlessly frustrating, experiences that trans people constantly have to deal with. For instance, friends who are fully accepting of me as trans will nevertheless sometimes accidentally slip up my pronouns, whereas people who assume that I am not trans have never once made this error. Upon finding out that I'm trans, well-meaning acquaintances will sometimes ask me intrusive questions about my sexuality and genitals that they would never in a million years presume to ask of a non-trans acquaintance. When trans women appear in TV and films, they are often depicted putting on cosmetics and clothing, or stumbling in high heels, even though such visuals rarely accompany images of non-trans women.

In early drafts of many of these chapters, I would address such tendencies in an ad hoc manner as they occurred to me. But ultimately, I realized that these were all part of the same pervasive mindset—one which we are all socialized to subscribe to—in which trans people's gender expressions, identities, and bodies are viewed differently (and less legitimately) than those of people who are not trans. And just as I was considering how best to present this mindset, I came across an Emi Koyama blog-post that introduced me to *cis terminology*—that is, language that uses the prefix "cis" to name the unmarked dominant majority (i.e., people who are not trans) in order to better articulate the ways in which trans people are viewed and treated in society.[8] According to this scheme, people who are not transgender would be described as *cisgender*, and people who are not transsexual would be described as *cissexual.* Because of the transsexual-focused nature of this book, I primarily used "cissexual" throughout this text, although "cisgender" is more frequently used today.

While cis terminology has become fairly commonplace, back when I first started using it, very few trans people were even aware of it, as it had only been used infrequently and sporadically up to that point. In fact, I believe that *Whipping Girl* was the first book to employ cis terminology on a consistent basis, and it is generally credited with popularizing this language.[9] While I initially worried about introducing language that most readers would find unfamiliar, I ultimately decided to use it, not only because "cis" is less awkward to use than "non-trans" (the term that I had been using up to that point in my writing and activism), but because it allowed me to discuss *cissexism*—the double standard that leads people to view, interpret, and treat trans people differently (and less legitimately) than they do our cis counterparts. And I devoted an entire chapter ("Dismantling Cissexual Privilege") to dissecting this double standard and explaining how it plays out in trans people's lives—upon completing it, I felt that it was the most important thing that I had written up to that point.

Finally, *Whipping Girl* has also become known for is its unapologetic defense of feminine gender expression. Once again, at the risk of overgeneralizing, feminism circa the '70s and '80s was largely disdainful of femininity, portraying it as a set of artificial behaviors that women were coerced into achieving in order to appease men. By the '90s, this view was increasingly challenged by third-wave feminism and the femme movement. While I was certainly influenced by these latter movements, I was often disappointed by how they only tended to defend certain "re-appropriations" of femininity. For instance, they would praise riot grrrl fashions, or femmes who are paired with butches, for being nontraditionally feminine and/or for re-working femininity toward feminist or queer ends. This, of course, implied that traditional and/or heterosexual expressions of femininity remain suspect. As a trans woman who was never socialized nor encouraged to be feminine, and who grew up trying to hide any feminine tendencies I had, the premise that femininity is inherently artificial and only exists for men's benefit struck me as not only false, but patently sexist. Drawing on my previously described vantage points (e.g., my intrinsic inclinations model, and how we project certain meanings and assumptions onto some expressions of gender but not others), I was able to make the case that the wholesale condemning of femininity is one of the more unfortunate missteps in the history of feminism. I have since expanded on these ideas in *Excluded* and in other subsequent writings.[10]

In preparation for writing this preface to the second edition, I reread *Whipping Girl*. While many of the problems that I chronicle (e.g., antifeminine sentiment, cissexism, trans-misogyny, oppositional and traditional sexism) still persist today, many of the specific details that I delve into have changed considerably. Some of them are of a personal nature—for instance, I now identify as bisexual rather than lesbian, and have written about that change in my identity and activism in *Excluded*.[11] Transgender identity labels are always evolving: Certain ones that I mention here (e.g., "trannyboi") have largely disappeared, whereas others not discussed in this text (e.g., "agender") have since become more common. The Michigan Womyn's Music Festival—which is cited in several chapters, as its trans woman-exclusion policy had been a focus of my early activism—apparently just held their final festival; sadly, they never did welcome trans women.[12] I talk at great length here about two trans-specific diagnoses in the *DSM* (the so-called "psychiatric bible"): *gender identity disorder* and *transvestic fetishism*. Recently, a new *DSM* (the fifth revision) has been published, and these diagnoses have morphed into *gender dysphoria* and *transvestic disorder*, respectively—I discuss this revision process and the resulting diagnoses at great length in my third book *Outspoken: A Decade of Transgender Activism and Trans Feminism*.[13] On a more positive front, the Harry Benjamin International Gender Dysphoria Association (HBIGDA) is now the World Professional Association for Transgender Health (WPATH) and they recently elected their first transgender president (Jamison Green); they still publish the Standards of Care, which are now far more flexible and trans-friendly than the archaic versions that I describe in Chapter 7. I also discuss Ray Blanchard's theory of "autogynephilia" at several points in this book—I went on to write several additional critical reviews of the theory, and numerous research papers have since been published by others, which together demonstrate that the theory is incorrect (although unfortunately and unsurprisingly, some people still cite the concept in order to invalidate trans women's identities).[14]

Perhaps the biggest change since *Whipping Girl* was published in 2007 has been media coverage and depictions of trans people. Back then, such considerations were not only few and far between, but they were almost exclusively the creations of cisgender people, and rarely included actual transgender perspectives. While trans-related media representations are still far from perfect, today's trans characters are more likely to have some basis in reality, and they are increasingly portrayed by trans actors.[15] News stories in mainstream publications about serious issues faced by trans people are not only far more frequent, they are often penned by trans writers. In recent years, mainstream audiences have heard celebrity trans people such as Laverne Cox, Janet Mock, Laura Jane Grace, Chaz Bono, and most recently Caitlyn Jenner, share their first-hand experiences and discuss issues that impact trans communities.

This influx of authentic trans voices and respectful trans depictions in the media did not exist when I was writing *Whipping Girl*. And it is clearly a sign of progress, albeit one that comes with certain limitations. As I write this preface in the wake of Caitlyn Jenner's recent mega-public coming out and transition, I am impressed by all the kind words of support and praise she has received, while simultaneously unsurprised by the constant pronoun slip-ups and references to "Bruce," the relentless use of "before and after" pictures in the coverage of her *Vanity Fair* cover story, and the scenes of her putting on make up used in promotional clips for her new show *I Am Cait*—these are all transgender tropes that I discuss over the course of this book. One way to make sense of this discrepancy is to say that while transphobia (i.e., fear of and aversion to trans people) is on the decline, cissexism still runs rampant and persists in the minds of many people who consider themselves to be trans-friendly or trans allies. Hopefully, *Whipping Girl* will continue to be a resource for those who wish to move beyond superficial expressions of tolerance or acceptance, and instead are willing to recognize and relinquish the many double standards that negatively impact transgender people.

Another major shift in the last decade has been an increased acknowledgement of differences among transgender people. As I discuss in the final chapter, "The Future of Queer/Trans Activism," by the early-to-mid-'00s, a very specific conceptualization of "transgender" seemed to be coalescing in the minds of many people. Rather than simply being a broad coalition of gender diverse people (as originally intended), "transgender" seemed to increasingly signify a particular aesthetic and political identity, and a set of shared values and preferred ways of being, that favored certain gender-variant individuals over others. *Whipping Girl* is most certainly a reaction to that trend, as I tried to explain how this monolithic view of "transgender" ignored the very different experiences, obstacles, and perspectives of both transsexuals and people on the trans female/feminine spectrum. But I was not the only person who was concerned with this growing presumption of transgender homogeneity. The mid-to-late-'00s also saw an increase in discussions about how racism, classism, and ableism intersect with the transgender experience, and how trans people who exist outside of queer communities, urban centers, and/or the United States, often had very different takes on trans activism and gender variance. In an essay I wrote the year after *Whipping Girl* was released, I christened this movement "second-wave transgender activism"—analogous to a similar increase in discussions about difference that occurred during the rise of third-wave feminism—although (perhaps for the best) that moniker never caught on.[16]

While I am proud of the fact that *Whipping Girl* was the first book to discuss trans-misogyny and the intersection of oppositional and traditional sexism, it seems clear in retrospect that it would have been a far stronger book had I extended my analysis to examine how these forces also intersect with other forms of marginalization (e.g., racism, classism, ableism, etc.). Today, numerous studies have been published that demonstrate how many forms of anti-trans discrimination (e.g., transphobic violence) disproportionately target people on the trans female/feminine spectrum, trans people of color, and poor and working class trans people, and that those who lie at the intersection of all three of these categories (as is the case for many trans women of color) are impacted the most severely.[17] But back when I was writing *Whipping Girl*, there was a paucity of research into such matters, which is why this book (like most trans activist writings of the '90s and '00s) relies so heavily on my own personal experiences and observations in order to bolster my arguments. The writer in me recognizes that this informal and personal approach probably made the book more accessible and compelling for many readers. But the activist in me now readily sees how this approach left significant holes in my analysis. After all, I am not simply a trans woman, but rather a white, middle class, able-bodied, "generation X," out, queer-identified transsexual woman who "passes" as cissexual living in a U.S. major city. Thus, while the anecdotes that I share here remain true and are potentially illuminating, it is important to keep in mind that they only tell part of a much larger story.

Similarly, when I was writing this book, I saw myself as an outsider who was rallying against the powers that be in the hope that people would start to take trans women's concerns seriously. But now, a decade later, *Whipping Girl* is often used as teaching materials in classrooms, and it is sometimes deemed to be an "authoritative" text about trans people. Knowing this now, I fear that the frequent forefronting of my own personal experiences, and the specific focus on transsexuals and trans female/feminine people may give some readers a skewed view of gender-variant communities and issues. For example, *Whipping Girl* does not provide similar in-depth discussions about the issues and experiences of intersex people, non-binary-identified and two-spirit people, trans male/masculine-spectrum people, straight-identified trans people, trans people of color and other cultures, and so on. Additionally, increasing numbers of trans children are socially transitioning prior to adulthood (which was still rare back when I was writing this book), and their perspectives will no doubt differ significantly from trans people (such as myself) who have not had that experience. So I encourage readers to view *Whipping Girl*, not as "the definitive book" about trans people and issues, but rather as one trans perspective among many, all of which should be explored in greater detail.

While I believe that it is important to recognize and accommodate the many differences that exist among gender variant people, I also think that it is vital that we try to understand and work together with one another rather than view ourselves as opposing factions, or as existing at differing hierarchical positions. I feel the need to stress this because, in the years since *Whipping Girl* was published, transgender activism has increasingly moved away from the broad goals of "shattering the gender binary" and eliminating all gender norms (which would benefit *all* of us), and more toward an identity politics approach focused primarily on the concerns of trans people. And unfortunately, "trans people" is increasingly used in a manner that is synonymous with "transsexuals-only." And the cis/trans distinction—which I forwarded here primarily to talk about double standards in how people's genders are perceived, interpreted, and treated—is now sometimes used to promote a unilateral "cis people are the oppressors, and trans people the oppressed, end of story" narrative. I have discussed the many problems that I see with these trends in my 2014 two-part essay series "Cissexism and Cis Privilege Revisited."[18]

Cissexism and trans-misogyny are pervasive problems in our society, and we most certainly should be focusing on them. But we should also recognize that they are both offshoots of much larger systemic forces—oppositional and traditional sexism—that to varying degrees impact everybody. And oppositional and traditional sexism are but two among a multitude of different forms of marginalization, and we should be working together to end all of them. Throughout Part 2 of my second book *Excluded,* I offer numerous strategies that I believe can help us challenge all forms of sexism and marginalization without erasing or ignoring any specific group's experiences and issues in the process.

What follows is the book as it was originally written, albeit with a few small clarifying changes and corrections. After much deliberation, I have decided not to change any of the trans-related terminology that I used in the first edition, for the following reasons. In recent years, I have written extensively about a phenomenon that I call the Activist Language Merry-Go-Round—briefly stated, because trans people are highly stigmatized and face undue scrutiny in our culture, all of the language associated with us will also eventually face similar stigma and scrutiny.[19] So even if I did try to update the original language, whatever supposedly new and fresh terms I might choose today in 2015 would probably be viewed as outdated or problematic (for some reason or another) within a few short years. Besides, all of the trans-related terms that I routinely use here (aside from words like "effemimania" or "subconscious sex," which I coined in the process of writing this book) have long histories of being used in a positive or neutral manner, despite recent or occasional objections to the contrary. For readers who have questions or concerns regarding my use of language and/or specific terms, I have probably addressed them in one of my many transgender terminology follow-up pieces.[20]

Finally, on a personal note: When I was first working on this project, I remember explicitly thinking to myself that I was trying to write the book that I wish that I had had as a teenager or young adult—one that would help me make sense of both my inexplicable feelings that I should be female rather than male, as well as the conflicting societal messages that were constantly telling me "boys are better than girls" and "women are only good for one thing." Given this, I am immensely grateful to have heard from many trans women and trans feminine people in subsequent years that *Whipping Girl* was that book for them. And quite honestly, I am astounded (in the best possible sense) that a book whose primary goal was explaining and empowering trans female/feminine perspectives has found praise and appreciation from so many readers who have not had that experience themselves.

Julia Serano
September 2015

Introduction

"If I didn't define myself for myself, I would be crunched into other people's fantasies for me and eaten alive."

—Audre Lorde

WHEN I FIRST TOLD people that I was working on a book based on my experiences and perspectives as a transsexual woman, many of them immediately assumed that I was writing an autobiography (rather than a political or historical account, a work of fiction, or a collection of personal essays). Perhaps they imagined that I would write one of those confessional tell-alls that non-trans people seem to constantly want to hear from transsexual women, one that begins with my insistence that I have always been a "woman trapped inside a man's body"; one that distorts my desire to be female into a quest for feminine pursuits; one that explains the ins and outs of sex reassignment surgery and hormones in gory detail; one that completely avoids discussions about what it is like to be treated as a woman and how that compares to how I was treated as a male; one that whitewashes away all of the prejudices I face for being transsexual; a book that ends not with me becoming an outspoken trans activist or feminist, but with the consummation of my womanhood in the form of my first sexual experience with a man. I am not surprised that many would assume that I was simply writing yet another variation of this archetype. Until very recently, this was the only sort of story that non-trans publishers and media producers would allow transsexual women to tell. And while I respect any trans woman who has been brave enough to share her story with the world, the media's narrow focus on the most palatable or sensationalistic transsexual storylines has resulted in making invisible the vast diversity of perspectives and experiences that exist among trans women. Further, this has dumbed down the intricate and difficult relationships many of us have with our own genders and physical bodies. It has also erased the difficulty we face in dealing with the gender stereotypes that other people project onto us because we are women and because we are transsexuals.

Other people who know me from my work as a transgender activist and trans-focused performance poet might have assumed that I was working on a "transgender revolution" book: one similar to those books by Kate Bornstein, Leslie Feinberg, and Riki Wilchins that influenced me so much when I was first coming out; one that challenges readers to look beyond the gender binary; one that encourages all transgender people (whether they are transsexuals, crossdressers, genderqueers, drag artists, etc.) to recognize that we are all in the same boat, all victims at the hands of the same rigid cultural gender norms. While I do believe that all transgender people have a stake in the same political fight against those who fear and dismiss gender diversity and difference in all of its wondrous forms, I do not believe that we are discriminated against in the same ways and for the exact same reasons. I have found that the ways people reacted to me back when I identified as a mostly closeted male crossdresser, or as a bigender queer boy, were very different from one another and yet again different from the way people react to me now that I am an out transsexual woman. The focus on "transgender" as a one-size-fits-all category for those who "transgress binary gender norms" has inadvertently erased the struggles faced by those of us who lie at the intersection of multiple forms of gender-based prejudice. And while I agree with many of the points "shattering-the-gender-binary"-themed books regularly make, I have come to the realization that they only tell part of the story.

The idea that all anti-trans discrimination arises from the fact that, as transgender people, we "transgress binary gender norms" does not resonate completely with my personal experiences. As a somewhat eccentric kid, I was given plenty of leeway to opt out of boys' activities and to cultivate an androgynous appearance and persona. I was sometimes teased for being different, for being an atypical or unmasculine boy, but it was nothing compared to venom that was reserved for those boys who acted downright feminine. And now, as an out transsexual woman, I find that those who wish to ridicule or dismiss me do not simply take me to task for the fact that I fail to conform to gender norms—instead, more often than not, they mock my femininity. From the perspective of an occasional gender bender or someone on the female-to-male spectrum, it might seem like binary gender norms are at the core of all anti-trans discrimination. But most of the anti-trans sentiment that I have had to deal with as a transsexual woman is probably better described as misogyny.

The fact that transsexual women are often singled out to bear the brunt of our culture's fascination with and demonization of transgenderism is a subject that has been ripe for feminist critique for about half a century now. Unfortunately, many feminists have been extraordinarily apathetic or antagonistic to the experiences and perspectives of transsexual women. In fact, the few non-trans feminists who have written about us in the past have usually based their theses upon the assumption that we are really "men" (not women), and that our physical transitions to female and our expressions of femininity represent an appropriation of female culture, symbolism, and bodies. Besides being disrespectful of the fact that we identify, live, and are treated by the world as women, such flawed approaches have overlooked an important opportunity to examine far more relevant issues: the ways in which traditional sexism shapes popular assumptions about transsexual women and why so many people in our society feel threatened by the existence of "men who choose to become women."

The intent of this book is to debunk many of the myths and misconceptions that people have about transsexual women, as well as gender in general. By turning the tables on the rest of the world and examining why so many different facets of our society have set out to dehumanize trans women, I hope to show that we are ridiculed and dismissed not merely because we "transgress binary gender norms," as many transgender activists and gender theorists have proposed, but rather because we "choose" to be women rather than men. The fact that we identify and live as women, despite being born male and having inherited male privilege, challenges those in our society who wish to glorify maleness and masculinity, as well as those who frame the struggles faced by other women and queers solely in terms of male and heterosexual privilege.

Examining the society-wide disdain for trans women also brings to light an important yet often overlooked aspect of traditional sexism: that it targets people not only for their femaleness, but also for their expressions of femininity. Today, while it is generally considered to be offensive or prejudiced to openly discriminate against someone for being female, discriminating against someone's femininity is still considered fair game. The idea that masculinity is strong, tough, and natural while femininity is weak, vulnerable, and artificial continues to proliferate even among people who believe that women and men are equals. And in a world where femininity is so regularly dismissed, perhaps no form of gendered expression is considered more artificial and more suspect than male and transgender expressions of femininity.

I have called this book *Whipping Girl* to highlight the ways in which people who are feminine, whether they be female, male, and/or transgender, are almost universally demeaned compared with their masculine counterparts. This scapegoating of those who express femininity can be seen not only in the male-centered mainstream, but in the queer community, where "effeminate" gay men have been accused of holding back the gay rights movement, and where femme dykes have been accused of being the Uncle Toms of the lesbian movement. Even many feminists buy into traditionally sexist notions about femininity—that it is artificial, contrived, and frivolous; that it is a ruse that only serves the purpose of attracting and appeasing the desires of men. What I hope to show in this book is that the real ruse being played is not by those of us who happen to be feminine, but rather by those who place inferior meanings onto femininity. The idea that femininity is subordinate to masculinity dismisses women as a whole and shapes virtually all popular myths and stereotypes about trans women.

In this book, I break with past attempts in feminism and queer theory to dismiss femininity by characterizing it as "artificial" or "performance." Instead, I argue that certain aspects of femininity (as well as masculinity) are natural and can both precede socialization and supersede biological sex. For these reasons, I believe that it is negligent for feminists to focus only on those who are female-bodied, or for transgender activists to only talk about binary gender norms. No form of gender equity can ever truly be achieved until we first work to empower femininity itself.

Perhaps the most difficult issue that I have had to contend with in writing this book is the varied backgrounds of the audiences I am hoping to reach. Some readers may be transsexual themselves, or may be very active in the transgender community, but may not be tuned in to the many discourses about gender and transsexuality that exist in academia, clinical settings, feminism, or queer politics. Others may take an interest in this book from a women's, queer, or gender studies perspective, being familiar with what non-trans academics have had to say about trans people, but without ever having been exposed to a transsexual woman's take on these many dialogues and debates. Still others may be completely new to the subject, having picked up the book because they want to learn more about transsexuality, how to be a trans ally, or because they have a particular interest in the subjects of femininity and/or sexism. For me, it has certainly been a challenge to write a substantial book about such complex topics that can simultaneously be easily understood and enjoyed by audiences who so greatly differ in their prior knowledge and their presumptions.

While I have written this book in "lay language" and with a general audience in mind, the use of transgender-specific or -related jargon is unavoidable. I have not only had to define a lot of preexisting terms for those who are new to this subject, but redefine or even create new terms to clear up confusion and to fill gaps left by the strange hodgepodge of clinical, academic, and activist language typically used to describe transgender people and experiences. While creating new terms can potentially be disconcerting to readers at first, I feel that it is necessary for addressing and challenging the many assumptions that are commonly made about gender and trans women.

"Trans Woman Manifesto," which follows this introduction, is the piece I've chosen to set the stage for many of the ideas put forward in this book. It is followed by Part 1, Trans/Gender Theory, which focuses largely on depictions and representations of transsexuals in the media, medicine and psychiatry, social sciences, academic gender studies, and queer and feminist politics. Because transsexuals make up a relatively small percentage of the population and have little to no power or voice in these fields, non-transsexual depictions regularly stand in for or trump the perspectives and experiences of actual transsexuals. This is highly problematic, as many of these depictions are sensationalizing, sexualizing, and/or outright hostile. Other depictions are not intended to be blatantly demeaning, yet they still have a drastic negative impact on the lives of transsexuals because they frame transsexuality in terms of non-trans people's assumptions and interests. This forces transsexuals to describe ourselves and our experiences in terms of non-trans terminology and values, which inevitably place us in a subordinate position (i.e., non-trans genders are seen as "normal," "natural," and "unquestionable," whereas transsexual genders are presumed to be "abnormal," "artificial," and perpetually in question and open to interpretation). This also has the rather dubious consequence of positioning non-trans people who merely study transsexuality as "experts" who somehow understand transsexuals better than we understand ourselves. I spend a great deal of this section debunking non-trans representations of transsexuality because they effectively silence trans people's political voices and prevent us from describing our lives the way we see and experience them.

Of course, it is impossible to discuss such issues without having to grapple with another gender binary of sorts—that between gender essentialists (who believe that women and men represent two mutually exclusive categories, each born with certain inherent, nonoverlapping traits) and social constructionists (who believe that gender differences are primarily or exclusively the result of socialization and binary gender norms). For this reason, I have included my own view of gender in this section, one that accommodates my experiences both as a trans person and as a practicing biologist; one that acknowledges that both intrinsic and extrinsic factors help to shape the way that we come to experience and understand our own genders.

Part 2, Trans Women, Femininity, and Feminism, brings together my experiences and observations—pre-, during, and post-transition—to discuss the many ways fear, suspicion, and dismissiveness toward femininity shape societal attitudes toward trans women and influence the way trans women often come to view ourselves. In the last two chapters of this section, I bring together several of the main themes in this book to suggest new directions for gender-based activism. In chapter 19, "Putting the Feminine Back into Feminism," I make the case that feminist activism and theory would be best served by working to empower and embrace femininity, rather than eschewing or deriding it, as it often has in the past. Such an approach would allow feminism to both incorporate transgender perspectives and reach out to the countless feminine-identified women who have felt alienated by the movement in the past. And in chapter 20, "The Future of Queer/Trans Activism," I show how certain taken-for-granted beliefs and assumptions that are prevalent in contemporary queer and transgender theory and politics ensure that trans women's perspectives and issues will continue to take a back seat to those of other queers and transgender people. I argue that, rather than focusing on "shattering the gender binary"—a strategy that invariably pits gender-conforming and non-gender-conforming people against one another—we work to challenge all forms of gender entitlement (i.e., when a person privileges their own perceptions, interpretations, and evaluations of other people's genders over the way those people understand themselves). After all, the one thing that all forms of sexism share—whether they target females, queers, transsexuals, or others—is that they all begin with placing assumptions and value judgments onto other people's gendered bodies and behaviors.

Trans Woman Manifesto

THIS MANIFESTO CALLS FOR the end of the scapegoating, deriding, and dehumanizing of trans women everywhere. For the purposes of this manifesto, *trans woman* is defined as any person who was assigned a male sex at birth, but who identifies as and/or lives as a woman. No qualifications should be placed on the term "trans woman" based on a person's ability to "pass" as female, her hormone levels, or the state of her genitals—after all, it is downright sexist to reduce any woman (trans or otherwise) down to her mere body parts or to require her to live up to certain societally dictated ideals regarding appearance.

Perhaps no sexual minority is more maligned or misunderstood than trans women. As a group, we have been systematically pathologized by the medical and psychological establishment, sensationalized and ridiculed by the media, marginalized by mainstream lesbian and gay organizations, dismissed by certain segments of the feminist community, and, in too many instances, been made the victims of violence at the hands of men who feel that we somehow threaten their masculinity and heterosexuality. Rather than being given the opportunity to speak for ourselves on the very issues that affect our own lives, trans women are instead treated more like research subjects: Others place us under their microscopes, dissect our lives, and assign motivations and desires to us that validate their own theories and agendas regarding gender and sexuality.

Trans women are so ridiculed and despised because we are uniquely positioned at the intersection of multiple binary gender-based forms of prejudice: transphobia, cissexism, and misogyny.

Transphobia is an irrational fear of, aversion to, or discrimination against people whose gendered identities, appearances, or behaviors deviate from societal norms. In much the same way that homophobic people are often driven by their own repressed homosexual tendencies, transphobia is first and foremost an expression of one's own insecurity about having to live up to cultural gender ideals. The fact that transphobia is so rampant in our society reflects the reality that we place an extraordinary amount of pressure on individuals to conform to all of the expectations, restrictions, assumptions, and privileges associated with the sex they were assigned at birth.

While all transgender people experience transphobia, transsexuals additionally experience a related (albeit distinct) form of prejudice: *cissexism,* which is the belief that transsexuals' identified genders are inferior to, or less authentic than, those of *cissexuals* (i.e., people who are not transsexual and who have only ever experienced their subconscious and physical sexes as being aligned). The most common expression of cissexism occurs when people attempt to deny the transsexual the basic privileges that are associated with the trans person's self-identified gender. Common examples include purposeful misuse of pronouns or insisting that the trans person use a different public restroom. The justification for this denial is generally founded on the assumption that the trans person's gender is not authentic because it does not correlate with the sex they were assigned at birth. In making this assumption, cissexists attempt to create an artificial hierarchy. By insisting that the trans person's gender is "fake," they attempt to validate their own gender as "real" or "natural." This sort of thinking is extraordinarily naive, as it denies a basic truth: We make assumptions every day about other people's genders without ever seeing their birth certificates, their chromosomes, their genitals, their reproductive systems, their childhood socialization, or their legal sex. There is no such thing as a "real" gender—there is only the gender we experience ourselves as and the gender we perceive others to be.

While often different in practice, cissexism, transphobia, and homophobia are all rooted in *oppositional sexism,* which is the belief that female and male are rigid, mutually exclusive categories, each possessing a unique and nonoverlapping set of attributes, aptitudes, abilities, and desires. Oppositional sexists attempt to punish or dismiss those of us who fall outside of gender or sexual norms because our existence threatens the idea that women and men are "opposite" sexes. This explains why bisexuals, lesbians, gays, transsexuals, and other transgender people—who may experience their genders and sexualities in very different ways—are so often confused or lumped into the same category (i.e., queer) by society at large. Our natural inclinations to be attracted to the same sex, to identify as the other sex, and/or to express ourselves in ways typically associated with the other sex blur the boundaries required to maintain the male-centered gender hierarchy that exists in our culture today.

In addition to the rigid, mutually exclusive gender categories established by oppositional sexism, the other requirement for maintaining a male-centered gender hierarchy is to enforce *traditional sexism*—the belief that maleness and masculinity are superior to femaleness and femininity. Traditional and oppositional sexism work hand in hand to ensure that those who are masculine have power over those who are feminine, and that only those born male will be seen as authentically masculine. For the purposes of this manifesto, the word *misogyny* will be used to describe this tendency to dismiss and deride femaleness and femininity.

Just as all transgender people experience transphobia and cissexism to differing extents (depending on how often, obvious, or out we are as transgender), we experience misogyny to differing extents too. This is most evident in the fact that, while there are many different types of transgender people, our society tends to single out trans women and others on the male-to-female (MTF) spectrum for attention and ridicule. This is not merely because we transgress binary gender norms per se, but because we, by necessity, embrace our own femaleness and femininity. Indeed, more often than not it is our expressions of femininity and our desire to be female that become sensationalized, sexualized, and trivialized by others. While trans people on the female-to-male (FTM) spectrum face discrimination for breaking gender norms (i.e., oppositional sexism), their expressions of maleness or masculinity themselves are not targeted for ridicule—to do so would require one to question masculinity itself.

When a trans person is ridiculed or dismissed not merely for failing to live up to gender norms, but for their expressions of femaleness or femininity, they become the victims of a specific form of discrimination: *trans-misogyny*. When the majority of jokes made at the expense of trans people center on "men wearing dresses" or "men who want their penises cut off," that is not transphobia—it is trans-misogyny. When the majority of violence and sexual assaults committed against trans people is directed at trans women, that is not transphobia—it is trans-misogyny.[1] When it's okay for women to wear "men's" clothing, but when men who wear "women's" clothing can be diagnosed with the psychological disorder transvestic fetishism, that is not transphobia—it is trans-misogyny.[2] When women's or lesbian organizations and events open their doors to trans men but not trans women, that is not transphobia—it is trans-misogyny.[3]

In a male-centered gender hierarchy, where it is assumed that men are better than women and that masculinity is superior to femininity, there is no greater perceived threat than the existence of trans women, who despite being born male and inheriting male privilege "choose" to be female instead. By embracing our own femaleness and femininity, we, in a sense, cast a shadow of doubt over the supposed supremacy of maleness and masculinity. In order to lessen the threat we pose to the male-centered gender hierarchy, our culture (primarily via the media) uses every tactic in its arsenal of traditional sexism to dismiss us:

1 The media hyperfeminizes us by accompanying stories about trans women with pictures of us putting on makeup, dresses, and high-heeled shoes in an attempt to highlight the supposed "frivolous" nature of our femaleness, or by portraying trans women as having derogatory feminine-associated character traits such as being weak, confused, passive, or mousy.

2. The media hypersexualizes us by creating the impression that most trans women are sex workers or sexual deceivers, and by asserting that we transition for primarily sexual reasons (e.g., to prey on innocent straight men or to fulfill some kind of bizarre sex fantasy). Such depictions not only belittle trans women's motives for transitioning, but implicitly suggest that women as a whole have no worth beyond their ability to be sexualized.

3. The media objectifies our bodies by sensationalizing sex reassignment surgery and openly discussing our "man-made vaginas" without any of the discretion that normally accompanies discussions about genitals. Further, those of us who have not had surgery are constantly being reduced to our body parts, whether by the creators of tranny porn who overemphasize and exaggerate our penises (thus distorting trans women into "she-males" and "chicks with dicks") or by other people who have been so brainwashed by phallocentricism that they believe that the mere presence of a penis can trump the femaleness of our identities, our personalities, and the rest of our bodies.

Because anti-trans discrimination is steeped in traditional sexism, it is not simply enough for trans activists to challenge binary gender norms (i.e., oppositional sexism)—we must also challenge the idea that femininity is inferior to masculinity and that femaleness is inferior to maleness. In other words, by necessity, trans activism must be at its core a feminist movement.

Some might consider this contention controversial. Over the years, many self-described feminists have gone out of their way to dismiss trans people and in particular trans women, often resorting to many of the same tactics (hyperfeminization, hypersexualization, and objectification of our bodies) that the mainstream media regularly uses against us.[4] These pseudofeminists proclaim, "Women can do anything men can," then ridicule trans women for any perceived masculine tendency we may have. They argue that women should be strong and unafraid of speaking our minds, then tell trans women that we act like men when we voice our opinions. They claim that it is misogynistic when men create standards and expectations for women to meet, then they dismiss us for not meeting their standard of "woman." These pseudofeminists consistently preach feminism with one hand while practicing traditional sexism with the other.

It is time for us to take back the word "feminism" from these pseudofeminists. After all, as a concept, feminism is much like the ideas of "democracy" or "Christianity." Each has a major tenet at its core, yet there are a seemingly infinite number of ways in which those beliefs are practiced. And just as some forms of democracy and Christianity are corrupt and hypocritical while others are more just and righteous, we trans women must join allies of all genders and sexualities to forge a new type of feminism, one that understands that the only way for us to achieve true gender equity is to abolish both oppositional sexism and traditional sexism.

It is no longer enough for feminism to fight solely for the rights of those born female. That strategy has furthered the prospects of many women over the years, but now it bumps up against a glass ceiling that is partly of its own making. Though the movement worked hard to encourage women to enter previously male-dominated areas of life, many feminists have been ambivalent at best, and resistant at worst, to the idea of men expressing or exhibiting feminine traits and moving into certain traditionally female realms. And while we credit previous feminist movements for helping to create a society where most sensible people would agree with the statement "women and men are equals," we lament the fact that we remain light-years away from being able to say that most people believe that femininity is masculinity's equal.

Instead of attempting to empower those born female by encouraging them to move further away from femininity, we should instead learn to empower femininity itself. We must stop dismissing it as "artificial" or as a "performance," and instead recognize that certain aspects of femininity (and masculinity as well) transcend both socialization and biological sex—otherwise there would not be feminine boy and masculine girl children. We must challenge all who assume that feminine vulnerability is a sign of weakness. For when we do open ourselves up, whether it be by honestly communicating our thoughts and feelings or expressing our emotions, it is a daring act, one that takes more courage and inner strength than the alpha male facade of silence and stoicism.

We must challenge all those who insist that women who act or dress in a feminine manner take on a submissive or passive posture. For many of us, dressing or acting feminine is something we do for ourselves, not for others. It is our way of reclaiming our own bodies and fearlessly expressing our own personalities and sexualities. It is not us who are guilty of trying to reduce our bodies to mere playthings, but rather those who foolishly assume that our feminine style is a signal that we sexually subjugate ourselves to men.

In a world where masculinity is assumed to represent strength and power, those who are butch and boyish are able to contemplate their identities within the relative safety of those connotations. In contrast, those of us who are feminine are forced to define ourselves on our own terms and develop our own sense of self-worth. It takes guts, determination, and fearlessness for those of us who are feminine to lift ourselves up out of the inferior meanings that are constantly being projected onto us. If you require any evidence that femininity can be more fierce and dangerous than masculinity, all you need to do is ask the average man to hold your handbag or a bouquet of flowers for a minute, and watch how far away he holds it from his body. Or tell him that you would like to put your lipstick on him and watch how fast he runs off in the other direction. In a world where masculinity is respected and femininity is regularly dismissed, it takes an enormous amount of strength and confidence for any person, whether female- or male-bodied, to embrace their feminine self.

But it is not enough for us to empower femaleness and femininity. We must also stop pretending that there are essential differences between women and men. This begins with the acknowledgment that there are exceptions to every gender rule and stereotype, and this simply stated fact disproves all gender theories that purport that female and male are mutually exclusive categories. We must move away from pretending that women and men are "opposite" sexes, because when we buy into that myth it establishes a dangerous precedent. For if men are big, then women must be small; and if men are strong then women must be weak. And if being butch is to make yourself rock-solid, then being femme becomes allowing yourself to be malleable; and if being a man means taking control of your own situation, then being a woman becomes living up to other people's expectations. When we buy into the idea that female and male are "opposites," it becomes impossible for us to empower women without either ridiculing men or pulling the rug out from under ourselves.

It is only when we move away from the idea that there are "opposite" sexes, and let go of the culturally derived values that are assigned to expressions of femininity and masculinity, that we may finally approach gender equity. By challenging both oppositional and traditional sexism simultaneously, we can make the world safe for those of us who are queer, those of us who are feminine, and those of us who are female, thus empowering people of all sexualities and genders.

Trans/Gender Theory

1

Coming to Terms with Transgenderism and Transsexuality

MOST NON-TRANS PEOPLE are unfamiliar with the words that we in the transgender community use to describe ourselves, our experiences, and our most pressing issues. Books and websites that discuss transgenderism and transsexuality often include some kind of glossary, where these terms are laid out and defined in a nice, orderly, alphabetical fashion. However, a potential problem with the glossary approach is that it gives the impression that all of these transgender-related words and phrases are somehow written in stone, indelibly passed down from generation to generation. This is most certainly not the case. Many of the terms used these days to describe transgender people did not exist a decade ago. Conversely, many of the terms that were commonly used a decade ago are now considered to be out of fashion, outdated, or even offensive to many people in the transgender community. Even the terms that are used frequently today are regularly disputed, as individual transgender people may define words in a slightly different manner or have aesthetic or political preferences for certain words over others. So in lieu of a glossary, I will use this chapter to define many of the transgender-specific terms used throughout the book and to explain why I chose these particular words and phrases rather than others.

It is difficult to talk about people who are trans*sex*ual or trans*gender* without first defining the words "sex" and "gender." "Sex" commonly refers to whether a person is physically female and/or male. Because the physical traits that we most often take into account when describing "sex" are biological in origin (e.g., sex chromosomes, hormones, reproductive systems, genitals, and so forth), there is a tendency to see sex as being a "natural" aspect of gender. However, this is not quite the case. Cultural expectations and assumptions play a large role in shaping how we determine and consider sex. For example, in our culture, such assumptions are very genital-centric: A person's sex is assigned at birth based on the presence or absence of a penis. Thus, our genitals play a far more important role in determining our legal sex than do our chromosomes (which in most cases are never actually examined) or our reproductive capacity. After all, a woman can have a hysterectomy, or a man can have a vasectomy, without changing or nullifying their legal sex. Indeed, the fact that we even have a "legal" sex demonstrates that society greatly shapes our understanding of sex. Thus, throughout this book, I will use the word "sex" primarily to refer to a person's physical femaleness and/or maleness, but I will also sometimes use it to refer to the social and legal classes that are associated with one's physical sex.

The word "gender" is regularly used in a number of ways. Most commonly, it's used in a manner that's indistinguishable from "sex" (i.e., to describe whether a person is physically, socially, and legally male and/or female). Other people use the word "gender" to describe a person's gender identity (whether they identify as female, male, both, or neither), their gender expression and gender roles (whether they act feminine, masculine, both, or neither), or the privileges, assumptions, expectations, and restrictions they face due to the sex others perceive them to be. Because of the many meanings infused into it, I will use the word "gender" in a broad way to refer to various aspects of a person's physical or social sex, their sex-related behaviors, the sex-based class system they are situated within, or (in most cases) some combination thereof.

Now that we understand "sex" and "gender," we can begin to consider the word *transgender,* which is perhaps one of the most confusing and misunderstood words in the English language. While the word originally had a more narrow definition, since the 1990s it has been used primarily as an umbrella term to describe those who defy societal expectations and assumptions regarding femaleness and maleness; this includes people who are transsexual (those who live as members of the sex other than the one they were assigned at birth), intersex (those who are born with a reproductive or sexual anatomy that does not fit the typical definitions of female or male), and genderqueer (those who identity outside of the male/female binary), as well as those whose gender expression differs from their anatomical or perceived sex (including crossdressers, drag performers, masculine women, feminine men, and so on). I will also sometimes use the synonymous term *gender-variant* to describe all people who are considered by others to deviate from societal norms of femaleness and maleness.

The far-reaching inclusiveness of the word "transgender" was purposely designed to accommodate the many gender and sexual minorities who were excluded from the previous feminist and gay rights movements. At the same time, its broadness can be highly problematic in that it often blurs or erases the distinctiveness of its constituents. For example, while male crossdressers and transsexual men are both male-identified transgender people, these groups face a very different set of issues with regards to managing their gender difference. Similarly, drag queens and transsexual women generally have very different experiences and perspectives regarding gender, despite the fact that they are often confused with one another by mainstream society.

Thus, the best way to reconcile the nebulous nature of the word is to recognize that it is primarily a political term, one that brings together disparate classes of people to fight for the common goal of ending all discrimination based on sex/gender variance. While useful politically, *transgender* is too vague of a word to imply much commonality between individual people's identities, life experiences, or understanding of gender.

Another point that is often overlooked in discussions about transgenderism is that many individuals who fall under the transgender umbrella choose not to identify with the term. For example, many intersex people reject the term because their condition is about physical sex (not gender) and the primary issues they face (e.g., nonconsensual "normalizing" medical procedures during infancy or childhood) differ greatly from those of the greater transgender community.[1] Similarly, many transsexuals disavow the term because of its anti-transsexual roots or because they feel that the transgender movement tends to privilege those identities, actions, and appearances that most visibly "transgress" gender norms.[2] This tendency renders invisible the fact that many of us struggle more with issues related to our physical femaleness or maleness than we do with our expressions of femininity or masculinity. Throughout this book, I will use the word *trans* to refer to people who (to varying degrees) struggle with a subconscious understanding or intuition that there is something "wrong" with the sex they were assigned at birth and/or who feel that they should have been born as or wish they could be the other sex. (It should be noted that the word "trans" is also often used in another manner, namely as a synonym or abbreviation for the word *transgender*). For many trans people, the fact that their appearances or behaviors may fall outside of societal gender norms is a very real issue, but one that is often seen as secondary to the cognitive dissonance that arises from the fact that their *subconscious sex* does not match their physical sex. This *gender dissonance* is usually experienced as a kind of emotional pain or sadness that grows more intense over time, sometimes reaching a point where it can become debilitating.

There are many different strategies that trans people may use to ease their gender dissonance. Perhaps the most common one is trying to suppress or deny one's subconscious sex. Others may allow their subconscious sex to come to the surface occasionally, for example through either crossdressing or role-playing. Still others may come to see themselves as *bigender* (having a mixture of both femininity and masculinity and/or femaleness and maleness), *gender-fluid* (moving freely between genders), or *genderqueer* (identifying outside of the male/female gender binary). And those of us who make the choice to live as the sex other than the one we were assigned at birth are commonly called *transsexuals.*

Perhaps the most underacknowledged issue with regard to the transgender community—and one that is a continuing source of both confusion and contention—is the fact that many of the above strategies and identities that trans people gravitate toward in order to relieve their gender dissonance are also shared by people who do not experience any discomfort with regards to their subconscious and physical sex. For example, some male-bodied crossdressers spend much of their lives wishing they were actually female, while others see their crossdressing as simply a way to express a feminine side of their personalities. While many drag artists view themselves primarily as entertainers or enjoy performing and parodying gender stereotypes, some trans people gravitate toward drag because it provides them with a rare opportunity to express aspects of their subconscious sex in a socially sanctioned setting. And while many trans people identify as genderqueer because it helps them make sense of their own experiences of living in a world where their understanding of themselves differs so greatly from the way they are perceived by society, other people identify as genderqueer because, on a purely intellectual level, they question the validity of the binary gender system.

Thus, not only do transgender people vary in their perspectives and experiences, but individuals within the same transgender subcategory (whether it be crossdresser, drag artist, genderqueer, etc.) may also differ greatly in what drives them to embrace that identity. And while this book primarily focuses on transsexuality, and more specifically on trans women (as that is my experience and perspective), it is not because I believe that transgender people who are not transsexual are any less important or legitimate; their expressions of gender are just as valid as mine and the discrimination they may face as a result of those expressions is just as real. It is also crucial for us to recognize that it is equally valid for a trans person to decide to transition and live as the other sex as it is for them to instead choose to blur gender boundaries and identify themselves outside the gender binary. There is no one right way to be trans. Each of us simply needs to figure out what works best for us and what allows us to best express who we feel we are.

When discussing transsexuals, it is often necessary to distinguish between those who transition from male to female—who are commonly referred to as *trans women*—and those who transition from female to male—who are called *trans men*. I prefer these terms over others because they acknowledge the lived and self-identified gender of the trans person (i.e., woman or man), while adding the adjective "trans" as a way to describe one particular aspect of that person's life experience. In other words, "trans woman" and "trans man" function in a way similar to the phrases "Catholic woman" or "Asian man." Because many trans people choose to relieve their gender dissonance in ways other than transitioning, I will often use the phrases *male-to-female (MTF) spectrum* and *female-to-male (FTM) spectrum* to describe all trans people (regardless of whether they are genderqueer, transsexual, crossdresser, etc.) who experience their gender as being different from or more complex than the gender they were assigned at birth.

Sometimes people have a tendency to dismiss or delegitimize trans women's and trans men's gender identities and lived experiences by relegating us to our own unique categories that are separate from "woman" or "man." This strategy is often adopted by non-trans folks who wish to discuss trans people without ever bringing into question their own assumptions and beliefs about maleness and femaleness. An obvious example of this phenomenon is the prevalence of the terms "she-males," "he-shes," and "chicks with dicks" in reference to trans women. Sometimes attempts to *third-sex* or *third-gender* trans people are more subtle or subconscious than that, such as when people merge the phrase "trans woman" to make one word, "transwoman," or use the adjectives MTF and FTM as nouns (for example, "Julia Serano is an MTF."). I do not identify as a "male-to-female"—I identify as a woman. These attempts to relegate trans people to "third sex" categories not only disregard the profoundly felt gender identity of the transsexual in question, but also ignore the very real experiences that trans person has had being treated as a member of the sex that they have transitioned to.

When discussing transsexuals' lives, it is important to find words that accurately describe their gendered experiences in both the past and present. Many trans people say they understood themselves to be female or male for most of their lives despite the fact that it wasn't the sex they were assigned at birth. Therefore, when a trans person transitions, their subconscious sex or gender identity essentially stays the same—rather, it is their physical sex that changes (hence the term trans*sex*ual). With regards to the trans person's original sex, I will often use the somewhat clunky phrase *the sex (or gender) they were assigned at birth* to emphasize the nonconsensual nature of how we are raised, socialized, and treated by society on the basis of our physical sex. For convenience, I may also refer to it as their *assigned gender/sex* or (to a lesser extent) their *birth sex*. I may refer to the sex that the trans person has transitioned to as their *preferred sex,* their *identified sex* (to emphasize the fact that it agrees with their gender identity), or their *lived sex* (to emphasize the fact that they now live and experience the world as a member of that sex).

It is common for people to assume that being or becoming a transsexual involves some kind of "sex change operation."

However, this is not necessarily the case. While some transsexuals undergo numerous medical procedures as part of their physical transitions, others either cannot afford or choose not to undergo such procedures. Indeed, attempts to limit the word "transsexual" to only those who physically transition is not only classist (because of the affordability issue), but objectifying, as it reduces all trans people to the medical procedures that have been carried out on their bodies. For these reasons, I will use the word *transsexual* to describe anyone who is currently, or is working toward, living as a member of the sex other than the one they were assigned at birth, regardless of what procedures they may have had. Further, because there are so many different paths that a transsexual person may take toward living in their identified sex, I will use the word *transition* to describe the process of changing one's lived sex, rather than in reference to any specific medical procedure.

The most common medical procedure for transsexuals to seek out is *hormone replacement therapy,* which involves taking testosterone in the case of trans men, or taking estrogen (and sometimes progesterone) in the case of trans women. These are the same sex hormones that kick in during puberty in all people and they produce many of the same bodily changes in adult transsexuals as they do in adolescents: Some effects are changes in skin complexion and muscle/fat distribution, breast growth in trans women, and deepened voices and facial hair growth in trans men. These hormone-produced body changes are often referred to as *secondary sex characteristics* (to distinguish them from so-called *primary sex characteristics* such as reproductive organs and genitals). Secondary sex characteristics are the cues that we most often use when we classify adults as being either women or men, which explains why hormone replacement therapy is often sufficient to allow trans people to live unnoticed in their identified sex.

While there are a number of possible surgeries that a trans person may undertake, the one that seems to most capture public imagination is *sex reassignment surgery (SRS),* which involves reconstruction of the genitals to better match that of the transsexual's identified sex. Some trans people object to the term *SRS* and instead prefer alternatives such as *genital reassignment surgery, gender confirmation surgery,* or *bottom surgery* (to contrast it with *top surgery:* the removal or enhancement of breasts). Personally, I am not bothered by the technical name of the surgery so much as I am by the fact that it gets so much attention in the media and the general public. After all, as someone who is not a cardiologist nor has ever had a heart condition, I really don't feel any compelling need to know all of the technical names or hear play-by-play accounts of heart surgeries. Nor do I need to know all of the specific names and doses of chemotherapies in order to be touched by the story of someone who has survived cancer. For this reason, I am rather disturbed by the fact that so many people—who are neither medical professionals nor trans themselves—would want to hear all of the gory details regarding transsexual physical transformations, or would feel that they have any right to ask us about the state of our genitals. It is offensive that so many people feel that it is okay to publicly refer to transsexuals as being "pre-op" or "post-op" when it would so clearly be degrading and demeaning to regularly describe all boys and men as being either "circumcised" or "uncircumcised."

While the specific details of transsexual-related medical procedures should be readily available for those contemplating sex reassignment, such information is neither relevant nor necessary for one to understand the experiences and perspectives of trans people. After all, while my physical transition occurred primarily over a period of a year and a half—a mere fraction of my life—what has remained constant and pervasive (both pre-, during, and post-transition) has been the resistance and prejudice that I have faced from those who are not transgender, those who become irrationally uncomfortable or disturbed by my gender expression and/or female identity, and those who presume that their identified gender is more natural or valid than my own. For this reason, I believe that one cannot begin to fully understand transsexuality without thoroughly examining and critiquing the prejudices and presumptions of the non-transsexual majority. So although I will be discussing transsexuals throughout this book, I will also be spending a great deal of time discussing the beliefs and attitudes common among *cissexuals* —that is, people who have only ever experienced their subconscious sex and physical sex as being aligned. Similarly, people who are not transgender may be described as being *cisgender* (although I will be using this term less often, since the focus of this book is on transsexual women rather than the transgender population as a whole).[3] I prefer these terms, but I occasionally use the synonymous terms *non-transsexual* and *non-transgender*.

Some might feel that all of these trans- and gender-related terms I've introduced are overwhelming or confusing. And others, particularly those in the fields of gender and queer studies, might dismiss much of this language as contributing to a "reverse discourse"—that is, by describing myself as a transsexual and creating trans-specific terms to describe my experiences, I am simply reinforcing the same distinction between transsexuals and cissexuals that has marginalized me in the first place. My response to both of these arguments is the same: I do not believe that transsexuals and cissexuals are inherently different from one another. But the vastly different ways in which we are perceived and treated by others, and the way those differences impact our unique physical and social experiences, lead many transsexuals to see and understand gender very differently than our cissexual counterparts. And while transsexuals are extremely familiar with cissexual perspectives of gender (as they dominate in our culture), most cissexuals remain largely unfamiliar with trans perspectives. Using only words that cissexuals are familiar with in order to describe my gendered experiences would be similar to a musician only choosing words that nonmusicians understand when describing music. It can be done, but something crucial would surely be lost in the translation. Just as musicians cannot fully explain their reaction to a particular song without bringing up concepts such as "minor key" or "time signature," there are certain trans-specific words and ideas that will appear throughout this book that are crucial for me to use in order to precisely convey my thoughts and experiences regarding gender. To have an illuminating and nuanced discussion about my experiences and perspectives as a trans woman, we must begin to think in terms of words and ideas that accurately describe that experience.

2

Skirt Chasers: Why the Media Depicts the Trans Revolution in Lipstick and Heels

AS A TRANSSEXUAL WOMAN, I am often confronted by people who insist that I am not, nor can I ever be, a "real woman." One of the more common lines of reasoning goes something like this: *There's more to being a woman than simply putting on a dress.* I couldn't agree more. That's why it's so frustrating that people often seem confused because, although I have transitioned to female and live as a woman, I rarely wear makeup or dress in an overly feminine manner.

Despite the reality that there are as many types of trans women as there are women in general, most people believe that all trans women are on a quest to make ourselves as pretty, pink, and passive as possible. While there are certainly some trans women who buy into mainstream dogma about beauty and femininity, others are outspoken feminists and activists fighting against all gender stereotypes. But you'd never know it by looking at the popular media, which tends to assume that all transsexuals are male-to-female, and that all trans women want to achieve stereotypical femininity.

The existence of transsexuals—who transition from one sex to the other and often live completely unnoticed as the sex "opposite" to the one we were assigned at birth—has the potential to challenge the conventional assumption that gender differences arise from our chromosomes and genitals in a simple, straightforward manner. We can wreak havoc on such taken-for-granted concepts as *woman* and *man, homosexual* and *heterosexual*. These terms lose their cut-and-dried meaning when a person's assigned sex and lived sex are not the same. But because we are a threat to the categories that enable traditional and oppositional sexism, the images and experiences of trans people are presented in the media in a way that reaffirms, rather than challenges, gender stereotypes.

Trans Woman Archetypes in the Media

Media depictions of trans women, whether they take the form of fictional characters or actual people, usually fall under one of two main archetypes: the "deceptive transsexual" or the "pathetic transsexual." While characters based on both models are presented as having a vested interest in achieving an ultrafeminine appearance, they differ in their abilities to pull it off. Because the "deceivers" successfully pass as women, they generally act as unexpected plot twists, or play the role of sexual predators who fool innocent straight guys into falling for other "men."

Perhaps the most famous example of a "deceiver" is the character Dil in the 1992 movie *The Crying Game*. The film became a pop culture phenomenon primarily because most moviegoers were unaware that Dil was trans until about halfway through the movie. The revelation comes during a love scene between her and Fergus, the male protagonist who has been courting her. When Dil disrobes, the audience, along with Fergus, learns for the first time that Dil is physically male. When I saw the film, most of the men in the theater groaned at this revelation. Onscreen, Fergus has a similarly intense reaction: He slaps Dil and runs off to the bathroom to vomit.

The 1994 Jim Carrey vehicle *Ace Ventura: Pet Detective* features a "deceptive transsexual" as a villain. Police lieutenant Lois Einhorn (played by Sean Young) is secretly Ray Finkle, an ex–Miami Dolphins kicker who has stolen the team's mascot as part of a scheme to get back at Dolphins quarterback Dan Marino. The bizarre plot ends when Ventura strips Einhorn down to her underwear in front of about twenty police officers and announces, "She is suffering from the worst case of hemorrhoids I have ever seen." He then turns her around so that we can see her penis and testicles tucked between her legs. All of the police officers proceed to vomit as *The Crying Game*'s theme song plays in the background.

Even though "deceivers" successfully "pass" as women, and are often played by female actors (with the notable exception of Jaye Davidson as Dil), these characters are never intended to challenge our assumptions about gender itself. On the contrary, they are positioned as "fake" women, and their "secret" trans status is revealed in a dramatic moment of "truth." At this moment, the "deceiver"'s appearance (her femaleness) is reduced to mere illusion, and her secret (her maleness) becomes the real identity.

In a tactic that emphasizes their "true" maleness, "deceivers" are most often used as pawns to provoke male homophobia in other characters, as well as in the audience itself. This phenomenon is especially evident in TV talk shows like *Jerry Springer,* which regularly runs episodes with titles like "My Girlfriend's a Guy" and "I'm Really a Man!" that feature trans women coming out to their straight boyfriends. On a recent British TV reality show called *There's Something About Miriam,* six heterosexual men court an attractive woman who, unbeknownst to them, is transsexual. The broadcast of the show was delayed for several months because the men threatened to sue the show's producers, alleging that they had been the victims of defamation, personal injury, and conspiracy to commit sexual assault. The affair was eventually settled out of court, with each man coming away with a reported 125,000 British pounds (over 200,000 U.S. dollars at the time).[1]

In the 1970 film adaptation of Gore Vidal's novel *Myra Breckinridge,* the protagonist is a trans woman who heads out to Hollywood in order to take revenge on traditional manhood and to "realign the sexes." This "realignment" apparently involves raping an ex–football player with a strap-on dildo, which she does at one point during the movie. The recurring theme of "deceptive" trans women retaliating against men, often by seducing them, seems to be an unconscious acknowledgment that both male and heterosexual privilege is threatened by transsexuals.

In contrast to the "deceivers," who wield their feminine wiles with success, the "pathetic transsexual" characters aren't deluding anyone. Despite her masculine mannerisms and five o'clock shadow, the "pathetic transsexual" will inevitably insist that she is a woman trapped inside a man's body. The intense contradiction between the "pathetic" character's gender identity and her physical appearance is often played for laughs—as in the transition of musician Mark Shubb (played as a bearded baritone by Harry Shearer) at the conclusion of 2003's *A Mighty Wind.*

Unlike the "deceivers," whose ability to "pass" is a serious threat to our culture's ideas about gender and sexuality, "pathetic transsexuals"—who barely resemble women at all—are generally considered harmless. Perhaps for this reason, some of the most endearing pop culture portrayals of trans women fall into the "pathetic" category: John Lithgow's Oscar-nominated portrayal of ex–football player Roberta Muldoon in 1982's *The World According to Garp,* and Terence Stamp's role as the aging showgirl Bernadette in 1994's *The Adventures of Priscilla, Queen of the Desert.* More recently, the 1998 indie film *The Adventures of Sebastian Cole* begins with its teenage protagonist learning that his stepdad Hank, who looks and acts like a roadie for a '70s rock band, is about to become Henrietta. A sympathetic character and the only stable person in Sebastian's life, Henrietta spends most of the movie wearing floral-print nightgowns and bare-shouldered tops with tons of jewelry and makeup. Yet despite her extremely femme manner of dress, she continues to exhibit only stereotypical male behaviors, overtly ogling a waitress and punching out a guy who calls her a "faggot" (after which she laments, "I broke a nail").

In the case of Henrietta, this extreme combination of masculinity and femininity does not seem designed to challenge audiences' assumptions about maleness and femaleness. On the contrary, Henrietta's masculine voice and mannerisms are meant to demonstrate that, despite her desire to be female, she cannot change the fact that she is really and truly a man. As with *Garp*'s Roberta and *Priscilla*'s Bernadette, the audience is encouraged to respect Henrietta as a person, but not as a woman. While we are supposed to admire their courage—which presumably comes from the difficulty of living as women who do not appear very female—we are not meant to identify with them or to be sexually attracted to them, as we are to "deceivers" like Dil.

Interestingly, while the obvious outward masculinity of "pathetic transsexual" characters is always played up, so too is their lack of male genitalia (or their desire to part with them). In fact, some of the most memorable lines in these movies are uttered when the "pathetic transsexual" character makes light of her own castration. At one point during *Priscilla,* Bernadette remarks that her parents never spoke to her again, "after [she] had the chop." In *Garp,* when a man is injured while receiving a blow job during a car accident, Roberta delivers the one-liner, "I had mine removed surgically under general anesthesia, but to have it bitten off in a Buick . . ." In the 1994 fictionalized biography *Ed Wood,* Bill Murray plays another "pathetic transsexual," Bunny Breckinridge. After seeing Wood's film *Glen or Glenda,* Bunny is inspired to go to Mexico to have a "sex change," announcing to Wood, "Your movie made me realize I've got to take action. Goodbye, penis!"

The "pathetic" transsexual's lighthearted comments about having her penis lopped off come in stark contrast to the revelation of the "deceiver," who is generally found out by someone else in an embarrassing, often violent way. A Freudian might suggest that the "deceptive" transsexual's dangerous nature is symbolized by the presence of a hidden penis, while the "pathetic" transsexual's harmlessness is due to a lack thereof. A less phallic interpretation is that the very act of "passing" makes any trans woman who can do so into a "deceiver." Ultimately, both "deceptive" and "pathetic" transsexual characters are designed to validate the popular assumption that trans women are truly men. "Pathetic" transsexuals may want to be female, but their masculine appearances and mannerisms always give them away. And while the "deceiver" is initially perceived to be a "real" female, she is eventually revealed as a wolf in sheep's clothing—an illusion that is the product of lies and modern medical technology—and she is usually punished accordingly.

The Fascination with "Feminization"

In virtually all depictions of trans women, whether real or fictional, "deceptive" or "pathetic," the underlying assumption is that the trans woman wants to achieve a stereotypically feminine appearance and gender role. The possibility that trans women are even capable of making a distinction between identifying as female and wanting to cultivate a hyperfeminine image is never raised. In fact, the media often dwells on the specifics of the feminization process, showing trans women putting on their feminine exteriors. It's telling that TV, film, and news producers tend not to be satisfied with merely showing trans women wearing feminine clothes and makeup. Rather, it is their intent to capture trans women *in the act* of putting on lipstick, dresses, and high heels, thereby giving the audience the impression that the trans woman's femaleness is an artificial mask or costume.

An excellent example of this phenomenon is *Transamerica* (2005), a "buddy" road-trip movie pairing up trans woman Bree Osbourne (played by Felicity Huffman) with a son that she was previously unaware she had. In the opening five minutes of the film, we see Bree practicing along with the instructional video *Finding Your Female Voice,* putting on stockings, padding her bra, donning a pink dress suit, painting her nails (also pink), and putting on lipstick, eye shadow, powder, and other cosmetics. This scene (not coincidentally) is immediately followed by the first dialogue in the movie, where Bree tells a psychiatrist that she's been on hormone replacement therapy for three years, has undergone electrolysis, feminine facial surgery, a brow-lift, forehead reduction, jaw recontouring, and a tracheal shave. This opening flurry of cosmetic and medical feminization is clearly designed to establish that Bree's female identity is artificial and imitative, and to reduce her transition to the mere pursuit of feminine finery.

Throughout the rest of the film, feminine apparel and cosmetics are repeatedly used as a device to highlight Bree's fakeness. There are excessive scenes in which Bree is shown in the act of dressing and undressing, as though her clothing represented some kind of costume. We also see her applying and fixing her makeup nearly every chance she gets, and it is difficult not to view the thick layers of foundation she constantly wears as a mask that is hiding the "real" (undoubtedly more masculine) Bree underneath. While many MTF crossdressers often wear heavy makeup to cover up their beard shadow, a trans woman like Bree—who has already undergone electrolysis and been on hormones for three years—would not need to do this. Indeed, the fact that her foundation begins to develop a sheen from perspiration at several points in the movie, and that she stumbles in her high heels on more than one occasion—faux pas that never seem to afflict cissexual women in Hollywood—makes it clear that the filmmakers purposely used these female accessories as props to portray Bree as "doing female" rather badly. And they certainly succeeded, as Felicity Huffman comes off seeming infinitely more contrived than the several real-life trans women (such as Andrea James and Calpernia Addams) who appear briefly in the film.

The media's willingness to indulge the audience's fascination with the surface trappings that accompany the feminization of "men" also tarnishes nonfiction and serious attempts to tell the stories of trans women. For example, the 2004 *New York Times* article "As Repression Eases, More Iranians Change Their Sex" is not sensationalistic, describing the rise of transsexual rights in Iran.[2] Yet, one of the two photos that accompany the piece depicts an Iranian trans woman putting on lipstick. In 2003, *The Oprah Winfrey Show* aired a two-part special on transsexual women and their wives. The entire first episode featured a one-on-one interview with Jennifer Finney Boylan, author of the autobiography *She's Not There: A Life in Two Genders.* While Oprah Winfrey's conversation with Boylan was respectful and serious, the show nonetheless opened with predictable scenes of women putting on eye makeup, lipstick, and shoes, and the interview itself was interspersed with "before" pictures of Boylan, as if to constantly remind us that she's really a man underneath it all.

Mass media images of "biological males" dressing and acting in a feminine manner could potentially challenge mainstream notions of gender, but the way they are generally presented in these feminization scenes ensures that this never happens. The media neutralizes the potential threat that trans femininities pose to the category of "woman" by playing to the audience's subconscious belief that femininity itself is artificial. After all, while most people assume that women are naturally feminine, they also (rather hypocritically) require them to spend an hour or two each day putting on their faces and getting all dressed up in order to meet societal standards for femininity (unlike men, whose masculinity is presumed to come directly from who he *is* and what he *does*). In fact, it's the assumption that femininity is inherently "contrived," "frivolous," and "manipulative" that allows masculinity to always come off as "natural," "practical," and "sincere" by comparison.

Thus, the media is able to depict trans women donning feminine attire and accessories without ever giving the impression that they achieve "true" femaleness in the process. Further, by focusing on the most feminine of artifices, the media evokes the idea that trans women are living out some sort of sexual fetish. This sexualization of trans women's motives for transitioning not only belittles trans women's female identities, but encourages the objectification of women as a whole.

Of course, what always goes unseen are the great lengths to which producers will go to depict lurid and superficial scenes in which trans women get all dolled up in pretty clothes and cosmetics. Shawna Virago, a San Francisco trans activist, musician, and director of the Tranny Fest film festival, has experienced several such incidents with local news producers. For instance, when Virago was organizing a forum to facilitate communication between police and the trans community, a newspaper reporter approached her and other transgender activists to write an article about them. However, the paper was interested not in their politics but in their transitions. "They wanted each of us to include 'before' and 'after' pictures," Shawna said. "This pissed me off, and I tried to explain to the writer that the before-and-after stuff had nothing to do with police abuse and other issues, like trans women and HIV, but he didn't get it. So I was cut from the piece."

A few years later, someone from another paper contacted Virago and asked to photograph her "getting ready" to go out: "I told him I didn't think having a picture of me rolling out of bed and hustling to catch [the bus] would make for a compelling photo. He said, 'You know, getting pretty, putting on makeup.' I refused, but they did get a trans woman who complied, and there she was, putting on mascara and lipstick and a pretty dress, none of which had anything to do with the article, which was purportedly about political and social challenges the trans community faced."[3]

Trans woman Nancy Nangeroni and her partner Gordene O. MacKenzie, who together host the radio program *GenderTalk,* described two similar incidents on one of their programs. In both cases, while they were being filmed, the media producers wanted to get footage of the two of them putting on makeup together (requests that Nangeroni and MacKenzie denied).[4] I myself had a similar experience back in 2001, just before I began taking hormones. A friend arranged for me to meet with someone who was doing a film about the transgender movement. The filmmaker was noticeably disappointed when I showed up looking like a somewhat normal guy, wearing a T-shirt, jeans, and sneakers. She eventually asked me if I would mind putting on lipstick while she filmed me. I told her that wearing lipstick had nothing to do with the fact that I was transgender or that I identified as female. She shot a small amount of footage anyway (sans lipstick) and said she would get in touch with me if she decided to use any of it. I never heard back from her.

When audiences watch scenes of trans women putting on skirts and makeup, they are not necessarily seeing a reflection of the values of those trans women; they are witnessing TV, film, and news producers' obsessions with all objects commonly associated with female sexuality. In other words, the media's and audience's fascination with the feminization of trans women is a by-product of their sexualization of all women.

The Media's Transgender Gap

There is most certainly a connection between the differing values given to women and men in our culture and the media's fascination with depicting trans women rather than trans men, who were born female but identify as male. Although the number of people transitioning in each direction is relatively equal these days, media coverage would have us believe there is a huge disparity in the populations of trans men and women.[5]

Jamison Green, a trans man who authored a 1994 report that led to the city of San Francisco's decision to extend its civil rights protections to include gender identity, once said this about the media coverage of that event: "Several times at the courthouse, when the press was doing interviews, I stood by and listened as reporters inquired who wrote the report, and when I was pointed out to them as the author I could see them looking right through me, looking past me to find the man in a dress who must have written the report and whom they would want to interview. More than once a reporter asked me incredulously, 'You wrote the report?' They assumed that because of my 'normal' appearance that I wouldn't be newsworthy."[6]

Indeed, the media tends to not notice—or to outright ignore—trans men because they are unable to sensationalize them the way they do trans women without bringing masculinity itself into question. And in a world where modern psychology was founded upon the teaching that all young girls suffer from penis envy, most people think striving for masculinity seems like a perfectly reasonable goal. Author and sex activist Patrick Califia, who is a trans man, addresses this in his 1997 book *Sex Changes: The Politics of Transgenderism:* "It seems the world is still more titillated by 'a man who wants to become a woman' than it is by 'a woman who wants to become a man.' The first is scandalous, the latter is taken for granted. This reflects the very different levels of privilege men and women have in our society. Of course women want to be men, the general attitude seems to be, and of course they can't. And that's that."[7]

Once we recognize how media coverage of transsexuals is informed by the different values our society assigns to femaleness and maleness, it becomes obvious that virtually all attempts to sensationalize and deride trans women are built on a foundation of unspoken misogyny. Since most people cannot fathom why someone would give up male privilege and power in order to become a relatively disempowered female, they assume that trans women transition primarily as a way of obtaining the one type of power that women are perceived to have in our society: the ability to express femininity and to attract men.

This is why trans women like myself, who rarely dress in an overly feminine manner and/or who are not attracted to men, are such an enigma to many people. By assuming that my desire to be female is merely some sort of femininity fetish or sexual perversion, they are essentially making the case that women have no worth beyond the extent to which they can be sexualized.

Feminist Depictions of Trans Women

There are numerous parallels between the way trans women are depicted in the media and the way that they have been portrayed by some feminist theorists. While many feminists—especially younger ones who came of age in the 1980s and 1990s—recognize that trans women can be allies in the fight to eliminate gender stereotypes, other feminists—particularly those who embrace gender essentialism—believe that trans women foster sexism by mimicking patriarchal attitudes about femininity, or that we objectify women by trying to possess female bodies of our own. Many of these latter ideas stem from Janice G. Raymond's 1979 book *The Transsexual Empire: The Making of the She-Male,* which is perhaps the most influential feminist writing on transsexuals. Like the media, Raymond virtually ignores trans men, dismissing them as "tokens," and instead focuses almost exclusively on trans women, insisting that they transition in order to achieve stereotypical femininity. She even argues that "most transsexuals conform more to the feminine role than even the most feminine of natural-born women."[8] This fact does not surprise Raymond, since she believes that femininity itself is an artificial by-product of a patriarchal society. So despite the fact that trans women may attain femininity, Raymond does not believe that they become "real" women. (To emphasize this, she refers to trans women as "male-to-constructed-females" and addresses them with masculine pronouns throughout the book.) Thus, Raymond builds her case by relying on the same tactics as the media: She depicts trans women as hyperfeminine (in order to make their female identities appear highly artificial) and she hypersexualizes them (by playing down the existence of trans people who transition to male).

Unlike the media, Raymond does acknowledge the existence of trans women who are not stereotypically feminine, albeit reluctantly. She writes, "I have been very hesitant about devoting a chapter of this book to what I call the 'transsexually constructed lesbian-feminist.'"[9] Because she believes that lesbian-feminists represent "a small percentage of transsexuals" (a claim that she never verifies), she does not seem inclined to discuss their existence at all except for the "recent debate and divisiveness [the subject] produced within feminist circles."[10] Being that Raymond believes that femininity undermines women's true worth, you might think that she would be open to trans women who denounce femininity and patriarchal gender stereotypes. However, this is not the case. Instead, she argues, "As the male-to-constructed-female transsexual exhibits the attempt to possess women in a bodily sense while acting out the images into which men have molded women, the male-to-constructed-female who claims to be a lesbian-feminist attempts to possess women at a deeper level."[11] Throughout the rest of the chapter, she discusses how lesbian-feminist trans women use "deception" in order to "penetrate" women's spaces and minds. She says, "although the transsexually constructed lesbian-feminist does not exhibit a feminine identity and role, he does exhibit stereotypical masculine behavior."[12] This essentially puts trans women in a double bind: If they act feminine they are perceived as being a parody, but if they act masculine it is seen as a sign of their true male identity. This damned-if-they-do, damned-if-they-don't tactic is reminiscent of the pop cultural "deceptive"/"pathetic" transsexual archetypes. Both Raymond and the media ensure that trans women—whether they are feminine or masculine, whether they "pass" or not—will invariably come off as "fake" women no matter how they look or act.

While much of *The Transsexual Empire* is clearly over the top (the premise of the book is that "biological woman is in the process of being made obsolete by bio-medicine"), many of Raymond's arguments are echoed in contemporary attempts to justify the exclusion of trans women from women's organizations and spaces. In fact, the world's largest annual women-only event, the Michigan

Womyn's Music Festival (often referred to simply as "Michigan"), still enforces a "womyn-born-womyn"-only policy that is specifically designed to prevent trans women from attending.[13] Many of the excuses used to rationalize trans women's exclusion are not designed to protect the values of women-only space, but rather to reinforce the idea that trans women are "real" men and "fake" women. For example, one of the most cited reasons that trans women are not allowed in the festival is that we are born with, and many of us still have, penises (many trans women either cannot afford to or choose not to have sex reassignment surgery). It is argued that our penises are dangerous because they are a symbol of male oppression and have the potential to trigger women who have been sexually assaulted or abused by men. So penises are banned from the festival, right? Well, not quite: The festival does allow women to purchase and use dildos, strap-ons, and packing devices, many of which closely resemble penises. So phalluses in and of themselves are not so bad, just so long as they are not attached to a trans woman.

Another reason frequently given for the exclusion of trans women from Michigan is that we supposedly would bring "male energy" into the festival. While this seems to imply that expressions of masculinity are not allowed, nothing could be further from the truth. Michigan allows drag king performers who dress and act male, and the festival stage has featured several female-bodied performers who identify as transgender and sometimes describe themselves with male pronouns.[14] Presumably, Lisa Vogel (who is sole proprietor of the festival) allows this because she believes that no person who is born female is capable of exhibiting authentic masculinity or "male energy." Not only is this an insult to trans men (as it suggests that they can never be fully masculine or male), but it implies that "male energy" can be measured in some way independent of whether the person expressing it appears female or male. This is clearly not the case. Even though I am a trans woman, I have never been accused of expressing "male energy," because people *perceive* me as a woman. When I do act in a "masculine" way, people describe me as a "tomboy" or "butch," and if I get aggressive or argumentative, people call me a "bitch." My behaviors are still the same; it is only the context of my body (whether people see me as female or male) that has changed.

This is the inevitable problem with all attempts to portray trans women as "fake" females (whether media or feminist in origin): They require one to give different names, meanings, and values to the same behaviors depending on whether the person in question was born with a female or male body (or whether they are perceived to be a woman or a man). In other words, they require one to be sexist. When people insist that there are essential differences between women and men, they further a line of reasoning that ultimately refutes feminist ideals rather than supporting them.

From my own experience in having transitioned from one sex to the other, I have found that women and men are not separated by an insurmountable chasm, as many people seem to believe. Actually, most of us are only a hormone prescription away from being perceived as the "opposite" sex. Personally, I welcome this idea as a testament to just how little difference there really is between women and men. To believe that a woman is a woman because of her sex chromosomes, reproductive organs, or socialization denies the reality that every single day, we classify each person we see as either female or male based on a small number of visual cues and a ton of assumption. The one thing that women share is that we are all *perceived* as women and treated accordingly. As a feminist, I look forward to a time when we finally move beyond the idea that biology is destiny, and recognize that the most important differences that exist between women and men in our society are the different meanings that we place onto one another's bodies.

3

Before and After: Class and Body Transformations

TRANSSEXUAL LIVES ARE full of obstacles—childhood isolation, denial, depression, coming out, and managing our gender difference in a less than hospitable world. We have to navigate the legal limbo that surrounds what "sex" appears on our driver's licenses and passports, which restrooms we can safely use, and who we are allowed to marry. Many of us face workplace discrimination, police harassment, and the constant threat of violence. Yet the media focuses very little on any of this. Instead, TV shows and documentaries about transsexuals tend to focus rather exclusively on one particular aspect of our lives: our physical transitions.

Such transition-focused programs always seem to follow the same format, which includes rigorous discussions of all of the medical procedures involved (hormones, surgeries, electrolysis, etc.) and plenty of the requisite before-and-after shots. Before I transitioned, I found these programs predictable and formulaic, but I also found them helpful to a certain extent. As someone who had often thought about changing my sex, they gave me a certain understanding of what I might be able to expect if I were to pursue such a path myself. But of course, I was a demographic anomaly. Clearly these shows were being made by and for people who did not identify with the trans person in the program and who were not contemplating sex reassignment themselves. Back then, I never really questioned why a non-trans audience might be so interested in the minutiae of the transitioning process and trans-related medical procedures.

Now, after five years of living as an out transsexual, I have come to realize that these documentaries and TV programs reveal an even deeper underlying compulsion on the part of many cissexual people, one that goes way beyond natural curiosity, to dwell almost exclusively on the physical aspects of the transition process when contemplating transsexuality. Like most transsexuals, I have scores of anecdotes that highlight this tendency: During the question and answer session at a literary event, after reading a piece about the murder of trans woman Gwen Araujo, I was asked by an audience member if I had any electrolysis done on my face; after I did a workshop for college students on binary gender norms and the way we project our ideals about gender onto other people, a young woman asked me several questions about whether or not I'd had a "sex change operation"; after creating switchhitter.net, my coming-out-as-trans website, I received an angry email from a stranger complaining that I did not put any before-and-after pictures up on the site, as if the 3,700-word question and answer section and the 4,500-word mini-autobiography describing my experiences being trans wasn't sufficient for that person to fully grasp my transsexuality—he needed to see the changes firsthand.

Of course, it's not just strangers who ask to see before-and-after shots of me. When friends, colleagues, or acquaintances find out that I am trans, it is not uncommon for them to ask if I have any "before" pictures they can see, as if I just so happen to keep a boy photo of myself handy, you know, just in case. I usually respond by telling them that before I transitioned I looked exactly like I do now, except that I was a boy. They never seem particularly satisfied with that answer.

The thing that strikes me the most about the desire to see before-and-after pictures, or to hear all of the gory details about sex reassignment procedures, is how bold people often are about it. After all, these people have to know that I felt uncomfortable as male, that it was a difficult and often miserable part of my life. So why on earth would they ask to see pictures of me from that time period? From my perspective, it is as thoughtless as if I had told someone that I was suffering from depression a few years ago and for them to have responded, "Oh, do you have any pictures of yourself from back then?" And really, is there anything more disrespectful and inappropriate than asking someone (in public, no less!) whether they have had any medical procedures performed on their genitals? So what drives these otherwise well-meaning people to want to know about the physical aspects of my transition so badly that they are willing to disregard common courtesy and discretion?

Well, I wasn't quite sure myself until about two years ago, during the height of the reality TV plastic surgery craze, when shows like *Extreme Makeover, The Swan,* and *I Want a Famous Face* filled the airwaves. These shows seemed to be catering to a very similar audience desire: to witness a dramatic physical transformation process replete with before-and-after photos of the subject. Also around that time, gastric bypass surgery began receiving a lot of media attention, and there were numerous programs dedicated to following people who were described as being "morbidly obese" through their surgery and recovery, ending of course with the mandatory before-and-after shots punctuating just how much weight the subjects had lost. On Discovery Health Channel, there is even a series that's called *Plastic Surgery: Before & After,* which often combines conventional plastic surgeries and gastric bypasses in the same episode.

What really impressed me about these shows was how similar they are in format to many of the transsexual documentaries I have seen: They feature subjects who are unhappy with their bodies in some way, sympathetic and able doctors who describe the forthcoming procedures in great detail, hospital shots on the day of surgery and immediately afterward, a final scene after full recovery where the subject talks about how happy they are with the results, and side-by-side before-and-after photos that demonstrate the remarkable transformation in its entirety. Sometimes these shows are even set to slightly disturbing music that, when combined with the narrator's dramatic voice-over, impresses upon the viewer that they are watching something that is simultaneously wondrous and taboo. The only significant difference between many transsexual documentaries and these plastic surgery shows is that the former require a little more background and explanation as to why the subject wants to change their sex in the first place (presumably, the desire to become thinner or more conventionally attractive needs no explanation).

So why do plastic surgeries, gastric bypasses, and sex reassignment procedures receive such similar treatment in these programs? It is not simply because they all portray cutting-edge medical procedures. After all, there are plenty of shows that feature various medical techniques and surgeries, but they are generally far more serious and less sensationalistic in tone. Nor can it be said that the rarity of these procedures leads to the public's fascination with them. While sex reassignment is still fairly rare, 9.2 million cosmetic plastic surgery procedures and an estimated 140,000 gastric bypass surgeries were performed in 2004.[1] It also can't simply be that these shows depict transformations of some kind. After all, one occasionally sees behind-the-scenes programs about Hollywood makeup artists and costume designers who can drastically change an actor's appearance, yet they are never given the sensationalistic spin that these other types of transformations receive. There are also plenty of programs that feature nonsurgical makeovers (for example, *Queer Eye for the Straight Guy* and *What Not to Wear*), but they tend to have a more laid-back and informative feel, seducing the audience with their you-can-do-this-yourself attitude, in contrast to plastic surgery and sex reassignment shows, which have a far more cold and voyeuristic feel to them. And while a woman who changes her hair color and style, or a man who shaves off his beard, undergoes a significant transformation, one that often leaves them looking like a completely different person, the audience is not encouraged to gawk over their before-and-after pictures in the same way they do with the subjects of plastic surgery and sex reassignment programs.

I would argue that the major reason that plastic surgeries, gastric bypasses, and sex reassignments are all given similar sensationalistic treatments is because the subjects cross what is normally considered an impenetrable class boundary: from unattractive to beautiful, from fat to thin, and in the case of transsexuals, from male to female, or from female to male.

Of course, attractiveness as a class issue permeates much of what we see on TV—it determines who gets to be the protagonist or love interest and who ends up being the nerdy next-door neighbor or comic relief. And while TV advertisements may encourage us to buy various beauty products that are supposed to make us look incrementally more attractive, or dieting and exercising programs that are supposed to help us lose that extra ten, twenty, even forty pounds, it is commonly accepted that we each have certain physical limits that we are unable to overcome, limits that generally determine our social status regarding attractiveness. In fact, the large amount of effort that many of us put into attaining the relatively small improvements in our appearance that are achievable by exercising, dieting, and purchasing beauty products is a testament to how much we are judged (and how we judge others) based on conventional standards of beauty and size. So when somebody does cross those supposedly impassable boundaries, essentially changing their social class from not-so-attractive to stunning, or from "morbidly obese" to thin, it can change our thinking about beauty and attraction.

As a transsexual, I find myself dealing with this same phenomenon all the time, only with gender. Whether people realize it or not, most of us value, treat, and relate to women and men very differently, although not necessarily in a conscious or malicious way. Rather, like our attitudes about beauty and attraction, these prejudices are practically invisible to us, as they are woven into our social fabric. So when I tell someone that I used to be male, they are often dumbfounded at first, as if they have difficulty reconciling that someone who seems so naturally female to them could have once been something they consider to be so completely different.

The fact that a single individual can be both female and male, or ugly and beautiful, at different points in their life challenges the commonly held belief that these classes are mutually exclusive and naturally distinct from one another.

Coming face-to-face with an individual who has crossed class barriers of gender or attractiveness can help us recognize the extent to which our own biases, assumptions, and stereotypes create those class systems in the first place. But rather than question our own value judgments or notice the ways that we treat people differently based on their size, beauty, or gender, most of us reflexively react to these situations in a way that reinforces class boundaries: We focus on the presumed "artificiality" of the transformation the subject has undergone. Playing up the "artificial" aspects of the transformation process gives one the impression that the class barrier itself is "natural," one that could not have been crossed if it were not for modern medical technology. Of course, it is true that plastic surgeries and sex reassignments are "artificial," but then again so are the exercise bikes we work out on, the antiwrinkle moisturizers we smear on our faces, the dyes we use to color our hair, the clothes we buy to complement our figures, and the TV shows, movies, magazines, and billboards that bombard us with "ideal" images of gender, size, and beauty that set the standards that we try to live up to in the first place. The class systems based on attractiveness and gender are extraordinarily "artificial"—yet only those practices that seem to subvert those classes (rather than reaffirm them) are ever characterized as such.

Shows depicting plastic surgery, gastric bypasses, and sex reassignments are designed (whether consciously or unconsciously) to single out and exaggerate the supposed "artificial" nature of these procedures, thus giving the audience the opportunity to enjoy the spectacle of these dramatic transformations without ever bringing into question the authenticity of the class barrier that is being crossed. The more dramatic the change, the more "artificial" the whole process will inevitably seem. This is why plastic surgery shows rarely depict people who are conventionally attractive from the outset, even though such people certainly represent a significant portion of those who seek out plastic surgery. Nor do they follow subjects who merely want a nose job or a tummy tuck. Rather, these programs almost always depict people of either average or less-than-average attractiveness, and who undergo multiple procedures at once, thus creating the most dramatic and extensive physical change possible.

Similarly, the subjects of sex reassignment programs rarely ever begin the process as very feminine males or as very masculine females, even though many pre-transition trans people fall into these categories. Showing such people transitioning to become trans women and trans men, respectively, would not only make their transformation seem less dramatic; it would give the impression that sex reassignment merely confirms the subject's "natural" gender identity, as opposed to "artificially" altering that person's biological sex.

Perhaps for this reason, the most commonly depicted subject on these programs is a trans woman who starts out as a seemingly masculine male. In addition to the reasons for the media's focus on trans women rather than trans men (which I discussed in chapter 2), there are additional physical reasons to account for this phenomenon. Trans women often have more difficulties "passing" as their identified sex than trans men do, not only because of limitations of the MTF transition process in reversing some of the irreparable effects of prolonged exposure to testosterone, but because people in our culture predominantly rely on male (rather than female) cues when determining the sex of other people.[2] Therefore, some trans women require more procedures if they wish to be taken seriously as their identified sex. Sex reassignment TV programs I have seen have followed trans women not only through electrolysis, hormone replacement therapy, and bottom surgery (which are all fairly common), but also somewhat less common procedures, such as top surgery to increase the size of their breasts, tracheal shaves to reduce the size of their Adam's apples, and voice lessons to overcome their deep voices. Such shows also frequently depict trans women working with movement coaches and fashion consultants, even though it is safe to say that the overwhelming majority of trans women never engage in such a step.

These programs' concentration on trans people who undergo multiple medical procedures, or who take lessons to help them "pass" as their identified sex, tends to make invisible the many trans men and women who "pass" rather easily after hormone replacement therapy alone, or who choose not to undergo all of the procedures commonly associated with transsexuality. Focusing primarily on those trans people who undergo the most procedures during their transitions not only shows a more dramatic change—one that reinforces the idea that sex reassignment is "artificial"—but also fosters the audience's assumption that trans people are merely mimicking or impersonating the other sex rather than expressing their natural gender identity or subconscious sex.

Perhaps no element in these sex reassignment and plastic surgery shows helps confirm the audience's assumptions about gender and attractiveness more than the before-and-after photos. These pictures are designed to overemphasize stereotypes. In the programs that feature plastic surgery and gastric bypass surgery, the subject is almost always wearing frumpy clothes and frowning in the "before" picture, and dressed smart and smiling in the "after" picture, adding to the perception that they have become more attractive. In the transsexual documentaries, "before" photos of trans women almost always depict them in the most masculine of ways: playing sports as a young boy, with facial hair and wearing a wedding tuxedo or military uniform as a young man. Similarly, "before" shots of trans men often include pictures of them wearing birthday dresses as a child, or high school yearbook photos of them with long hair. The purpose for choosing these more stereotypically female and male images over other potential "before" pictures (for instance, ones where the subject looks more gender-variant or gender-neutral) is to emphasize the "naturalness" of the trans person's assigned sex, thereby exaggerating the "artificiality" of their identified sex.

In real life, before-and-after photos don't always depict such clear-cut gender differences. One time, a friend who has only known me as a woman visited our apartment and saw wedding photos of me and my wife, Dani, for the first time. Despite the fact that I am physically male and wearing a tuxedo in the pictures (as we were married before I physically transitioned), I do not look very masculine; instead, I look like the small, long-haired, androgynous boy that I used to be. My friend seemed a little let down by the photos. She muttered, "It's weird, because it looks just like you in the pictures, except that you're a guy." Similarly, whenever old friends meet up with me for the first time since my transition, they almost invariably comment on how strange it is that I seem like the exact same person to them, except that now I am female. It's as if our compulsion to place women and men into different categories of our brain, to see them as "opposite" sexes, is so intense that we have trouble imagining that it is possible for a person to change their sex without somehow becoming an entirely different person.

These days, whenever people ask me lots of questions about my previous male life and the medical procedures that helped facilitate my transition to female, I realize that they are making a desperate and concerted effort to preserve their own assumptions and stereotypes about gender, rather than opening their minds up to the possibility that women and men do not represent mutually exclusive categories. When they request to see my "before" photos or ask me what my former name was, it is because they are trying to visualize me as male in order to anchor my existence in my assigned sex. And when they focus on my physical transition, it is so they can imagine my femaleness as a product of medical science rather than something that is authentic, that comes from inside me.

I know that many in the trans community believe that these TV shows and documentaries following transsexuals through the transition process serve a purpose, offering us a bit of visibility and the rare chance to be depicted on TV as something other than a joke. But in actuality, they accomplish little more than reducing us to our physical transitions and our anatomically "altered" bodies. In other words, these programs objectify us. And while it has become somewhat customary for trans people to allow the media to use our "before" pictures whenever we appear on TV, this only enables the cissexual public to continue privileging our assigned sex over our subconscious sex and gender identity. If we truly want to be taken seriously in our identified sex, then we must not only refuse to indulge cissexual people's compulsion to pigeonhole us in our assigned sex, but call them out on the way that they continuously objectify our bodies while refusing to take our minds, our persons, and our identities seriously.

4

Boygasms and Girlgasms: A Frank Discussion About Hormones and Gender Differences

THOUGH I AM OFTEN RELUCTANT to indulge people's fascination with the details of my physical transition from male to female, I will often make an exception regarding the psychological changes I experienced due to hormones. The reason for this is quite simple: Sex hormones have become horribly politicized in our culture, evident in the way that people blatantly blame testosterone for nearly all instances of male aggression and violence, or the way that women who become legitimately angry or upset often have their opinions dismissed as mere symptoms of their body chemistry. Such hormonal folklore has strongly influenced medicine, as evidenced by the countless shoddy, pseudoscientific studies claiming to verify popular assumptions about testosterone and estrogen. Of course, such overt politicization has created a significant backlash of people who now play down the role of hormones in human behavior, who argue that most of their presumed effects (making men overly aggressive and women overly emotional) are better explained by socialization—after all, young boys are encouraged to be aggressive and discouraged from showing emotions, and vice versa for girls.

Having experienced both female and male hormones firsthand, I feel it's my duty to spoil this nature-versus-nurture debate by offering the following description and interpretation of my personal experiences "transitioning" from testosterone to estrogen and progesterone. But before I begin, there are two important points that must be made prior to any discussion regarding hormones. First, contrary to popular belief, hormones do not simply act like unilateral on/off switches controlling female/feminine or male/masculine development. All people have both androgens (which include testosterone) and estrogens in their systems, although the balance is tipped more toward the former in men and the latter in women. Not only are there different types of androgens and estrogens, but these hormones require different steroid receptors to function, are metabolized by numerous enzymes that can shift the balance by converting one hormone to another, and function by regulating the levels of scores of "downstream genes," which are more directly responsible for producing specific hormonal effects. Because of all these variables, there's an extensive amount of natural variation built into the way individual people experience and process specific hormones.

The second issue to keep in mind is the difficulty in distinguishing "real" hormone effects from their perceived or presumed effects. For example, shortly after I began hormone therapy, I had a strong craving for eggs. I immediately attributed this to the hormones until other trans women told me that they never had similar cravings. So perhaps that was an effect of the hormones only I had. Or maybe I was going through an "egg phase" that just so happened to coincide with the start of my hormone therapy. Hence, the problem: Not only can hormones affect individuals differently, but we sometimes attribute coincidences to them and project our own expectations onto them.

For these reasons, I will limit my discussion here to those hormonal changes I have experienced that have been corroborated by other trans women I have spoken with. Also, rather than get into the more physical effects of hormones (i.e., muscle/fat distribution, hair growth, etc.) which are not in dispute, I will focus primarily on the "psychological" changes—in my emotions, senses, and sexuality—that I experienced early on when I began taking estrogen along with an anti-androgen, which suppresses endogenous testosterone levels, to shift my hormonal balance into the range that most adult women experience.

People often say that female hormones make women "more emotional" than men, but in my view such claims are an oversimplification. How would I describe the changes I went through, then? In retrospect, when testosterone was the predominant sex hormone in my body, it was as though a thick curtain were draped over my emotions. It deadened their intensity, made all of my feelings pale and vague as if they were ghosts that would haunt me. But on estrogen, I find that I have all of the same emotions that I did back then, only now they come in crystal clear. In other words, it is not the actual emotions, but rather their intensity that has changed—the highs are way higher and the lows are way lower. Another way of saying it is that I feel my emotions more now; they are in the foreground rather than the background of my mind.

The anecdote that perhaps best captures this change occurred about two months after I started hormone therapy. My wife, Dani, and I had an argument and at one point I started to cry—something that was not all that uncommon for me when I was hormonally male. What was different was that after about a minute or so, I began to laugh while simultaneously continuing to cry. When Dani asked me why I was laughing, I replied, "I can't turn it off." Back when I was hormonally male, I felt as though I was always capable of stopping the cry, of holding it all in, if I really wanted to. Now, I find it nearly impossible to hold back the tears once I start crying. I've learned instead to just go with it, to let myself experience the cry, and it feels a lot more cathartic as a result.

In general, even though my emotions are much more intense these days, I certainly do not feel as though they get in the way of my logic or reasoning, or that they single-handedly control my every thought or decision. I remain perfectly capable of acting on rational thought rather than following my feelings. However, what I can no longer do (at least to the extent that I used to) is completely ignore my emotions, repress them, or entirely shut them out of my mind.

The change in the intensity of my emotions is paralleled in my sense of touch as well. I cannot say for sure that my sense of touch has improved—that I am able to feel things that I couldn't before—but it surely plays a greater role in how I experience the world. Whenever I am interested in something, whether it's a book, a piece of artwork, an article of clothing, or an object or material of any kind, I feel compelled to touch it, to handle it, as though my understanding of it would be incomplete without the tactile knowledge of how it physically feels to me. In contrast, when hormonally male, I generally felt satisfied with simply seeing an object of interest.

Unlike my emotions and sense of touch, which seem to have primarily increased in *intensity,* my sense of smell has definitely increased in *sensitivity*. That is to say, I now can smell things that I was previously unable to detect. Though it sounds like a cliché, during the first spring after my transition I was blown away by how flowers smelled to me. While I'd always found them very fragrant, I suddenly smelled all of these subtle notes and perfumes that I had never been aware of before. I also had similar experiences with the aroma of certain foods. Perhaps the most interesting facet of this change for me has been sensing new smells in people. I find that men now sometimes have a really strong, somewhat sweet smell to them that I had never been privy to before. But it is not simply that I have gained the ability to pick up on male odors or "pheromones," because I also now detect new smells with women. During my transition, I noticed that when I would kiss Dani or nuzzle my nose into her neck, it felt as though fireworks were going off in my brain. I was barraged with amazingly sweet, soothing, and sensual smells that not only sexually stimulated me, but also made me feel closer to her, as if I were connected to her in a way that I hadn't been before. Indeed, the increase in my senses of smell and touch, and the way I feel more "in touch" with my emotions, has led me to feel more in tune with the world, and with other people.

Without a doubt, the most profound change that has come with my hormonal transition has been in my sexuality. In fact, the very first change that I noticed—which came during my first few weeks on estrogen/anti-androgens—was a sharp decrease in my sex drive. I noticed this for the first time at the end of a really busy week, after working many hours and being out late most nights. It suddenly occurred to me, only after the fact, that I had neither had sex nor masturbated during the entire week. While this may not seem impressive to some readers, for me, at the time, it was completely unheard-of. I could barely go a day, let alone two days, without some form of release (in fact, for much of my adult male life, masturbating was an activity that I typically indulged in one to three times a day). While my sex drive may have decreased, this surely does not mean that I have lost interest in sex entirely. I still intensely enjoy masturbation and sex, it's just that I crave it about three to four times a week rather than one to three times a day.

While the quantity of my sexual experiences has decreased significantly, the quality of those experiences has increased exponentially. Indeed, I called this chapter "Boygasms and Girlgasms" because, for me, the differences in how my body responds to sexual stimuli—how I "get off," if you will—has been the most dramatic (and in many ways most enjoyable) hormonal change that I've experienced. I began to notice these changes within the first few weeks of starting hormone therapy. Even before I lost the ability to maintain erections, I found that what used to excite me—that back-and-forth stroking action that males typically prefer—really wasn't doing the trick anymore. I just felt like I needed something more. So I started experimenting with Dani's vibrators. When I had tried them in the past, they always felt like too much stimulation, but now they suddenly felt absolutely incredible. And back when I was hormonally male, sexual stimulation would cause me to climb rather rapidly toward the peak of orgasm; if I wanted the experience to last longer, I had to keep pulling back just before I hit that precipice. But now I found that I could go way beyond what used to be the point of orgasm, writhing for fifteen minutes in a sexual state that was far more intense than I had ever experienced before. Now, my orgasms are way more in the female rather than male range: They typically take longer to achieve (but are well worth the wait), each one has a different flavor and intensity, they are less centralized and more diffuse throughout my body, and they are often multiple.

Not surprisingly, changes in my senses have also greatly influenced my sexuality. Not only am I more sexually excited by the scent of my partner, but the increase in my tactile senses make my whole body feel alive—electric—during sex. Nowhere is this more obvious than in my nipples, which seem to have a direct connection to my groin. It also has become apparent to me that I am less visual with regard to my sexuality. I don't think that I recognized this at first, probably because it is harder to notice the gradual loss of a sensation than the appearance of a new one. I only realized it about a year later, when I began taking progesterone for ten days out of the month to simulate the endogenous expression of progesterone in most women. The first thing I noticed upon taking progesterone is that my sex drive, particularly in response to visual input, sharply increased. In fact, the visual effects of progesterone very much reminded me of how I responded to visual stimuli when I was hormonally male.

Upon hearing my experience, I am sure that some people—particularly those who favor social, rather than biological, explanations of gender difference—will be somewhat disappointed at the predictable nature of my transformation. Some may even assume that I am buying into female stereotypes when I describe myself becoming a more weepy, touchy-feely, flower-adoring, less sexually aggressive person. Not only are similar experiences regularly described by other trans women, but trans men typically give reciprocal accounts: They almost universally describe an increase in their sex drives (which become more responsive to visual inputs), male-type orgasms (more centralized, quicker to achieve), a decrease in their sense of smell, and more difficulty crying and discerning their emotions.[1]

On the other hand, those who are eager to have popular presumptions about hormones confirmed will probably be just as disappointed to hear what has *not* noticeably changed during my hormonal transition: my sexual orientation; the "types" of women I am attracted to; my tastes in music, movies, or hobbies; my politics; my sense of humor; my levels of aggression, competitiveness, nurturing, creativity, intelligence; and my ability to read maps or do math. While it would be irresponsible for me to say that these human traits are entirely hormone-independent (as it is possible that fetal hormones potentially play some role in predisposing us to such traits), they clearly are not controlled by adult hormone levels to the extent that many people argue or assume.

While transsexual accounts of hormones are largely in agreement with one another, I also find it illuminating to examine the more subtle differences between our individual experiences. For example, I have heard several trans men describe how they started to consume porn voraciously upon taking testosterone. While my sexuality was definitely more visual when I was hormonally male, and I certainly enjoyed looking at porn on occasion, I still always preferred erotic stories and fantasies to pictures of naked bodies. Similarly, I have heard some trans men say that they almost never cry since taking testosterone, whereas I used to cry somewhat often (although not nearly as often as I do now) when I was hormonally male. Some trans men have also described becoming more aggressive or competitive since taking testosterone (although many others describe themselves as becoming more calm).[2] However, when I was hormonally male, I typically found myself to be the least aggressive or competitive guy in any room that I entered. This is not to say that I was passive, as I have always been motivated and eager to succeed at any task I have taken on. Rather, I have never really felt any desire to have my success come at the expense of others.

Thus, it is clear that typical male levels of testosterone, in and of itself, are insufficient to produce many of these stereotypically male behaviors, most likely because of the variability that exists from person to person in the way this hormone is processed and experienced. While a part of me is tempted to attribute my apparent imperviousness to testosterone to the fact that I am trans—that on some level, I was never fully or completely male—I also realize that many cissexual people are exceptions in this regard as well. I know plenty of non-trans men who are not particularly into porn, who are not very aggressive, and/or who often cry. I have also met women who have high sex drives, who enjoy porn, and/or who are just as aggressive and competitive as the average alpha male. Thus, there seems to be more variation among women and among men than there is between the averages of these two groups.

Acknowledging this variation is absolutely crucial in order for us to finally move beyond overly simplistic (and binary) biology-versus-socialization debates regarding gender. After all, there are very real *biological* differences between hormones: Testosterone will probably make any given person cry less frequently and have a higher sex drive than estrogen will. However, if one were to argue that this biological difference represents an *essential* gender difference—one that holds true for all women and all men—they would be incorrect. After all, there are some men who cry more than certain women, and some women who have higher sex drives than certain men. Perhaps what is most telling is that, as a society, we regulate these hormonally influenced behaviors in a way that seems to exaggerate their natural effects. We actively discourage boys from crying, even though testosterone itself should reduce the chance of this happening. And we encourage men to act on their sex drives (by praising them as "studs") while discouraging women from doing the same (by dismissing them "sluts"), despite the fact that most women will end up having a lower sex drive than most men anyway.

While many gender theorists have focused their efforts on attempting to demonstrate that this sort of socialization *produces* gender differences, it seems to me more accurate to say that in many cases socialization acts to exaggerate biological gender differences that already exist. In other words, it coaxes those of us who are exceptional (e.g., men who cry often or women with high sex drives) to hide or curb those tendencies, rather than simply falling where we may on the spectrum of gender diversity. By attempting to play down or erase the existence of such exceptions, socialization distorts biological gender difference to create the impression that essential differences exist between women and men. Thus, the primary role of socialization is not to produce gender difference de novo, but to create the illusion that female and male are mutually exclusive, "opposite" sexes.

Recognizing the distinction between biological and essential gender differences has enormous ramifications for the future of gender activism. Since there is natural variation in our drives and the way we experience the world, attempts to minimize gender differences (i.e., insisting that people strive to be unisex or androgynous) are rather pointless; we should instead learn to embrace all forms of gender diversity, whether typical (feminine women and masculine men) or exceptional (masculine women and feminine men). Further, since some attributes that are considered feminine (e.g., being more in tune with one's emotions) or masculine (e.g., being preoccupied with sex) are clearly affected by our hormones, attempts by some gender theorists to frame femininity and masculinity as being entirely artificial or performative seem misplaced. Rather than focus on how femininity and masculinity are produced (an issue that has unfortunately dominated the field of gender studies of late), we should instead turn our attention to the ways these gender traits are interpreted.

The issue of interpretation becomes obvious when considering transsexuals. For example, one cannot help but notice how much more empowering trans male descriptions of hormonal transition tend to sound compared to those of trans women. Trans men experience an increase in their sex drive, become less emotional, and their bodies become harder and stronger—all of these changes having positive connotations in our society. In contrast, I have experienced a decrease in my sex drive and become more emotional, softer, and weaker—all traits that are viewed negatively. The reason for these differing connotations is obvious: In our culture, femininity and femaleness are not appreciated nor valued to the extent that masculinity and maleness are. And while embracing my own femaleness and femininity during my transition was personally empowering and rewarding, I nevertheless felt overwhelmed by all of the negative connotations and inferior meanings that other people began to project onto me. These meanings were not only projected onto my female body, but onto the hormones themselves: from the warning label on my progesterone prescription that read, "May cause drowsiness or dizziness" and "Avoid operating heavy machinery," to the men who have hinted that my female hormones were responsible for the fact that I disagreed with their opinion, and the women who sneered, "Why would you ever want to do that?" upon finding out that I have chosen to cycle my hormones.

Once we start thinking about gender as being socially exaggerated (rather than socially constructed), we can finally tackle the issue of sexism in our society without having to dismiss or undermine biological sex in the process. While biological gender differences are very real, most of the connotations, values, and assumptions we associate with female and male biology are not.

5

Blind Spots: On Subconscious Sex and Gender Entitlement

One of the most frustrating aspects about being a transsexual is that I'm frequently asked to explain to other people why I decided to transition. Why did I feel it was necessary to physically change my body? How could I possibly know that I'd be happier as a woman when I had only ever experienced being male? If I don't believe that women and men are "opposite" sexes, then why change my sex at all? Unfortunately, while these are among the most common questions people ask, they are also the ones to which people are the least open to hearing my answer. After having fielded these sorts of questions from my friends and family, at high school and college classes where I've been invited to speak, and from fellow queers and feminists with whom I've shared discussions about gender, I have come to the conclusion that most cissexuals have a particular blind spot at the source of their seemingly endless curiosity (and often doubt) about how someone who is born into a certain physical sex can come to know themselves as a member of the other sex. This blind spot has to do with what has been commonly called *gender identity*.

Personally, I have always found the term "gender identity" to be rather misleading. After all, identifying as something, whether it be as a woman, a Democrat, a Christian, a feminist, a cat person, or a metalhead, seems to be a conscious, deliberate choice on our part, one that we make in order to better describe how we think we fit into the world. Thus, with regard to transsexuals, the phrase "gender identity" is problematic because it seems to describe two potentially different things: the gender we consciously choose to identify as, and the gender we subconsciously feel ourselves to be. To make things clearer, I will refer to the latter as *subconscious sex*.

The main reason I make this distinction between gender identity and subconscious sex is that it best explains my own personal experiences. I did not have the quintessential trans experience of always feeling that I should have been female. For me, this recognition came about more gradually. The first memories I have of being trans took place early in my elementary school years, when I was around five or six. By this time, I was already consciously aware of the fact that I was physically male and that other people thought of me as a boy. During this time, I experienced numerous manifestations of my female subconscious sex: I had dreams in which adults would tell me I was a girl; I would draw pictures of little boys with needles going into their penises, imagining that the medicine in the syringe would make that organ disappear; I had an unexplainable feeling that I was doing something wrong every time I walked into the boys' restroom at school; and whenever our class split into groups of boys and girls, I always had a sneaking suspicion that at any moment someone might tap me on the shoulder and say, "Hey, what are you doing here? You're not a boy."

I wasn't sure what to make of these feelings at the time. After all, I was obviously a boy—everybody thought so. And unlike other MTF spectrum children, I never really wanted to take part in girlish activities, such as playing house. Being that, like most elementary school children, my understanding of "girl" and "boy" was largely based on gender preferences in toys, activities, and interests, it wasn't clear to me how to reconcile my vague, subconscious feelings with my passion for dinosaurs and my desire to be a major league baseball player when I grew up.

It wasn't until the age of eleven that I consciously recognized these subconscious feelings as an urge or desire to be female. The first incident that led to this discovery happened late one night, after engaging in a losing battle with insomnia. I found myself inexplicably compelled to remove a set of white, lacy curtains from the window and wrap them around my body like a dress. I walked toward the mirror. Since I was a prepubescent boy with one of those longish boy haircuts that were popular in the late '70s, the curtains alone were sufficient to complete my transformation: I looked like a girl. I stared at my reflection for over an hour, stunned. It felt like an epiphany because, for some unexplainable reason, seeing myself as a girl made absolutely perfect sense to me.

The second discovery happened shortly thereafter. Every day after school, I used to play by myself in my bedroom, making up little adventure stories that I would act out. For a while (most likely inspired by my mirror epiphany), the adventures I created had a plot twist where my imaginary nemesis would turn me into a girl and I would spend the rest of the story trying to find him so that he could turn me back into a boy. After a while, I got bored with that last part of the story, so I would simply continue throughout the rest of the adventure as a girl. I did this for a couple weeks before I realized that the "being a girl" part of the story was much more than just play. It became obvious to me that I actually wanted to be a girl and that, on some level, it felt right.

Trying to translate these subconscious experiences into conscious thought is a messy business. All of the words available in the English language completely fail to accurately capture or convey my personal understanding of these events. For example, if I were to say that I "saw" myself as female, or "knew" myself to be a girl, I would be denying the fact that I was consciously aware of my physical maleness at all times. And saying that I "wished" or "wanted" to be a girl erases how much being female made sense to me, how it felt right on the deepest, most profound level of my being. I could say that I "felt" like a girl, but that would give the false impression that I knew how other girls (and other boys) felt. And if I were to say that I was "supposed to be" a girl, or that I "should have been born" female, it would imply that I had some sort of cosmic insight into the grand scheme of the universe, which I most certainly did not.

Perhaps the best way to describe how my subconscious sex feels to me is to say that it seems as if, on some level, my brain expects my body to be female. Indeed, there is some evidence to suggest that our brains have an intrinsic understanding of what sex our bodies should be.[1] For example, there have been numerous instances in which male infants have been surgically reassigned as female shortly after birth due to botched circumcisions or cloacal exstrophy (a non-intersex medical condition). Despite being raised female and appearing to have female genitals, the majority of such children eventually come to identify as male, demonstrating that brain sex may override both socialization and genital sex.[2] There have also been studies that have examined a small, sexually dimorphic region of the brain known as the BSTc. Researchers found that the structure of the BSTc region in trans women more closely resembles that of most women, while in trans men it resembles that of most men.[3] Like all brain research, such studies have certain limitations and caveats, but they do suggest that our brains may be hardwired to expect our bodies to be female or male, independent of our socialization or the appearance of our bodies.

Personally, I am drawn to the brain-hardwiring hypothesis, not because I believe that it has been proven scientifically beyond a doubt, but because it best explains why the thoughts I have had of being female always felt vague and ever-present, like they were an unconscious knowing that always seemed to defy conscious reality. It would also account for how I knew there was something wrong with me being a boy before I ever could consciously put it into words; why I had dreams about being or becoming a girl well before I experienced any conscious desire to be female or feminine; why my first experiences masturbating as a teen (which happened before I had ever seen or heard anything about what happens when people have sex) involved me spreading my legs, placing my hand on my crotch, and rocking my hand back and forth the way many girls instinctively do it.

The brain-hardwiring hypothesis can also account for why thinking of myself as female has always been beyond my conscious reach, why I was unable to repress it or rationalize it away no matter how hard I tried. A lot of people assume that trans people have an addict-like obsession with being the other sex: The more we think about it, the more we want it or convince ourselves into believing it to be true. I have found that being trans is quite the opposite: The more I tried to ignore the thoughts of being female, the more persistently they pushed their way back into the forefront of my mind. In that way, they felt more like other subconscious feelings, such as hunger or thirst, where neglecting the urge only makes the feeling more intense with time.

I am sure that some people will object to me referring to this aspect of my person as a subconscious "sex" rather than "gender." I prefer "sex" because I have experienced it as being rather exclusively about my physical sex, and because for me this subconscious desire to be female has existed independently of the social phenomena commonly associated with the word "gender." As mentioned previously, my initial experience with my female subconscious sex was not accompanied by any corresponding desire to explore female gender roles or to express femininity. Nor was it the result of me trying to "fit in" to societal gender norms because, by all accounts, I was considered to be a fairly normal-acting young boy at the time. And my female subconscious sex was most certainly not the result of socialization or social gender constructs, as it defied everything I had been taught was true about gender, as well as the constant encouragement I received to think of myself as a boy and to act masculine.

Although I believe that my female subconscious sex originated within me (i.e., that it is an intrinsic part of my person), things were inevitably complicated once my conscious mind began processing these feelings, coming up against the reality of not only my physical maleness, but the fact that I had to function in a world where everybody else related to me as male. This intersection of subconscious and conscious sex is what I prefer to think of as gender identity.

When one's subconscious and conscious sexes match, as they do for cissexuals, an appropriate gender identity may emerge rather seamlessly. For me, the tension I felt between these two disparate understandings of myself was wholly jarring. Even as a youngster, I realized that there were really only three ways to potentially resolve the problem: I could suppress my subconscious sex (which I tried to do, but was never fully successful), accept my subconscious sex as my conscious sex (which would entail not only denying my physical maleness, but announcing to my family and friends that I was a girl—an action that I knew would be both dangerous and devastating for everyone involved), or learn to manage the difference between my conscious and subconscious sexes, finding novel ways of relating to my gender that would allow me to straddle both maleness and femaleness to certain extents.

While I have found my subconscious sex to be impervious to conscious thought or social influence, my gender identity (i.e., the way I consciously relate to my gender) has been very much shaped by cultural norms and my own personal beliefs and experiences. For example, even though my initial realization of wanting to be female occurred prior to me experiencing sexual attraction and independent of any desire to take part in stereotypically girlish activities and interests, that realization led me to question (and eventually experiment with) my sexuality and gender expression. After all, like most children, I was raised to believe that men were supposed to be masculine and attracted to women, and that women were supposed to be feminine and attracted to men. The fact that I wanted to be female necessarily threw these other gender-related facets into flux. In fact, the first thought that crossed my mind when I discovered that I wanted to be female was that I must be gay, an idea no doubt inspired by flamboyantly feminine gay male stereotypes that regularly appeared on TV in the '70s. However, once I hit puberty and my sexual desire kicked in, I found myself attracted to women and not men, which only served to confuse me more, since at the time I hadn't even heard the word "lesbian."

As time went on, I latched onto all sorts of other gender identities and theories that seemed to hold potential explanations for my subconscious feelings. For quite a while, I thought of myself as a crossdresser and viewed my female subconscious sex as a "feminine side" that was trying to get out. But after years of crossdressing, I eventually lost interest in it, realizing that my desire to be female had nothing to do with clothing or femininity per se. There was also a period of time when I embraced the word "pervert" and viewed my desire to be female as some sort of sexual kink. But after exploring that path, it became obvious that explanation could not account for the vast majority of instances when I thought about being female in a nonsexual context. And after reading Kate Bornstein's and Leslie Feinberg's writings for the first time, I embraced the words "transgender" and "queer." I began to think of myself as bigender, viewing my female subconscious sex as being just as legitimate as my physical maleness. In the years just prior to my transition, I started to express my femaleness as much as possible within the context of having a male body; I became a very androgynous queer boy in the eyes of the world. While it felt relieving to simply be myself, not to care about what other people thought of me, I still found myself grappling with a constant, compelling subconscious knowledge that I should be female rather than male. After twenty years of exploration and experimentation, I eventually reached the conclusion that my female subconscious sex had nothing to do with gender roles, femininity, or sexual expression—it was about the personal relationship I had with my own body.

For me, the hardest part about being trans has not been the discrimination or ridicule that I have faced for defying societal gender norms, but rather the internal pain I experienced when my subconscious and conscious sexes were at odds with one another. I think this is best captured by the psychological term "cognitive dissonance," which describes the mental tension and stress that occur in a person's mind when they find themselves holding two contradictory thoughts or views simultaneously—in this case, subconsciously seeing myself as female while consciously dealing with the fact that I was male. This gender dissonance can manifest itself in a number of ways. Sometimes it felt like stress or anxiousness, which led to marathon battles with insomnia. Other times, it surfaced as jealousy or anger at other people who seemed to enjoy taking their gender for granted. But most of all, it felt like sadness to me—a sort of gender sadness—a chronic and persistent grief over the fact that I felt so wrong in my body.

Sometimes people discount the fact that trans people feel any actual pain related to their gender. Of course, it is easy for them to dismiss gender dissonance: It's invisible and (perhaps more relevantly) they themselves are unable to relate to it. These same people, however, do understand that being stuck in a bad relationship or in an unfulfilling job can make a person miserable and lead to a depression so intense that it spills over into all other areas of that person's life. These types of pain can be tolerated temporarily, but in the long run, if things do not change, that stress and sadness can ruin a person. Well, if that much despair can be generated by a forty-hour-a-week job, then just imagine how despondent and distressed one might become if one was forced to live in a gender that felt wrong for twenty-four hours a day, seven days a week.

Unlike most forms of sadness that I've experienced, which inevitably ease with time, my gender dissonance only got worse with each passing day. And by the time I made the decision to transition, my gender dissonance had gotten so bad that it completely consumed me; it hurt more than any pain, physical or emotional, that I had ever experienced. I know that most people believe that transsexuals transition because we want to be the other sex, but that is an oversimplification. After all, I wanted to be female almost my whole life, but I was far too terrified of the label "transsexual," or of having potential regrets, to seriously consider transitioning. What changed during that twenty-some-year period was not my desire to be female, but rather my ability to cope with being male, to cope with my own gender dissonance. When I made the decision to transition, I honestly had no idea what it would be like for me to live as female. The only thing I knew for sure was that pretending to be male was slowly killing me.

Transsexuals will often say that they can never know for sure whether they should physically transition until they begin taking hormones—if they find that they like the changes in their body and the way they feel, then it was the right decision; if not, then it was the wrong one. While not a particularly helpful bit of advice, it is consistent with my own personal experience. I honestly was not 100 percent sure that transitioning would ease my gender dissonance until after my first few weeks of being on female hormones. The way they made me feel, and the subsequent changes they brought about in my body, just felt . . . *right*. There is really no other word to describe it.

It is typical for cissexuals to assume that trans people transition in order to obtain gender-related privileges of some sort. Such assumptions are undermined by the fact that post-transition transsexuals may end up being either female or male; being bisexual, homosexual, or heterosexual; or appearing gender-normative or gender-nonconforming. In my case, I went from being a straight man to a lesbian woman in the eyes of the world. And while I have lost the significant benefits of male and heterosexual privilege, I still consider my transition to be well worth it. Because for the first time in my life, I now regularly experience what I consider to be the most important gender privilege of all: feeling at home in my own sexed body. Rather than living with gender dissonance, I now experience gender concordance.

Many cissexual people seem to have a hard time accepting the idea that they too have a subconscious sex—a deep-rooted understanding of what sex their bodies should be. I suppose that when a person feels right in the sex they were born into, they are never forced to locate or question their subconscious sex, to differentiate it from their physical sex. In other words, their subconscious sex exists, but it is hidden from their view. They have a blind spot.

I do believe that it is possible for cissexuals to catch a glimpse of their subconscious sex. When I do presentations on trans issues, I try to accomplish this by asking the audience a question: "If I offered you ten million dollars under the condition that you live as the other sex for the rest of your life, would you take me up on the offer?" While there is often some wiseass in the audience who will say "Yes," the vast majority of people shake their heads to indicate "No." Their responses clearly have nothing to do with gender privileges, because both women and men, queers and straights insist that they wouldn't be willing to make that change. When I ask individuals why they answered no, they usually get a bit flustered at first, as if they are at a loss for words. Eventually, they end up saying something like, "Because I just *am* a woman (or man)," or, "It just wouldn't be *right*."

Let's face it: If cissexuals didn't have a subconscious sex, then sex reassignment would be far more common than it is. Women who wanted to succeed in the male-dominated business world would simply transition to male. Lesbians and gay men who were ashamed of their queerness would simply transition to the other sex. Gender studies grad students would transition for a few years to gather data for their theses. Actors playing transsexuals would go on hormones for a few months in order to make their portrayals more authentic. Criminals and spies would physically transition as a way of going undercover. And contestants on reality shows would be willing to change their sex in the hope of achieving fifteen minutes of fame.

Of course, such scenarios seem absolutely ridiculous to us. They are unfathomable because, on a profound, subconscious level, we all understand that our physical sex is far more than a superficial shell we inhabit. For me, this is the most frustrating part about cissexuals who express confusion or disbelief as to why transsexuals choose to transition. They are unable to see that their disbelief stems directly from their own experience of feeling at home in the sex they were born into, their own gender concordance. In other words, it is their own subconscious sex—and their inability to recognize it—that makes it difficult for them to understand why anyone would want to change their sex.

All of this reminds me of when I was growing up in the '70s and early '80s, when most straight people had a similar blind spot regarding sexual orientation. People often expressed an inability to fathom how someone could be attracted to the same sex. They said ridiculous things like, "It's just not natural," "It must be a phase," and "I just don't understand it." They actually had the nerve (or naiveté) to ask queer people, "But how do you know that you're really gay?" without ever thinking to ask themselves the reciprocal question: "How do I know that I'm really straight?"

Perhaps the most important conceptual change that has facilitated the gradual acceptance of LGB folks over the last twenty-five years is that straight people are no longer able to take their attraction to the other sex completely for granted, to assume that it is the one "natural" form of sexuality. They now recognize that, like queer people, they have a sexual orientation too—they are heterosexual. Similarly, I do not believe that trans people will be fully accepted in this society until cissexual people recognize that they also have a subconscious sex and that, if they are not battling a constant barrage of subconscious thoughts about being the other sex, then their subconscious sex most likely matches their physical one.

Recognizing our own blind spots—our inability to fully comprehend gender and sexual inclinations that we have not experienced firsthand—is an important first step toward eliminating all of the *gender entitlement* that exists in the world. Unlike gender dissonance, which is only experienced by trans people, gender entitlement can affect anyone. It is best described as the arrogant conviction that one's own beliefs, perceptions, and assumptions regarding gender and sexuality are more valid than those of other people. Gender entitlement often leads to *gender anxiety*, the act of becoming irrationally upset by or being made uncomfortable by the existence of those people who challenge or bring into question one's gender entitlement.

There are many different (but often overlapping) forms of gender entitlement and gender anxiety. For example, one of the most frequently discussed forms of gender entitlement is heterosexism, the belief that heterosexuality is the only "natural," legitimate, or morally acceptable form of sexual desire. Heterosexist gender entitlement can lead to homophobia, which is an expression of gender anxiety directed against those people who engage in same-sex relationships. Similarly, the gender-entitled belief that all women are (or should be) feminine and men masculine—which some have called *cisgenderism*—gives rise to transphobia, a gender anxiety that is directed against people who fall outside of those norms. While homophobia and transphobia have both received mainstream attention, thinking in terms of gender entitlement and gender anxiety also allows us to consider less well-known (but just as disparaging) forms of gender and sexual discrimination. For example, many gays and lesbians who believe that all people are "naturally" either homosexual or heterosexual often express biphobia, a gender anxiety directed toward bisexual people because they challenge the presumption that people can only be attracted to one sex or the other. I have also met some people in the transgender community who feel that identifying outside of the male/female binary is superior to, or more enlightened than, identifying within it. Such people often express gender anxiety (binary-phobia?) at people who identify strongly as either female or male.

What should be obvious by now is that all forms of gender entitlement and gender anxiety are, at their core, expressions of insecurity. After all, people who are truly comfortable with their own desires and expressions of gender and sexuality do not have any need to be bothered or concerned by dissimilar expressions and desires in others. However, when we indulge in our own insecurities and resort to gender entitlement, we not only deny the variation that exists in human gender and sexuality, but we arrogantly presume that other people should curb or conform *their* inclinations and desires in order to meet *our* expectations.

The most productive way that we as individuals can overcome our gender entitlement is by coming to terms with our own blind spots, acknowledging that there are certain gender and sexual expressions and desires that we cannot know, that we will never experience firsthand. Thus, the path toward overcoming homophobia or biphobia is to become more in touch with our own sexual orientations, to recognize that other people's sexual orientations have no bearing on our own. The transgender movement has taken a similar approach to confronting transphobia, by encouraging cisgender people to become comfortable with their own expressions of femininity and/or masculinity in order to be respectful of those expressions in others. This approach has most certainly benefited many transsexuals, as it has helped convince some of the public that we should be allowed to express our genders without being discriminated against. Unfortunately, confronting transphobia has done very little to ease cissexism, i.e., the belief that transsexual genders are less "real" or legitimate that cissexual genders. For me, this is most evident when I interact with people who accept my feminine behavior and female identity but adamantly draw the line when it comes to accepting my transsexual body.

Because most people have not come to terms with their own subconscious sex and its relation to their physical sex, they tend to experience unwarranted distress regarding sex/gender-variant bodies. Many people who say they favor transgender rights tend to balk when it means that they have to share a locker room or public shower with a transsexual. And plenty of people are supportive of their transgender friends and colleagues, but, hypocritically, would be disturbed if the person they were dating, sleeping with, or partnered to were to come out to them as transsexual. It is high time for gender-anxious cissexuals to look deep within themselves and ask why they *choose* to view transsexual bodies as unsettling or disturbing. How can they consider a physical body to be attractive or innocuous when it is assumed to be cissexual, then suddenly find it to be horrific or threatening upon the discovery that it is transsexual? And if such dramatically different responses can be elicited by the same human being under different circumstances, doesn't that indicate that the real difference resides in the cissexual mind and not in the transsexual body?

Once again, I am reminded of the 1980s, when it was popular for people in the earliest stages of accepting homosexuality to say, "I don't care what other people do in the privacy their own bedrooms, just as long as they don't flaunt it in front of me." Today, it is obvious to most of us that such remarks are merely prejudice disguising itself as tolerance. Similarly, it is time for gender-anxious cissexuals to start coming to terms with their own thinly veiled cissexism, to ask themselves why they feel entitled to "flaunt" their cissexual bodies (e.g., to shamelessly talk about their femaleness or maleness, their body parts and their functions) or to take certain gendered rights for granted (e.g., using public restrooms, freely sharing their bodies with lovers without having to confess, come out, or explain anything) while simultaneously insisting that transsexual bodies remain hidden from their view or be held to different standards. Gender-anxious cissexuals must begin to admit that the issues they have with our transsexual bodies stem directly from their own insecurities, from their fear of having their own genders and sexualities be brought into question. So long as most cissexuals refuse to come to terms with their own blind spots—specifically their own subconscious sex—the countless subtle and not-so-subtle ways in which they objectify trans people and treat us as second-class citizens will remain forever out of their view.

6

Intrinsic Inclinations: Explaining Gender and Sexual Diversity

IN THE LAST CHAPTER, I stated that recognizing subconscious sex as separate from physical sex is crucial to furthering a better understanding of transsexuality and anti-trans discrimination. There is at least one other aspect of gender that we must come to terms with before we can discuss the entire spectrum of gender and sexual diversity: *gender expression,* which refers to whether our presentation, behaviors, interests, and/or affinities are considered feminine, masculine, or some combination thereof.[1]

Gender expression is regularly confused with subconscious sex and/or sexual orientation. For example, people often assume that transsexuals transition not to align our physical and subconscious sexes, but because we want to express either femininity or masculinity. Similarly, it is common for some people to be mistaken for being lesbian or gay simply because they are somewhat masculine as women go or feminine as men go, respectively. Unlike our sexual orientation and subconscious sex, which are usually invisible to the rest of the world, other people can readily view our gender expression, making it perhaps the most widely commented on, critiqued, and regulated aspect of gender.

Indeed, the fact that gender expression is so highly regulated in our society has led many to argue that femininity and masculinity are merely social constructs (i.e., they do not occur naturally, but rather are inventions or artifacts of human culture). According to this social constructionist model, boys are socialized to become masculine and girls feminine; we learn to produce these gender expressions via a combination of positive and negative reinforcement, and through imitation, practice, and performance. Social constructionists point to the fact that the words "femininity" and "masculinity" do not merely describe human behavior, but represent ideals that all people are encouraged to meet. To demonstrate this, they focus much of their attention on socially influenced manifestations of gender expression (often called *gender roles*), which include feminine and masculine differences in speech patterns and word choice, mannerisms, roles in relationships, styles of dress, aesthetic preferences, interests, occupations, and so on. Social constructionists also argue that the fact that these gender roles can vary over time, and from culture to culture, is indicative of their constructed nature.

On the other side of this debate are gender essentialists, who believe that those born male are simply preprogrammed to act masculine, and those born female are preprogrammed to act feminine. Evidence to support their case includes the predominance of femininity in women and masculinity in men, in our culture and other cultures; the fact that girls tend to behave in a girlish manner and boys in a boyish manner from a very early age; that even in prehistoric humans, women and men seemed to perform different sets of tasks; and that species other than humans also show signs of gender dimorphic behavior. Among gender essentialists, it's generally assumed that genetic (and subsequent anatomical and hormonal) differences between females and males are the ultimate source for these behavioral differences. Despite their insistence, such direct links between specific genes and specific gendered behaviors in humans continue to remain elusive.

As someone who both is a geneticist and has experienced firsthand the very different ways in which women and men are treated and valued in our society, I believe that both social constructionists and gender essentialists are wrong (or at least they are both only partially right). The fatal flaw of the gender essentialist argument is the obvious fact that not all men are masculine and not all women are feminine. There are *exceptional* gender expressions: There are masculine women, feminine men, and people of both sexes who express combinations of femininity and masculinity. People who have exceptional gender expressions (like those with exceptional subconscious sexes and sexual orientations) exist in virtually all cultures and throughout history, which suggests that they represent a natural phenomenon. Gender essentialists often try to dismiss such exceptions as anomalies, the result of biological errors or developmental defects. However, exceptional gender expressions, subconscious sexes, and sexual orientations all occur at frequencies that are several orders of magnitude higher than one would expect if they represented genetic "mistakes."[2] Further, the fact that we actively encourage boys to be masculine, and ostracize and ridicule them if they act feminine (and vice versa for girls), strongly suggests that were it not for socialization, there would be even more exceptional gender expression than there is now.

Unfortunately, a strict social constructionist model does not easily account for exceptional gender expression either. Many girls who are masculine and boys who are feminine show signs of such behavior at a very early age (often before such children have been fully socialized with regard to gender norms), and generally continue to express such behavior into adulthood (despite the extreme amount of societal pressure that we place on individuals to reproduce gender expression appropriate for their assigned sex). This strongly suggests that certain expressions of femininity and masculinity represent deep, subconscious inclinations in a manner similar to those of sexual orientation and subconscious sex. (I use the word "inclination" here as a catchall phrase to describe any persistent desire, affinity, or urge that predisposes us toward particular gender and sexual expressions and experiences.) While I believe that such inclinations are likely to be hardwired into our brains (as they exist on a subconscious level and often remain constant throughout our lives), I hesitate to define them as purely biological phenomena, as social factors clearly play a strong role in how each individual interprets these inclinations. In fact, in most cases it is impossible to distinguish our inclinations from our socialization, since they both typically point us in the same direction. Generally, we only ever notice our inclinations when they are exceptional—when they deviate from both biological and social norms.

Further evidence that gender inclinations represent naturally occurring phenomena can be found in other species. If one looks across a wide spectrum of mammals and birds (whose gender and sexual expressions are presumably not shaped by social constructs to the extent that ours are), one generally finds certain behaviors and affinities that seem to predominate in one sex, but which also occur at lower but substantial frequencies in the other sex as well.[3] Thus, any model that attempts to explain human gender expression, sexual orientation, and subconscious sex must take into account the fact that both typical and exceptional forms of these inclinations occur naturally (i.e., without social influence) to varying degrees.

In order to reconcile this issue, I would like to put forward what I call an *intrinsic inclination* model to explain human gender and sexual variation. Here are the basic tenets of this model:

1 Subconscious sex, gender expression, and sexual orientation represent separate gender inclinations that are determined largely independently of one another. (This model does not preclude the possibility that these three inclinations may themselves be composed of multiple, separable inclinations, or that additional gender inclinations may exist as well.)

2 These gender inclinations are, to some extent, intrinsic to our persons, as they occur on a deep, subconscious level and generally remain intact despite social influences and conscious attempts by individuals to purge, repress, or ignore them.

3 Because no single genetic, anatomical, hormonal, environmental, or psychological factor has ever been found to directly cause any of these gender inclinations, we can assume that they are quantitative traits (i.e., multiple factors determine them through complex interactions). As a result, rather than producing discrete classes (such as feminine and masculine; attraction to women or men), each inclination shows a continuous range of possible outcomes.

4 Each of these inclinations roughly correlates with physical sex, resulting in a bimodal distribution pattern (i.e., two

> overlapping bell curves) similar to that seen for other gender differences, such as height.[4] While it may be true that, on average, men are taller than women, such a statement becomes virtually meaningless when one examines individual people, as any given woman may be taller than any given man. Most people have heights that are relatively close to the average, but others fall in outlying areas of the range (for instance, some women are 6 feet 2 inches and some men are 5 feet 4 inches). Similarly, while women on average are more feminine than men, some women are more masculine than certain men, and some men more feminine than certain women.

Because these inclinations appear to have multiple inputs and show a continuous range of outcomes, it is incorrect to assume that those with exceptional sexual orientations, subconscious sexes, or gender expressions represent developmental, biological, or environmental "errors"; rather, they are naturally occurring examples of human variation.

Reconciling Intrinsic Inclinations with Social Constructs

The beauty of the intrinsic inclinations model is that it simultaneously explains why most people appear to have typical genders (e.g., most men come to identify as male, act masculine, and are attracted to women, and the inverse for women) and accounts for the vast diversity of gender and sexuality that exists in the world. It explains why gay men and lesbians may be butch or femme or androgynous; why masculine girls can grow up to be lesbians, trans men, or heterosexual women; and why trans women can be bisexual, straight, or lesbian.

In addition to the variation that exists within these three gender inclinations, there is additional diversity with regard to physical sex itself. Physical sex can be further divided into multiple, separable characteristics: chromosomal sex (XX and XY), gonadal sex (ovaries and testes), genital sex (clitoris, vagina, and penis), hormonal sex (estrogens and androgens), and a host of secondary sex characteristics (such as breast growth in women, beard growth in men, etc.). While we like to think of females and males as constituting discrete, mutually exclusive classes, about two in one hundred people are born intersex.[5]

So there is a vast amount of naturally occurring sexual and gender variation in the world. The question becomes: How do we make sense of it all? That's where social constructs come in. While variation in our sex characteristics and gender inclinations may occur naturally, the way we interpret those traits, and the identities and meanings we associate with them, can vary significantly from culture to culture. In our society, what it means to be a woman or a man—the symbols, customs, expectations, restrictions, and privileges associated with those classes—are very different today than they were fifty years ago. This holds true for both typical and exceptional gender inclinations. For example, in this time and place I am able to identify as a woman, a dyke, a transsexual, and a transgender person—to me, each of these identities represents a slightly different (but somewhat overlapping) aspect of my gender and sexuality. However, had I been born a half century earlier—before most of these labels were commonly used or even existed—it would be impossible for me to identify the way that I do now. Perhaps my female subconscious sex would have led me to try "passing" and living as a woman, as trans people often did before medical means of transitioning became widely available. Or perhaps I would have taken part in the homosexual underground of the time, which was an amalgamation of people who would probably be considered lesbian, gay, bisexual, and transgender today. Or maybe, unaware of the existence of any other gender-variant people, I might have remained closeted for lack of any obvious alternative.

Further, had I been born in some other country, I might have developed a very different transgender identity. Examples of MTF spectrum transgender people in other cultures include Indian hijras, Brazilian transvestis, Thai katoeys, and Native American "berdaches," or "two-spirit" people.[6] These transgender identities differ not only in name but in their customs, practices, and social roles. Part of the reason these groups differ relates to the fact that their cultures place more emphasis on certain gender inclinations over others. In some cultures, a person's gender expression plays a larger role in determining gender than we experience in the United States. Other cultures seem to place more emphasis on whether the person in question engages in sexual relationships with women or men. In our culture, we divide people into two groups—females and males—almost exclusively based on their physical sex. Of course, many physical sex characteristics are not readily visible to us, so it is more correct to say that we tend to rely exclusively on genital sex when assigning a person's sex at birth; with children, we rely on gender expression and roles; with adults, we rely primarily on secondary sex characteristics.

The fact that we perceive two major categories of gender enables us to view women and men as "opposites"—a premise that is founded on a series of egregiously incorrect assumptions. First, in order for the two sexes to be "opposites," they must first be mutually exclusive. Therefore, on a societal level, we purposefully ignore the variation that exists in sex characteristics and create the illusion that there is absolutely no overlap between the physical sexes. Second, we ignore the reality that intrinsic inclinations produce a continuous range of possibilities, and instead assume that each inclination produces only one of two possible outcomes, mirroring the two sexes. Thus, we assume that people can only be attracted to women or men (not both), they can only be feminine or masculine (not both), and they can only identify as female or male (not both). The third assumption we make is to presume that the typical inclination for each sex holds true for all people of that sex. Thus, all female-bodied people are assumed to be feminine, to be attracted to men, and to identify as female (and vice versa for male-bodied people).

The very idea that there are "opposite" sexes unnecessarily polarizes women and men; it isolates us from one another and exaggerates our differences. It provides the framework for us to project other "opposite" pairs onto female and male (and femininity and masculinity). Thus, we assume that men are aggressive and women are passive; men are tough and women are weak; men are practical and women are emotional; men are big and women are small; and so on. As a culture, we regularly buy into this way of thinking despite the fact that we all encounter countless exceptions that prove these assumptions incorrect: women who are aggressive, tough, practical, and/or big, and men who are passive, weak, emotional, and/or small. This idea of "opposites" creates expectations for femaleness/femininity and maleness/masculinity that all people are encouraged to meet, and simultaneously delegitimizes all behaviors that do not fit these ideals. For example, people regularly make comments about women who are aggressive, while male acts of aggression are rarely commented on (as aggression is built into our preconception of maleness and masculinity). Similarly, people often make a big deal over men who cry in public, but not over women who do the same (as expressing emotion is built into our presumptions of femininity and femaleness). Sometimes these exceptional behaviors are further dismissed as illegitimate and unnatural through the use of gender-specific insults (e.g., an aggressive woman might be called a "bitch"; an emotional man might be called a "wimp" or a "sissy").

Many opponents of this view of gender refer to it as the *binary gender system,* which implies that its problematic nature stems primarily from the fact that it consists of only two classes: male and female. Personally, I do not think that there is necessarily any harm in us recognizing that there are two major categories of sex, so long as we realize that these categories are neither discrete nor mutually exclusive, and that we remain respectful of the fact that many people have exceptional sex characteristics and gender inclinations. In fact, as a trans person, having spent most of my life battling gender dissonance, I don't have the privilege that others have of being able to presume that the femaleness or maleness of my body or mind is entirely meaningless, superficial, or unimportant. I have found that my physical sex, and how it relates to my subconscious sex, is incommensurably important to me.

I would argue that the major problem with the binary gender system is not that it is binary (as most physical sex characteristics and gender inclinations appear to be bimodal in nature) but rather that it facilitates the naive and oppressive belief that women and men are "opposites." Because the idea that women and men are "opposite" sexes automatically creates assumptions and stereotypes that are differently applied to each sex, I call this view of gender *oppositional sexism.*

Not only does oppositional sexism form the framework that fosters the entrenchment of *traditional sexism* (the idea that maleness and masculinity are superior to femaleness and femininity), it marginalizes those of us who have exceptional sexual and gender traits. It accomplishes this, in part, by invalidating our natural gender inclinations and sex characteristics: A gay man's attraction to men is not seen to be as legitimate as that of a heterosexual woman; a trans man's male identity is not seen to be as valid as that of a cissexual man; a male-bodied transgender person's femininity is not seen to be as authentic as a cisgender woman's; and intersex bodies are not considered to be as natural as non-intersex female and male bodies.

Oppositional sexism delegitimizes exceptional gender and sexual traits, and can also create hostility and fear toward those who display them. For example, the fact that I am a lesbian or a transsexual really shouldn't have any bearing on anyone else's gender or sexuality (after all, gender inclinations are not contagious). However, people who have not given any critical thought to their own sexual orientation, subconscious sex, and/or gender expression—and who therefore derive their own identities from oppositional assumptions about gender—may feel that their sexuality and gender are threatened by my existence. After all, if you believe that a woman is defined as someone who is not male, masculine, or attracted to women, and that a man is defined as someone who is not female, feminine, or attracted to men, then the fact that I have changed my sex, or that I'm a woman who is attracted to other women, will inevitably bring everyone else's gender and sexuality into question. Because my lesbian and trans status appears to blur the very meaning of "woman," other women might feel that

I somehow undermine their own sense of femaleness, while some men might fear that if they were to become attracted to me, it might undermine their own maleness. So in a sense, the notion of "opposite sexes" intertwines all of our genders and sexualities with one another.

This interconnectedness of genders helps explain why we are encouraged to modify our own behaviors to better fit gender norms, and why we go out of our way to encourage gender-appropriate (and to discourage gender-inappropriate) behaviors in others. The countless approving or disapproving comments that we make about other people's gender presentations, identities, and behaviors create an atmosphere in which many people with exceptional gender and sexual traits feel that they have to remain closeted. It also causes people with typical gender inclinations and sex characteristics to become self-conscious and on guard, as their gender may be brought into question at any time. Thus, oppositional sexism exacerbates gender anxiety in all people, and is a major factor responsible for most of the prejudice and discrimination directed at sexual minorities.

Unfortunately, one of the most common ways people with exceptional gender and sexual traits try to counter such discrimination is by neutralizing the significance of their particular exceptional traits while simultaneously emphasizing the ways in which they otherwise uphold oppositional sexist ideals. For example, many people who are attracted to members of their own sex have tried to convince the predominantly straight mainstream public that "we're just like you except for our sexual orientation." This, of course, plays down the reality that many people who identify as bisexual, gay, or lesbian also have exceptional gender expressions, sex characteristics, and/or subconscious sexes. At the same time, many people in the transgender community have tried to neutralize their exceptional gender traits by stressing their heterosexuality: Some transsexuals insist that their goal is to become "normal" women or men (i.e., straight, with appropriate gender expression); and male crossdressers often emphasize the fact that they identify as men and are attracted to women (i.e., "normal" subconscious sex and sexual orientation).

The obvious problem with all of these approaches is that they marginalize those who have multiple exceptional gender and sexual traits. And their limited success is ultimately due to the fact that they attempt to cure the symptom (homophobia, transphobia, etc.) rather than the source of the problem (oppositional sexism). After all, the reason the mainstream public regularly confuses homosexuals, bisexuals, transgender people, and intersex people is that, in their eyes, we all represent the same thing. We are all often lumped together as "queer"—exceptions that challenge the mainstream oppositional assumptions about gender. Therefore, while it is important to educate people about the distinctions between different gender inclinations and sex characteristics, and the unique identities, issues, and challenges each minority group faces because of those specific differences, it is also important to stand together to challenge the myth that women and men are "opposites."

In my experience as a trans activist, I have found that the biggest obstacle facing those who fall under the "queer" or "LGBTIQ" umbrella, with regards to coming together to challenge oppositional sexism, is primarily a conceptual one. Over the years, different queer subgroups have each developed their own theories and language to describe and communicate their particular struggles.

Many of these concepts, while effective in single-inclination activism, are counterproductive in the fight against oppositional sexism because they marginalize and make invisible the experiences of other queers.

For example, the gay rights movement has historically framed much of their activism around the premise that heterosexuals oppress homosexuals. This oversimplification creates the false impression that homosexual and heterosexual people are "opposites"—an idea that marginalizes bisexuals. Further, the terms most commonly used to describe the prejudice faced by lesbians and gay men—"homophobia" and "heterosexism"—mistakenly imply that queer people are primarily discriminated against because of their sexual orientation. This is a false assumption, as those in the lesbian and gay communities who arguably face the harshest discrimination from the straight world are those who also exhibit exceptional gender expression (i.e., outwardly feminine gay men and butch lesbian women). This privileging of sexual orientation over other gender inclinations has allowed some gay rights activists to exclude gender-variant people from their movement (under the premise that they are focused on sexual orientation, not gender identity or expression), while simultaneously claiming that the prejudice and violence faced by transgender people is the result of "homophobia." This appropriation of gender-variant experiences and struggles by single-issue gay rights activists seems to serve the sole purpose of placing cisgender gays and lesbians atop the queer pecking order. Any movement whose goal is to truly end prejudice against all queer people must begin by replacing gay-specific phrases (like "heterosexism") with more inclusive ones (such as "oppositional sexism") that are equally respectful of all exceptional gender and sexual traits, and which acknowledge the fact that, in many cases, homophobia and transphobia are indistinguishable phenomena.

The transgender movement, which was primarily made up of those excluded by mainstream gay rights groups, has conceptual and linguistic problems of its own. The fact that at least two overlapping classes of people—those with exceptional gender expressions and those with exceptional subconscious sexes—have been subsumed by the category "transgender" has created a lot of unnecessary tension and confusion. The result is that at least two different (and largely incompatible) views of gender have gained hold in this community. The first one, which is forwarded by many transsexuals, can be summed up by the popular phrase "sex is in the body, and gender is in the mind." While this saying is useful to convey why a transsexual might want to change their physical sex to match their identified sex, it oversimplifies the concept of gender. The fact that the word "gender" is shorthand for subconscious sex inadvertently privileges subconscious sex over gender expression. Further, it mistakenly implies that more socially influenced aspects of gender (such as gender identity and gender roles), as well as one's ability or willingness to conform to oppositional sexist ideals, stem directly from one's subconscious sex, which is most certainly not true. People who espouse this view often look down on those people who identify outside of the male/female binary, or who express combinations of masculinity and femininity, presuming that these groups do not represent "serious" or "true" transgender people.

A different view is held by those transgender people who insist that gender itself is entirely constructed. Many feel empowered by this idea because it frees their exceptional gender traits from the social stigma inherent in oppositional sexism. But it also oversimplifies the concept of "gender" by dismissing the possibility that there are any intrinsic inclinations, such as subconscious sex and gender expression, that contribute to our gender identities and gender roles, respectively. This sort of thinking, when taken to the extreme, can privilege those people who are predisposed toward being bigender and bisexual. In this scenario, someone who feels comfortable identifying outside the male/female gender binary, expressing combinations of both femininity and masculinity, and/or having sexual relations with both male- and female-bodied people, may falsely assume that their "bi" inclinations represent a natural state that is present in all other people. From this "bi-sexist" perspective, people who identify exclusively as either female or male, feminine or masculine, homosexual or heterosexual, are assumed to have developed such preferences as the result of being duped by binary gender norms and socialization. This view has also led to the creation of another oppositional binary of sorts, pitting those transgender people who identify outside the gender binary (and who are therefore presumed to challenge gender norms) against transsexuals (who are accused of supporting the gender status quo by transitioning to their identified sex). Such arguments—that bigender and genderqueer people are more "radical" or "queer" than transsexuals—are highly reminiscent of similarly naive accusations made in the past by homosexuals who argued that they were more "radical" or "queer" than bisexuals. The creation of such radical/conservative gender binaries are both self-absorbed and anti-queer, as they dismiss the very real discrimination transsexuals and bisexuals face in favor of establishing pecking orders within the queer community.

These examples demonstrate how gender theories designed to free certain people from gender-related stigma or oppression can often inadvertently marginalize other sexual minorities, or even worse, create new gender hierarchies that are just as oppressive as the initial system. There are several telltale signs of flawed gender theories. First, we should beware of any gender theory that makes the assumption that there is any one "right" or "natural" way to be gendered or to be sexual. Such theories are typically narcissistic in nature, as they merely reveal their designers' desire to cast themselves on top of the gender hierarchy. Further, if one presumes there is only one "right" or "natural" way to be gendered, then the only way to explain why some people display typical gender and sexual traits while others display exceptional ones is by surmising that one of those two groups is being intentionally led astray somehow. Indeed, this is exactly what the religious right argues when they invent stories about homosexuals who actively recruit young children via the "gay agenda." Those who claim that we are all born with bisexual, androgynous, or gender-neutral tendencies (only to be molded into heterosexual, masculine men and feminine women via socialization and gender norms) use a similar strategy.

I take issue with any theory that suggests that people are so easily duped into leading such contrived sexual and gendered lives, as my own exceptional gender inclinations have been too strong and persistent to be ignored or reshaped by society. And while oppositional sexism certainly leads many people to closet their gender inclinations, I find it difficult to believe that the vast majority of people are hiding their true genders and sexualities or have resigned themselves to accepting wholly artificial ones. I would argue that our culture's oppositional gender system can only be held so firmly in place because it resonates with the majority's gender inclinations (that most—but not all—men gravitate toward masculinity and women to femininity).

Second, we should beware of any theory that attempts to oversimplify gender. It is common for articles or books about gender to begin by defining gender in an exclusive way, such as whether a person is feminine or masculine (i.e., gender expression/gender roles), whether they identify as female or male (i.e., subconscious sex/gender identity), or whether they behave according to the social norms associated with each sex. These assumptions severely limit the terms of the debate. The truth is that any dialogue about gender must begin with the acknowledgment that the word "gender" has scores of meanings, and all of them must be seriously considered if we hope to have an honest and fruitful discussion on the subject. Thus, theories that rely on either strictly gender essentialist or social constructionist definitions of gender, or that privilege certain gender inclinations over others, are destined to be inadequate in explaining the vast diversity of gender and sexual traits that exist in the world, and will inevitably make invisible certain sexual minorities.

Finally, we should question any view of gender founded on gender entitlement. When we project our own gender-based assumptions and opinions onto other people's behaviors and bodies, we necessarily erase the distinctness of their individual genders and sexualities. Each of us has a unique experience with gender, one that is influenced by a host of extrinsic factors, such as culture, religion, race, economic class, upbringing, and ability, as well as intrinsic factors including our anatomy, genetic and hormonal makeup, subconscious sex, sexual orientation, and gender expression. Together, these factors help determine the gendered experiences we are exposed to, as well as the ways we process and make sense of them. For this reason, no person is capable of fully understanding our own gendered perspectives and experiences, nor are we able to presume the gendered histories, desires, motives, and perceptions of others.

As a transsexual, I have been fortunate enough to have had the rather rare (and surreal) experience of being perceived by others as both a woman and a man, as homosexual and heterosexual, as feminine, masculine, and gender-ambiguous at different points in my life. People treated me in vastly different ways in each case, and the assumptions they made about my gender and sexuality often had little to do with my own identity and life history. As a gender activist, I believe that it's crucial for us to finally recognize this massive difference that exists between perception and personal experience. While I do not believe that there is an impenetrable wall that separates women from men, or queers from straights, I do believe that one exists between our own *experiential gender*, which we live, feel, and experience firsthand, and the genders of others, which we merely perceive or make presumptions about but can never truly know in a tangible way. It is time for discourses in gender and sexuality to acknowledge this great divide, to move beyond the insolent rhetoric of gender entitlement and one-size-fits-all gender theories. We must stop projecting what we wish were true about gender and sexuality onto other people, and instead learn to yield to their unique individual identities, experiences, and perspectives.

7

Pathological Science: Debunking Sexological and Sociological Models of Transgenderism

THE RISE OF MODERN MEDICINE and psychology over the last two centuries has generated a large amount of interest and investigation into the origins and expressions of human gender and sexuality. Researchers in what is sometimes called the field of "sexology" have tried to take a multidisciplinary approach, applying their various expertise in psychology, medicine, epidemiology, endocrinology, and sociology to better understand the nature of both typical and exceptional forms of sex, gender, and sexuality. However, in a climate so permeated by traditional and oppositional sexism, it's virtually impossible to completely separate scientific inquiry from one's own personal and political views. While some sexologists, such as Magnus Hirschfeld and Alfred Kinsey, seemed to have been driven by a desire to make the world safe for those who differ from sexual and gender norms, others have sought to erase or eradicate those exceptional genders and sexualities instead. While these latter researchers likely considered themselves well-intentioned, they have left a legacy in which naturally occurring, exceptional sex characteristics and gender inclinations are routinely viewed as abnormalities, paraphilias, and pathologies.

One of the most active areas of sexological study has been transsexuality, and that work was possible because trans people have often been required to subject themselves to research in order to gain access to hormones and surgery. This dependent relationship was instituted by the Harry Benjamin International Gender Dysphoria Association (HBIGDA), a professional organization that sets the guidelines for the "psychiatric, psychological, medical, and surgical management of gender identity disorders."[1] Until 1998, *The HBIGDA Standards of Care* stated that "[a]ny and all recommendations for sex reassignment surgery and hormone therapy should be made only by clinical behavioral scientists."[2] Because these medical procedures are prerequisites for obtaining legal change of sex in the United States, the psychiatric community (as well as other psychologists, physicians, and sexologists who had a hand in establishing the standards of care) has become positioned as "gatekeepers" of medical and legal sex reassignment. During the last half century, this group has amassed a large body of research on the subjects of transsexuality and transgenderism that has very much shaped the way our culture views and values transgender people, as well as how transgender people come to understand themselves. However, this body of research, though presented as "scientific" and "objective," reveals more about the researchers' biases and assumptions than it does about the transgender population.

Oppositional Sexism and Sex Reassignment

As I mentioned in previous chapters, trans people (who have a subconscious sex that is not in concordance with their physical sex) often suffer from gender dissonance, which is best thought of as the psychological strain of having to constantly pretend to be a member of a gender with which they do not identify. Over the years, sexologists have tried everything imaginable to "cure" trans people of gender dissonance, including psychoanalysis, aversion and electroshock therapies, administering assigned-sex-consistent hormones (i.e., androgens for male-bodied trans people, estrogens for female-bodied trans people) and psychotropic drugs—all to no avail. The only thing that has ever been shown to successfully alleviate gender dissonance is allowing the trans person to live in their identified gender.[3] There is an extraordinary amount of historical and anthropological evidence to further support this strategy, as trans people across cultures and throughout history have chosen to live as members of the other sex, often taking on the roles, manner of dress, and/or occupations associated with their identified genders and, in some cases, physically and hormonally altering their bodies via castration.[4]

In the last century, advances in medicine have offered trans people the opportunity to physically transition (via hormones and surgery) in addition to socially transitioning. One of the most prominent advocates for allowing this option was endocrinologist Harry Benjamin (for whom HBIGDA was later named).

Benjamin's first encounter with trans people took place in the early 1920s, when an MTF spectrum individual sought his help in obtaining female hormones in order to induce female development—a request which Benjamin eventually fulfilled and which led to "emotional improvement" on the part of the trans person.[5] Over the years, Benjamin met with countless trans people, often through referrals from other sexologists, and was apparently struck by their desperation, the failure of conventional therapies (such as psychotherapy) to relieve their pain, the medical and psychiatric community's general unwillingness to take their requests to physically transition seriously, and the fact that many turned to suicide or self-castration when their only option was to remain in their assigned sex.

Since sex reassignment surgery was not generally available in the United States at the time, Benjamin focused on the use of hormone replacement therapy, which he found went a long way toward easing gender dissonance in trans people. While he believed that sex reassignment surgery should be made available in the "more serious and intense cases," he also advocated the use of hormones to relieve gender dissonance in those trans people who were not able to or did not want to fully transition to the other sex.[6] In his 1966 book, *The Transsexual Phenomenon,* Benjamin outlined a seven-point, Kinsey-esque scale to describe people on the MTF spectrum, ranging from what he called "pseudo transvestites" to "true transsexuals." Though it was flawed in some respects, his scale did acknowledge that there was a large variation among trans people in terms of their wanting to temporarily, partially, or completely transition to the other sex, and whether that transition would be of a social, hormonal, and/or surgical nature.[7]

But as transsexuality gained more attention—almost all of it negative—from the mainstream media and the psychiatric and medical establishments, there was increasing pressure to placate the public's prejudices and fears about sex reassignment.[8] In response, many of those who were positioning themselves as gatekeepers argued in favor of an approach that was quite different from the one Benjamin initially advocated, one that would regulate and limit the availability of hormones and sex reassignment procedures only to those trans people who would be able to successfully blend into society as "normal" women and men. According to this strategy, the gatekeepers' job was to sort out the "true" transsexuals (who would be allowed to fully transition) from all other trans people (who would be denied any medical intervention other than psychotherapy). This highly dichotomous approach to treating trans people reflected the fact that most other sexologists who became involved in transsexuality—such as John Money, who pioneered the use of nonconsensual genital surgeries on intersex infants, and Richard Green, who is renowned for his use of behavioral modification to eliminate femininity in young boys—seemed to be primarily interested in "curing" (i.e., eliminating) sex-, gender-, and sexuality-related ambiguities.

By the late 1960s—with the establishment of several U.S. gender identity clinics and the publication of Green and Money's medical anthology *Transsexualism and Sex Reassignment*—a standard protocol for dealing with people who requested sex reassignment had started to emerge.[9] These guidelines for treatment were later codified with the release of the original *HBIGDA Standards of Care* in 1979, and while they have evolved somewhat over time—especially since the mid-1990s, when HBIGDA finally began to incorporate changes suggested by the transgender community—they follow the same basic outline today.[10] While this chapter is largely written in past tense (to maintain grammatical consistency), it should be said that most gatekeepers today still follow this same basic protocol, and many still evaluate their trans clients based on the oppositional and traditional sexist criteria that I discuss throughout this chapter. The first step in this process was a period of psychotherapy (lasting at least three months, often more), during which time a mental health professional would evaluate the client. If the trans person received a recommendation from that therapist (which today comes in the form of a diagnosis of gender identity disorder, or GID), they would then be allowed to begin their "real-life test"—a one- or two-year period during which they were required to live full-time in their identified sex. If the real-life test was deemed successful by both the transsexual and the therapist, the trans person would be eligible for hormone replacement therapy (in those cases where hormones were not prescribed before or concurrent with the real-life test) and sex reassignment surgery (which usually required a recommendation from a second mental health professional).

While the gatekeepers consistently argued that these methods were designed to protect the transsexual, the way they were executed (especially prior to the mid-1990s) reveals an underlying agenda. Whether unconscious or deliberate, the gatekeepers clearly sought to (1) minimize the number of transsexuals who transitioned, (2) ensure that most people who did transition would not be "gender-ambiguous" in any way, and (3) make certain that those transsexuals who fully transitioned would remain silent about their trans status. These goals were clearly disadvantageous to transsexuals, as they limited trans people's ability to obtain relief from gender dissonance and served to isolate trans people from one another, thus rendering them invisible. Rather, these goals were primarily designed to protect the cissexual public from their own gender anxiety by ensuring that most cissexuals would never come face-to-face with someone they knew to be transsexual.

The gatekeepers' attempts to suppress the number of trans people allowed to transition occurred at virtually every step of the sex reassignment process. For example, the gender identity clinics that were established to treat (and carry out research on) trans people often accepted only a small percentage of those who applied to their programs (for example, the program at Johns Hopkins University only approved twenty-four of the first two thousand requests they received for sex reassignment surgery).[11] And simply being accepted into one of these programs was not a guarantee that one would be allowed to transition. First, the trans person had to undergo extensive, sometimes indefinite, periods of psychotherapy designed to evaluate whether or not they met the psychiatrist's criteria for "true" transsexuals, rather than the arguably more important task of preparing the trans person for the emotional and physical changes associated with transitioning. Those who received recommendations were required to continue in therapy through the entire transitioning process (i.e., until after surgery). This requirement of several years of psychotherapy—in addition to the expenses of hormones, surgery, and other procedures that were generally not covered by health insurance—created a huge financial burden that severely limited the number of people who would have the economic means to transition in the first place.

Those who were allowed to begin the real-life test often faced additional obstacles, as some gender identity clinics (and early versions of *The HBIGDA Standards of Care*) required trans people to begin their tests prior to starting hormone replacement therapy.[12] Since an extraordinarily small percentage of trans people are physically able to "pass" as their identified sex without the aid of hormones, this unnecessarily exposed the transsexual to all sorts of discrimination, harassment, and potential violence. This postponing of hormones essentially perverted the real-life test, turning it into little more than a hazing period designed to weed out transsexuals who were the least "passable" in their identified sex.

The gatekeepers also kept the number of transitioned transsexuals low by requiring them to conform to oppositional sexist ideals regarding gender. This was primarily achieved by making "passing" a prerequisite for transitioning.[13] Such criteria ensured that cissexual prejudices about the preferred sizes and shapes of female and male bodies would be the ultimate arbiters of whether a trans person would be allowed to transition or not. Not only did the trans person have to physically "pass" as their identified sex, they needed to exhibit the "appropriate" sexual orientation (heterosexual) and gender expression (masculinity for trans men; femininity for trans women) for that sex as well. Many critics have pointed to these restrictions—particularly the fact that trans people who professed an attraction to members of their identified sex were regularly denied recommendations for transitioning—as evidence of "heterosexism" or "homophobia" among the gatekeepers. Unfortunately, such accusations are overly simplistic and somewhat misplaced. If anything, the gatekeepers were first and foremost cissexist rather than heterosexist. After all, the requirement that trans people had to be heterosexual in their identified sex was enforced long after "homosexuality" had been removed from the *DSM*.[14] Furthermore, the gatekeepers were not only restricting exceptional sexual orientation in transsexuals, but exceptional gender expression as well. So while the gatekeepers generally acknowledged that cissexuals varied significantly in their sexual orientations and gender expressions, they chose to hold transsexuals to a completely different (and more rigid) set of standards.

By focusing so intensely on the transsexual's ability to "pass" and conform to oppositional sexist notions of gender, the gatekeepers reduced the issue of relieving trans people's gender dissonance to a secondary, if not marginal, concern. For example, prominent and frequently cited research articles that attempted to assess the efficacy of sex reassignment often relied on factors designed to measure the transsexual's ability to "pass," without considering whether or not transitioning improved the emotional well-being of the trans person.[15] The tendency to dismiss the profound pain associated with gender dissonance can also be found in the countless condescending remarks that appear in research articles referring to transsexuals as being "impatient" and characterizing their desire for sex reassignment as "obsessive/compulsive."[16] This insensitivity toward trans people's pain indicates that the gatekeepers were far more concerned with protecting the cissexual world from the existence of transsexuality than they were with treating trans people's gender dissonance. Perhaps nothing demonstrates this better than the gatekeepers' willingness to deny trans people treatment (despite knowing how common it was for this group to become depressed and suicidal when unable to transition) solely based on the superficial criteria of trans people's appearances.

Because relief from gender dissonance depended on one's ability to live up to these rigid and oppositional sexist expectations, trans people quickly learned (both by reading the research articles and through conversations with other transsexuals) exactly what they needed to say and how they needed to act in order to procure a recommendation for hormones and sex reassignment. For example, most trans women understood that they needed to show up for their psychotherapy appointments wearing dresses and makeup, expressing stereotypically feminine mannerisms, insisting that they had always felt like women trapped inside men's bodies, that they'd identified as female since they were small children, that they were attracted to men but currently avoided intimate relations because they did not see themselves as homosexual, and that they were repulsed by their own penises. Those who did not follow this script risked having their requests for sex reassignment denied. Of course, the gatekeepers eventually realized that many, if not most, trans people were merely telling them what they wanted to hear, and their resentment around this can be found in the articles they published, which often contain descriptions of transsexuals as being "deceptive" and "liars."[17] Apparently, they found it more productive to vent about their experiences in the medical literature rather than question the legitimacy of their "true transsexual" archetype or acknowledge the role that their own oppositional sexist assumptions played in forcing trans people to lie in order to obtain relief from gender dissonance.

It is particularly hypocritical that gatekeepers accused trans people of being "liars," as their own protocols typically directed transsexuals to lie about their pasts after transitioning. In what seems to be complete contradiction of the most basic tenets of psychotherapy, trans people were required to invent gender-consistent (i.e., cissexual) histories for themselves, so that if they were ever questioned about their pasts, they would not have to reveal their trans status.[18] While this requirement was purportedly put into place to protect the transsexual from the cissexual public, it is clear that what concerned the gatekeepers the most was protecting the cissexual public from the transsexual. Proof of this exists in documents of trans people who were open about being transsexual, or who attempted to financially capitalize on that status (for example, by becoming entertainers or revealing their stories to the public), being described as "sociopathic" in the medical literature.[19] Canonical writings on transsexuality also argued that, for transsexuals embarking on their transitions, a "change in geographic location is almost mandatory," and that "continued association with an employer . . . should be terminated so as to *avoid any embarrassment to the employer.*" (Emphasis mine.)[20] Regarding family, gatekeepers suggested, "Young children are better told that their parents are divorcing and that Daddy will be living far away and probably unable to see them."[21] At every turn, the gatekeepers prioritized their concern for the feelings of cissexuals who were related to, or acquainted with, the transsexual over those of the trans person.

The gatekeepers' requirement that transsexuals so completely hide their trans status created innumerable obstacles for trans people: the shame and self-loathing that is associated with living in the closet; having to cut off relationships with family and friends, thus eliminating any possible social support system they may have had previously; having to look for a new job, in a new location, without being able to reference their past employment history and while continuing to pay the therapy and medical bills necessary to complete their transition—all of this on top of having to navigate their way through the world in their identified gender for the first time. Because of the combination of all of these stresses, it was not uncommon for transsexuals to become highly depressed or suicidal post-transition. Often, gatekeepers would assume that such problems stemmed from the transsexual's own gender issues rather than from the closeted and isolated lives they were forced to lead. For example, one transsexual who became depressed, primarily because of her fears that others would discover her trans status and that she would be rejected if she were found out, was described by the gatekeepers as "still struggling with the problem of gender identification."[22]

What became lost in gatekeeper discourse regarding transsexuality (especially with regard to incidents of post-transition depression and "transsexual regret") was any distinction between the trans person's gender dissonance (an intrinsic matter) and the emotional stress the transsexual experienced as a result of having to deal with the gender anxiety of the cissexual public (which was an extrinsic matter). Indeed, the blurring of these separate issues was codified with the invention of the psychological term *gender dysphoria,* which made invisible cissexual gender anxiety by conflating it with the trans person's intrinsic gender dissonance.[23] The regular use of the phrase by gatekeepers illustrates their assumption that it was the transsexuals' responsibility to shape their lives around the cissexual public's prejudice against them. And while most gatekeepers surely saw themselves as "treating" trans people, their own insistence that trans people "pass" as cissexual and hide their trans status after transitioning only enabled societal cissexism.

Traditional Sexism and Effemimania

Gatekeepers also practiced traditional sexism, as evident in the way their research and writings focused almost exclusively on MTF spectrum trans people. This occurred even though their own estimates typically showed MTF transsexuality to be merely three-times more prevalent than in the FTM direction.[24] Of course, as previously discussed, gatekeeper statistics were often just a reflection of their own biases (i.e., if they chose not to examine or treat you, you would not be counted as a transsexual). Today (now that information and access to transitioning is more widely available), trans people seem to be transitioning in both directions at roughly equal rates. This strongly suggests that the higher rates of MTF transsexuality cited in the past were simply an artifact of the gatekeepers' preferences for studying and "treating" it.

Many attempts to explain the gatekeepers' focus on trans women over trans men have centered on the assumption that traditional sexism was occurring based on the trans person's assigned sex. For example, many have pointed out that trans women, having been raised male, tended to have more financial resources to afford the extremely costly therapies and procedures associated with transitioning. Others have argued that a female-bodied person who wanted to transition to male would be taken far less seriously than a male-bodied person who expressed a desire to transition to female.[25] While the idea that a gatekeeper would take a "man" more seriously than a "woman" probably played some role in fostering this discrepancy, I would argue that, more often than not, traditional sexism tended to work in the other direction. In other words, the gatekeepers focused on MTF spectrum individuals not because of that group's male privilege per se, but because they considered male expressions of femininity to be more disturbing and potentially threatening to society than female expressions of masculinity.

The idea that "male femininity" is more psychopathological than "female masculinity" can be found throughout the transgender-specific diagnoses in the most recent edition of the *DSM (DSM-IV-TR)*. For example, the entry for transvestic fetishism (which exempts FTM spectrum trans people) is listed in the *DSM* as a paraphilia, a psychiatric category for sexual behaviors described as involving "(1) nonhuman objects, (2) the suffering or humiliation of oneself or one's partner, or (3) children or other nonconsenting persons." The transvestic fetishism diagnosis is written in such a vague way as to include most, if not all, heterosexual men who routinely crossdress.[26] Kelley Winters (writing under the pen name Katherine Wilson) of GID Reform Advocates (an organization that works to reform the psychiatric classification of gender diversity as mental disorder), has pointed out how this diagnosis, while targeting male-bodied people, is mired in traditional sexism:

> *Curiously, women and gay men are free to wear whatever clothing they choose without a label of mental illness. This criterion serves to enforce a stricter standard of conformity for straight males than women or gay men. Its dual standard not only reflects the social privilege of heterosexual males in American culture, but promotes it. One implication is that biological males who emulate women, with their lower social status, are presumed irrational and mentally disordered, while biological females who emulate males are not. A second implication stereotypically associates femininity and crossdressing with male homosexuality and serves to punish straight males who transgress this stereotype.*[27]

A similar tactic of punishing femininity in boys more vigorously than masculinity in girls can be found in the *DSM*'s gender identity disorder (GID) in children diagnosis. As Winters points out, "Boys are inexplicably held to a much stricter standard of conformity than girls in their choice of clothing and activities. A simple preference for crossdressing or simulating female attire meets the diagnostic criterion for boys but not for girls, who must insist on wearing only male clothing to merit diagnosis."[28]

The GID in children diagnosis has come under a lot of scrutiny since it was instituted in 1980, as it is often used as the justification for carrying out behavioral modification (including aversion and electroshock therapies) on children in an attempt to eliminate their exceptional gender expression and prevent them from growing up to be queer.[29] While children of both sexes have been subjected to these procedures, the lion's share of the research and funding for such projects has targeted femininity in boys rather than masculinity in girls. In fact, the largest grant awarded to this sort of research has gone to the "Feminine Boy Project," which was conducted by Richard Green and summarized in his 1987 book *The "Sissy Boy Syndrome" and the Development of Homosexuality*.[30] Green (who is also a former HBIGDA president and coeditor of the book *Transsexualism and Sex Reassignment*) is just one of many researchers whose work seems to be primarily focused on studying all varieties of feminine or female-associated behaviors and inclinations in male-bodied people. I would describe much of this research as stemming from *effemimania*—an obsession with "male femininity."

One of the characteristic traits of effemimanic research is that it tends to conflate feminine gender expression, male homosexuality, and MTF transsexuality with one another, often treating them as though they were different symptoms of the same "disease." This is evident in the theories psychiatrists and sexologists have offered to explain the etiology of these phenomena. The most common of these theories is that the combination of a dominant or smothering mother and a passive or distant father leads young boys to identify with their mothers and emulate their mothers' behaviors.[31] (This theory, which was fiercely forwarded by effemimanic psychiatrist Robert Stoller, has been regularly applied to both male homosexuality and MTF transsexuality.) Variations on this theory remained popular in the psychiatric community for many decades, despite psychiatrists' inability to explain all, or even most, instances of "male femininity." Another common theory is that a male child's developing brain may be inappropriately influenced by the mother's female hormones in utero. Others have suggested that both male homosexuality and MTF transsexuality may arise from X chromosome–specific mutations or genomic imprinting events that a mother passes on to her son (who is susceptible due to the fact that he has a single X chromosome).[32] Of course, the one thing that these theories all have in common—besides the fact that they all blame the mother for her son's feminine inclinations—is that they cannot be applied to (nor do they even attempt to account for) the existence of exceptional gender inclinations in those born and raised female.

Effemimania in sexology has led to the creation of additional labels and subcategories for MTF spectrum trans people that are rarely, if ever, applied to FTM spectrum individuals. The most common of these is the distinction between transvestites and transsexuals. According to gatekeeper lore, transvestites are male-identified, are attracted to women, and show no interest in transitioning, while MTF transsexuals are female-identified, attracted to men, and wish to fully transition. Some gatekeepers continue to rely on such stereotypes despite the overwhelming evidence that such cut-and-dried categories do not exist: Some male transvestites are bisexual or gay, and many who seem heterosexual often fantasize about having sex with men; many MTF transsexuals are bisexual or lesbian; some MTF trans people choose to live full-time as women without undergoing sex reassignment; and a significant percentage of transvestites eventually come to identify as transsexual and seek out sex reassignment.

Another common classification system specifically designed to describe variations among MTF spectrum individuals is the distinction between primary and secondary transsexuals.[33] According to this model, primary transsexuals fit the classic archetype of "true" transsexuals: They tend to become aware of their female gender identity very early in childhood, they are often very feminine throughout their lives, and they are generally attracted to men. Secondary transsexuals tend to discover their female gender identity much later in life (usually during puberty), they are typically less feminine than primary transsexuals, and they are usually attracted to women. A hypersexualized version of this model recently garnered attention with the publication of J. Michael Bailey's 2003 book *The Man Who Would Be Queen.*[34] Bailey refers to primary-type MTF transsexuals as being "homosexual" and claims that they are merely feminine men whose decision to transition to female arises from their desire to be intimate with men. Bailey further claims that secondary-type transsexuals are "autogynephilic"—essentially men who are attracted to women and who seek sex reassignment because they are turned on by the idea of having female bodies themselves. Despite the fact that the concept of autogynephilia (which was originally coined by fellow gatekeeper Ray Blanchard in the late 1980s) is based on dubious evidence and has never been scientifically substantiated, it also appears in the *DSM.*[35]

Of course, anyone who has spent any significant time in the transgender community—beyond interviewing folks at a nearby gender identity clinic, a local crossdressing support group, or the tranny bar scene (where Bailey apparently conducted much of his research)—realizes that there are countless exceptions to all of these models.[36] Rather than trying to shove all trans people into some rigid, dichotomous model, one could instead easily explain the vast diversity that exists in the transgender population by assuming that gender expression, subconscious sex, and sexual orientation are determined largely independently of one another (as I did in chapter 6, "Intrinsic Inclinations"). This would not only account for the variation seen among transgender people, but can also explain why some trans people consciously identify as the other sex from their earliest memories, while others come to this realization later in life. After all, prior to puberty, social distinctions between girls and boys are almost solely based on gender expression and gender roles. Thus, a physically male child who has both a feminine gender expression and a female subconscious sex is likely to come to the conclusion that they are (or should be) a girl rather than a boy. On the other hand, if that same child were masculine in gender expression, they might initially identify as a boy—both because of their physical sex and their tendency to exhibit stereotypically masculine behaviors—and might not become consciously aware of their female subconscious sex until puberty, when physical sex becomes the predominant distinguishing characteristic between females and males. This model can also explain why many cross-gender-identified boys grow up to be gay or bisexual rather than transsexual: Their early cross-gender identification arises from their feminine gender expression rather than from a female subconscious sex.

So if a relatively straightforward intrinsic inclination model can explain all of the variation among trans people on both the MTF and FTM spectrums, then why have so many gatekeepers continued to put forward effemimanic, MTF-specific models to describe transgenderism? Because effemimania is first and foremost an expression of traditional sexism. And because the gatekeepers often work from the implicit assumption that femininity is inferior to masculinity, it should be no surprise that they view "male femininity" to be a greater concern than "female masculinity." Such assumptions are illuminated in Phyllis Burke's 1996 book *Gender Shock*, which focuses heavily on Richard Green's Feminine Boy Project. Burke describes Green's line of reasoning as involving "a devaluation of all that is traditionally feminine when it appears strongly in a boy. Girls are not chosen [as playmates] by boys because they like them; they are chosen because they can be dominated, or are not a threat. Activities are chosen not because they are enjoyed, but because boys fail at masculine activities, because if the boys could succeed at masculine activities, why would they bother with feminine activities?"[37]

Some might be inclined to view effemimania as simply a manifestation of homophobia or transphobia, but this would be inaccurate. Effemimania specifically targets femininity rather than homosexuality or transsexuality as a whole. For example, in her 1991 essay "How to Bring Your Kids Up Gay: The War on Effeminate Boys," Eve Kosofsky Sedgwick discusses how Richard C. Friedman, a psychoanalyst and the author of *Male Homosexuality: A Contemporary Psychoanalytic Perspective*, speaks rather admirably about gay men who exhibit masculine traits, while correlating "adult gay male effeminacy with 'global character psychopathology' and what he calls 'the lower part of the psychostructural spectrum.'"[38] And while all forms of transsexuality are still formally pathologized, it has been quite common for gatekeepers to claim that trans men are more psychologically "stable" than trans women.[39] Often, such comments are made without any further explanation, leading one to suspect that these characterizations stem from the gatekeepers' unspoken assumption that masculinity and the desire to be male are, in and of themselves, more rational and healthy tendencies than femininity and the desire to be female.

Another issue that seems to fuel effemimania is our cultural tendency to sexualize femininity and femaleness in all its forms. While countless feminist writers and theorists have analyzed the ways in which the sexualization of femaleness and femininity permeates virtually every aspect of our culture and has a negative impact on most women's lives, they have typically ignored the way this tendency creates an environment in which "male femininity" is almost always considered in purely sexual terms. For example, most popular images and impressions of trans women revolve around sexuality: from "she-male" and "chicks with dicks" pornography to media portrayals of us as sexual deceivers, prostitutes, and sex workers. And of course, there are the recurring themes of trans women who transition in order either to gain the sexual attention of men or to fulfill some kind of bizarre sex fantasy (both of which appear regularly in the media, and also in Bailey and Blanchard's model of MTF transgenderism).

In this context, it's easy to understand why Bailey and Blanchard were able to get away with proposing a homosexual/autogynephilic model for MTF spectrum trans people without ever being challenged by their professional peers to apply their theories to FTM spectrum trans people. To do so would require these predominantly straight- and male-identified gatekeepers to view masculinity and maleness in purely erotic terms—in other words, to reduce maleness to the status of mere sexual object (something that they would be loath to do in the unlikely event that this line of reasoning ever crossed their minds). This unwillingness to sexualize masculinity to the extent that femininity is sexualized explains why the gatekeepers endlessly dwelled on every perceived nuance and variation that occurred in the sexual practices and fantasies of the MTF spectrum population while simultaneously adamantly claiming that there was no such thing as female transvestism, no erotic component to FTM crossdressing, and no such thing as a gay-identified trans man.[40] Of course, such identities and experiences have always existed, and have been documented by members of the transgender community and by researchers outside the field of sexology.

The sexualization of trans women has also had a profound effect on the criteria used to determine which transsexuals have been allowed to transition. While both trans men and trans women were historically required to meet the gatekeepers' oppositional sexist ideals, trans women often faced an additional standard: They had to be sexually desirable in their identified sex as well. In the 1970s, Suzanne J. Kessler and Wendy McKenna came across several instances in which gatekeepers were rather blatant about this practice: "A clinician during a panel session on transsexualism at the 1974 meeting of the American Psychological Association said that he was more convinced of the femaleness of a male-to-female transsexual if she was particularly beautiful and was capable of evoking in him those feelings that beautiful women generally do. Another clinician told us that he uses his own sexual interest as a criterion for deciding whether a transsexual is really the gender she/he claims."[41]

While not all gatekeepers relied on their own sexual attraction to assess whether trans women would gain their approval for sex reassignment, it is clear that most took the issue of sexual desirability into consideration. For example, in 1969, gatekeeper John Randell stated, "In both sexes, the individuals chosen for operation were selected because they were credible in their impersonation or, in the case of some males, had won sexual acceptance in the female role despite minor incongruous features."[42] Thus, being sexually desirable often superseded other transitioning criteria. Further, as one reads through MTF transsexual case studies, it becomes readily apparent that the word "attractive" is regularly used in conjunction with trans women whom the gatekeepers consider to be successful in their transitions. Those who would argue that this emphasis on the sexual desirability of trans women is a thing of the past might want to take a look at J. Michael Bailey's book, which I mentioned previously (published in 2003), in which he comments, "There is no way to say this as sensitively as I would prefer, so I will just go ahead. Most homosexual transsexuals are much better looking than most autogynephilic transsexuals."[43]

While not all gatekeepers are guilty of sexualizing their trans female clients to this extent, it is clear that many, if not most, expect trans women to make themselves as conventionally pretty as possible. In Anne Bolin's 1988 book *In Search of Eve,* a trans woman she interviewed put it this way: "Shrinks have the idea that to be a transsexual you must be a traditionally feminine woman: skirts, stockings, the whole nine yards."[44] Another trans woman sums up the problem this way: "You must conform to a doctor's idea of a woman, not necessarily yours."[45]

Viviane Namaste's 2000 book *Invisible Lives* includes an interview with a trans woman who was initially denied hormones by a gatekeeper because she showed up for her therapy appointment wearing "male" clothes. She recounts: "I just went back, and this time I did all my kohl [makeup], inside and outside my eyes, [wore] my little fake fur jacket and my tight black pants. And she said, 'You've come a long way since I saw you first. And now I am convinced that you're transsexual.' It was like three weeks later!"[46]

In my own conversations with trans women, I've found that such expectations are still quite prevalent. On a trans-woman-focused email list that I was a member of in the early 2000s, a new member posted that she had just scheduled her first therapy appointment and she asked if anyone had any advice for her. Sadly, there were about twenty responses, mostly from trans women who'd had the experience of being turned down because they had worn "male" or unisex clothing to their visits, and then later being approved after showing up to their appointments wearing dresses and makeup. While such standards are clearly traditionally sexist, it should once again be pointed out that they are also cissexist, as they require transsexual women to meet a more rigid standard of femininity than cissexual women in order to be considered female.

In chapter 2, "Skirt Chasers," I discussed the ways in which trans women are often required to prove their femaleness through superficial means—particularly by wearing dresses, heels, makeup, etc.—and then are dismissed as being "fake" women or "female impersonators" because of the perceived artifice involved. The same criticism can be applied to the gatekeepers who complained or commented on trans women's "exaggeration" of their femininity without ever considering that their own criteria virtually required trans women to maintain a hyperfeminine appearance in order to gain access to the means of transitioning. In 1969, Money (and coauthors) discussed the results of tests they had administered to transsexuals to measure their feminine and masculine tendencies.[47] The authors praised trans men for giving answers that were "masculine," but not any more "masculine" than those of the average cissexual man. At no time did the authors consider the possibility that the trans men's unexaggerated masculine responses were made possible by the fact that most gatekeepers, being male themselves, understood that there was more than one way to be a man. In contrast, trans women were derided for having scores that were higher on the feminine range than that of the average woman. Yet trans women were required to act more feminine than the average woman in order to be taken seriously as transsexuals. Evidence to support the idea that trans women's hyperfeminine test scores were merely an attempt to appease the traditionally sexist biases of the gatekeepers can be found in Anne Bolin's 1988 work *In Search of Eve*. When Bolin—who is not a gatekeeper and whose interactions with trans women occurred entirely outside of a clinical setting—administered a similar test, she found that trans women's scores were a lot more varied and closer to the norm of cissexual women. She commented, "The importance of fulfilling caretaker expectations . . . may be the single most important factor responsible for the prevalent medical-mental health conceptions of transsexualism."[48]

This, of course, is the major problem with most medical, psychiatric, and sexological research into transgenderism. While generally presented under the guise of objective science, the body of research compiled by the gatekeepers has been so undermined by their own biases that their results are nothing more than a research artifact. The gatekeepers consistently claimed that transsexuality was a "rare" phenomenon without acknowledging that they themselves played an active role in restricting the number of trans people who would be allowed to transition; they believed that crossdressing and transsexuality primarily "afflicted" those assigned a male sex at birth without realizing that their own effemimania rendered FTM spectrum individuals invisible. Indeed, the majority of research on transgenderism and transsexuality they produced clearly fit the criteria for "pathological science," a term used to describe work that initially conforms to the scientific method, but then unconsciously veers from that method and begins a pathological process of wishful data interpretation.[49]

Critiquing the Critics

Sexologists have greatly shaped the way the public at large views transsexuals (as well as the way many transsexuals come to view themselves), but they are not the only group to position themselves as "authorities" on transsexuality. Over the years, many academics in the social sciences and in gender studies have also written extensively on the subject. Unlike the gatekeepers, who have often expressed consternation and condemnation for those transsexuals who fail to live up to society's traditional and oppositional sexist expectations regarding gender, many academics have had the reciprocal concern—namely, that transsexuals work too hard to achieve gender normalcy. This concern typically arises from the assumption (embraced by many in the humanities) that transsexuality is a modern construction, something that would not exist if it were not for medical technology, psychological pathology, patriarchy, heterosexism, capitalism, and/or our culture's rigid binary gender norms. Because academics in the fields of sociology and gender studies have been disposed toward seeking out the societal causes of transsexuality, they have tended to overlook or dismiss the possibility that intrinsic inclinations (i.e., subconscious sex) drive trans people toward transitioning. Framing the issue this way has ensured that transsexuality can only be understood as a form of "false consciousness" and that transsexuals themselves can only be conceptualized in one of two ways: as "dupes" (who are misled into transitioning by gatekeepers) or as "fakes" (who are so distressed by their own exceptional gender expressions and/or sexual orientations that they are willing to go to the extreme lengths of surgically altering their bodies and unquestioningly embracing sexist ideals in order to fit into straight mainstream society).

While sociological models of transsexuality and transgenderism have not had as direct an impact on the lives of trans people as sexological models have, both models foster the false impression that cissexual "experts" (whether academic or clinical) are capable of understanding transsexuality better than transsexuals themselves—an idea that is as problematic as suggesting that male "experts" can understand womanhood better than women, or that heterosexual "experts" can understand homosexuality better than gays and lesbians. Further, while sociological and gender studies accounts of transsexuality have not garnered the public attention that their sexological counterparts have, they have profoundly shaped the manner in which trans people are discussed and considered in academia and in feminism. In this section, I will debunk many of the most common academic misconceptions regarding transsexuality. While some of the arguments I critique may seem unfamiliar, even esoteric, to readers outside the fields of sociology and gender studies, it is vital to address these points here, as they are encountered repeatedly in queer and feminist politics.

One of the most prevalent academic misconceptions regarding transsexuality is that the gatekeepers actively promote the use of sex reassignment and prey on gender-variant people, enticing them with the promise of assimilating them into "normal" women and men. One of the more influential research articles espousing this view was written by sociologists Dwight B. Billings and Thomas Urban in 1982, in which they claimed that "transsexualism is a socially constructed reality which *only* exists in and through medical practice." (Emphasis theirs.)[50] In Billings's and Urban's eyes, "transsexual therapy . . . pushes patients toward an alluring world of artificial vaginas and penises rather than toward self-understanding and sexual politics."[51] Janice G. Raymond has a similar view. In her 1979 book *The Transsexual Empire* (discussed previously in chapter 2), she described sex reassignment as a "male interventionist technology" in which "[t]ranssexuals surrender themselves to . . . therapists and technicians."[52] She goes on to suggest that trans people would be better off if they were counseled using the same "consciousness-raising" methods that she experienced in the feminist movement.[53] So, in other words, both sets of authors believe that transsexuality would not exist if trans people simply became more educated and involved in feminism and sexual politics.

So how do Raymond, Billings, and Urban explain why trans people are so easily "duped" into transitioning when transsexuality itself is considered taboo by society at large? Their rationale is that transsexuality has become socially acceptable, a rather outrageous claim considering they were writing during the late 1970s and early 1980s, respectively.[54] Of course, the idea that transsexuals are highly susceptible to suggestion and easily yield to medical authority would surely come as a surprise to many gatekeepers, who regularly complained about how transsexuals were "stubborn," highly resistant to psychotherapy, and usually came to appointments having already made up their minds.[55]

Another major flaw with these theses is that they rest on the assumption that people identifying and living as members of the sex other than the one they were assigned at birth was a novel phenomenon, one that did not exist prior to the invention of sex reassignment procedures. However, numerous historians and anthropologists have described the existence of trans people in other eras and cultures.[56] In fact, many of the original gatekeepers, including Harry Benjamin, only "discovered" the existence of transsexuality after trans people approached them about the possibilities of physically transitioning, and many of the earliest transsexuals, such as Christine Jorgensen (the first transsexual to gain mainstream attention) and "Agnes" (who is discussed in more detail in chapter 9), self-administered hormones prior to consulting with doctors about their desire to physically transition.[57] Indeed, the gatekeepers didn't "invent" sex reassignment, but were dragged into it kicking and screaming. And the fact that the gatekeepers almost universally favored strict restrictions that greatly reduced the number of people undergoing sex reassignment clearly indicates that they were, at best, reluctant advocates.

A similar attempt to remove transsexuals from any historical or cross-cultural context can be found in Bernice L. Hausman's

1995 book *Changing Sex*. Despite the fact that Hausman is aware of people throughout history who have lived as members of the other sex, or who do so today without using hormones or surgery, she nevertheless chooses to narrowly define transsexuality as the act of changing one's sex via physically transitioning.[58] This allows her to put forward the thesis that "developments in medical technology and practice were central to the establishment of the necessary conditions for the emergence of the demand for sex change."[59] The amateurish nature of this argument is astounding; it's akin to discounting the existence of all nonmotorized vehicles (bicycles, sailboats, horse-drawn carriages, etc.) to make the claim that transportation is a modern construction dependent on the discovery of fossil fuel and combustion engines.

Of course, there is an obvious reason why Hausman chose to define transsexuality so narrowly: To do otherwise would subvert her entire thesis. After all, if she were to acknowledge that trans people have existed in varied cultures and throughout history, her readers might view transsexuality as part of a natural rather than culture-specific phenomenon and thus understand trans people's desire to live in their identified sex as being primarily driven by their own intrinsic inclinations rather than by social forces. From such a perspective, one would be inclined to see sex reassignment as a modern option for trans people, similar to how recent advances in medicine now enable cissexual women and men to undergo similar procedures, such as hormone replacement therapy, breast or penis enhancement or reconstruction, and infertility treatments. Instead, by removing transsexuality from this trans-historical and cross-cultural context, Hausman misleads her readers into believing that trans people suddenly appeared out of nowhere, almost overnight—a fabrication that practically strong-arms her readership into seeing transsexuality as a culturally specific and socially derived phenomenon.

The intellectual inconsistencies in Hausman's thesis become even more blatant when she makes it clear that she accepts that same-sex desire has always existed (and therefore precedes social construction). This allows her to claim that transsexuality is not analogous to homosexuality because of its "special *conceptual* and *material* relation to medical discourse and practice." (Emphasis hers.)[60] This is a rather convenient argument for Hausman to make considering that she has already dismissed the existence of those transsexuals who do not physically transition. Indeed, Hausman seems oblivious to the fact that, were she able to wave away the existence of same-sex attraction throughout history (as she does with transsexuality), she could easily make the analogous claim that homosexuality is just as much a product of modern medicine as transsexuality. After all, both words, "homosexuality" and "transsexuality," were coined within the last 150 years, gained prominence as concepts with the rise of sexology in the twentieth century, and emerged as identities and political movements both because of and in response to their psychological pathologization. And if one were hell-bent on portraying homosexuality as entirely constructed, one could easily reach the same shortsighted conclusion that Hausman has reached. The argument would go: The rise in the number of people openly calling themselves homosexuals over the past half century is not due to political and cultural changes that have allowed them to finally "come out of the closet," but rather that the medical invention of homosexuality itself generated a "demand" for people to become homosexual.

Hausman's book demonstrates the misinformation academics can generate when they narrowly define transsexuality based on psychiatric or medical parameters, or attempt to isolate transsexuals who do physically transition from the broader population of trans people who identify and live as members of the other sex without medical intervention. These very same mistakes are regularly made by anthropologists who focus on what are sometimes called "third," "multiple," or "alternate" genders—categories designed to describe people who are viewed by their cultures as being not quite male and not quite female. Because these groups appear to exist outside the gender binary, and blur distinctions between what Westerners would call transsexuality, homosexuality, and transgenderism, they are subjects of interest among academics who believe that gender is primarily socially constructed.

One such anthropologist is Serena Nanda, who has studied Indian hijras and authored several books, including *Gender Diversity: Crosscultural Variations*. This 2000 book is an overview of gender variation across the world, and highlights examples of social categories and gender roles that challenge our Western tendency to define gender exclusively based on one's physical sex. For the most part, Nanda remains respectful and refrains from placing value judgments on the cultures and gender-variant people she describes—that is, until she gets to the chapter titled "Transsexualism." Here, she seems to go into diatribe mode, describing transsexuals as a medical "invention" who are shaped by Western doctors' and psychologists' stereotyped view of gender.[61]

Nanda goes on to make the broader point that transsexuals, "far from being an example of gender diversity, both reflected and reinforced the dominant Euro-American sex/gender ideology in which one had to choose to be either a man or a (stereotypical) woman."[62] For Nanda to make this sort of blanket generalization when there are countless examples of transsexuals who were involved in the early days of the gay rights and the lesbian-feminist movements, or who are at the forefront of today's transgender and genderqueer movements, suggests that either she is completely ignorant of the existence of any transsexuals who do not fit her stereotype, or she purposefully ignores or discounts them in order to create the false impression that all transsexuals are stamped from the same medical establishment cookie cutter.

Nanda's motives for painting such a rigid and distorted picture of transsexuals becomes obvious in the following chapter, "Transgenderism." Despite the fact that virtually all organizations and communities that call themselves "transgender" generally include transsexuals, Nanda has somehow taken it upon herself to redefine "transgender" in opposition to "transsexual." She describes transgenderism as being based on the principle of androgyny, explaining that (unlike transsexuals) transgender people do not limit themselves to a single gender.[63] It seems rather obvious why she is so determined to deny the overlap between these two groups. A running theme throughout the book is that transgender people who are defined as being separate from female and male necessarily challenge our Western assumptions that the male/female binary gender system is "natural." Transsexuals complicate this issue by virtue of the fact that we are gender-variant yet typically identify within the binary. By dismissing us as a medical invention that "upholds the status quo of the binary sex/gender system," Nanda seems to be establishing a gender binary of her own, one in which "third gender," androgynous, and visibly queer people who blur distinctions between female and male are considered radical and natural, while those who identify as or appear to be clearly female or male are considered conservative and contrived.[64]

This radical/conservative gender binary is also forwarded by Will Roscoe, an anthropologist who has focused much of his research on reconstructing the lives of what he refers to as "berdaches" (a Western umbrella term for Native American gender-variant people) from the historical record. As a strict social constructionist, Roscoe refuses to believe that these gender-variant identities represent merely "a compromise between nature and culture or a niche to accommodate 'natural' variation."[65] He also denounces the view held by many anthropologists that some of these individuals "crossed" genders (from male to female or female to male) because they could then (in his eyes) be "interpreted as upholding a heterosexist gender system."[66]

Because Roscoe is determined to demonstrate that Native American gender-variant people represent "third genders," he plays up the ways in which these groups showed signs of being separate from and/or a mix of female and male, while playing down evidence that some may have actually seen themselves as, or wanted to be, the other gender. While this is not difficult to do for certain groups (as these roles varied significantly between Native American nations), Roscoe sticks to his "third gender" hypothesis even when analyzing the historical record of the Mohave alyha (MTF spectrum) and hwame (FTM spectrum) identities (reviewed in his 1994 essay "How to Become a Berdache"). Despite the fact that the alyha "insisted on being referred to by female names and with female gender references," used "the Mohave word for clitoris to refer to their penises," received female facial tattoos, and took part in rituals where they simulated pregnancy, Roscoe still argues that they should be considered "third gender" because they were given a unique name (i.e., alyha) to distinguish them from other women.[67] Other evidence that Roscoe uses to undermine the Mohave alyha's apparent self-identified gender is that they were not always fully accepted in that gender by other Mohaves: He references accounts of individual Mohaves commenting that alyha were less womanly than other women and cites rare occasions when some Mohaves used pronouns that referenced these individuals' birth (rather than identified) sex.[68] Thus, to make his point that Mohave alyha and hwame represent "third genders," Roscoe resorts to giving more credence to the judgments of non-gender-variant Mohave than to the way these individuals saw themselves. Perhaps this shouldn't be a surprise, as Roscoe himself purposely uses inappropriate pronouns and favors birth sex over identified sex when writing about these groups.

The strict dichotomy that Nanda and Roscoe attempt to make between "third genders" and trans people who "cross" from one gender to the other seems rather dubious. After all, some people who are members of non-Western "third gender" traditions do identify fully as the other sex and/or choose to physically transition when given the opportunity.[69] Furthermore, as a Western transsexual, I may identify squarely within the male/female gender binary if I want to, but once other people discover my transsexual status, they usually start slipping up on pronouns and referring to me as a MTF, boy-girl, s/he, she-he, or a she-male. In other words, people try to third-gender me. Both Roscoe and Nanda seem to have so much invested in promoting the theoretical significance of "third genders" that they're oblivious to the ways in which these categories—rather than shattering the gender binary—may actually contribute to its stabilization by marking and segregating those people who have exceptional gender inclinations from gender-normative women and men. If you want to convince me that a culture truly has multiple genders that are dissociated from binary sex, show me one where male- and female-bodied people are both included in every gender category.

Unfortunately, the mistaken notion that some genders are inherently more "radical" or "subversive" than others, which is seen throughout much of the anthropological literature on "third genders," has also flourished throughout much of the anthropological literature on "third genders," has also flourished throughout the social sciences, in women's and gender studies departments, and the humanities in general. And in the social constructionists' radical/conservative gender binary, no group is more regularly discredited and maligned than transsexuals—we are often portrayed as gender sellouts, and our attempts to live as and/or physically transition to our identified sex are often misread as being driven not by our own intrinsic inclinations, but by a desire to "fit in" or assimilate into gender normalcy. Such misconceptions are evident in the following series of quotes:

> *Transsexualism is a response to the rigid, socially prescribed gender dichotomy of heterosexual men and women.*
>
> —Frank Lewins (1995)[70]

> *The idea is that societal pressure . . . leads the transsexual to surmount the problem by changing the body to fit the norm of dichotomous gender.*
>
> —David E. Grimm (1987)[71]

Transsexual patients have an excessively narrow image of what constitutes "sex-appropriate" behaviour. . . . Were the notions of masculinity and femininity less rigid, sex change operations should be unnecessary.

—Margrit Eichler (1980)[72]

Sex-change surgery is profoundly conservative in that it reinforces sharply contrasting gender roles by shaping individuals to fit them.

—Germaine Greer (1999)[73]

While transsexuals may be deviants in terms of cultural norms about how one arrives at being a man or a woman, they are, for the most part, highly conformist about what to do once you get there.

—Judith Shapiro (1991)[74]

Ironically, transsexuals wish to be women but end up approximating men's sexual conservatism . . . most can still be typified as the Uncle Toms of the sexual liberation movement, in sharp contrast with other sexual minorities.

—Thomas Kando (1974)[75]

The implication that transsexuals transition in order to hide their exceptional gender expression and/or sexual orientation is only made possible by the social constructionist practice of dumbing down gender to exclude subconscious sex. This exclusion is notable, since virtually all transsexuals describe experiencing a profound, inexplicable, intrinsic self-knowing regarding their own gender. Because such accounts of transsexual subconscious sex/gender identity are nearly ubiquitous, one can only conclude that either the above critics have made their conclusions without bothering to read or listen to what transsexuals have said about their own lives and experiences, or they have chosen to ignore or discount such accounts, presumably out of an unwillingness to consider the possibility that trans people have an understanding about gender that cissexual academics do not. Not only do these "transsexual-as-assimilationist" accusations blatantly dismiss transsexual perspectives, but they are also unabashedly cissexist in other ways. They erase the existence of the many transsexuals who are unrelenting feminists and queer activists, and hold those transsexuals who do identify as heterosexual feminine women and masculine men more accountable for gender-based oppression than the overwhelming majority of cissexual people who identify the same way.

Another dehumanizing tactic used by these academic critics is the assumption that they are capable of fully understanding and speaking authoritatively about transsexuality despite the fact that they are not transsexual themselves; in fact, rarely do they get to know any transsexuals personally. When Shapiro, Nanda, Grimm, and Eichler speak disparagingly about transsexuals, their arguments rely almost entirely on other people's research. Hausman boasts about attending one transgender conference, then liberally (and extensively) quotes from transsexual autobiographies without any consideration given to the role that non-trans book publishers and audiences play in deciding which transsexual stories get told and which do not.

Those sociologists who do base their critiques on interviews with transsexuals seem to have no qualms about drawing firm conclusions despite the many caveats inherent in their research: They generally rely on pathetically small sample sizes from the same geographic location, and their sample populations consist of trans people from similar (middle-class) economic dispositions who are all in the earliest stages of transition. This latter point is particularly salient, as the perspectives of transsexuals who are in the process of actively managing their physical transitions (and other people's reactions to those changes) tend to differ greatly from those who have already been living in their identified sex for a number of years. Further, many sociologists make the common mistake of deriving their sample population from patients at gender identity clinics (GICs). While such clinics may seem a boon for sociologists—as they provide a rare place where one can find a relatively large number of transsexuals—they are also likely to provide the most biased research population.[76] GICs are notorious for enforcing particularly strict oppositional and traditional sexist norms for their trans patients. Thus, research populations derived entirely from GICs have already been selected for those transsexuals who are most able or willing to conform to cissexual expectations regarding gender. Further, because GICs regularly carry out research on transsexuals, sociologists who conduct interviews in association with GICs are likely to be viewed by the transsexual as part of the gatekeeper establishment. As a result, the sociologists will likely receive pat and predictable answers to their interview questions.

Because transsexuals often have to submit themselves to the rigorous interrogation of gatekeepers, and constantly have to explain and justify their existence to a reluctant cissexual public, many are weary and suspicious of any cissexual—whether gatekeeper or academic—who wishes to turn trans people into research subjects. This reluctance is evident in the vast difference between the conclusions of superficial sociological interviews and those where the interviewers worked to gain the transsexual's trust, such as in the work of Anne Bolin and Viviane K. Namaste.

Bolin's study is particularly telling because she starts out with a small and biased sample population similar to that which many sociologists rely on: The bulk of her data came from twelve members of the same transgender support group, all of whom were in the early stages of transitioning.[77] However, because she got to know these trans women over several years and eventually gained their trust, she got to see a very different perspective of the trans female experience: "Contrary to the stereotype of transsexuals as hyperfeminine, reveling in traditional notions of womanhood to a greater extent than genetic women, the transsexuals in this population were not admirers of stereotypical womanhood. They were keenly aware of the feminist movement, wanted careers as well as someone to share their lives with, and represented styles of dressing as diverse as the female population emulated."[78]

If more academics would actually get to know transsexuals as people (rather than as mere research subjects), they would find that the assumption that we transition in order to "fit in" to the gender binary has virtually no relevance in most transsexuals' lives. For many of us, the decision to transition comes after years of successfully "passing" as "normal" members of our assigned sex—for us, transitioning entails the complete antithesis of trying to fit in. Those of us who are attracted to members of our identified sex transition despite the fact that we will no longer be considered heterosexual.

The variation in our gender expression ensures that some of us will be considered somewhat masculine women or feminine men after our transitions. And all transsexuals run the risk of being unable to physically "pass" (in the short term or the long term) in our identified sex upon transitioning.

Perhaps the most condescending aspect of the "transsexual-as-assimilationist" argument is that it presumes that transsexuals are accepted by society more than cissexuals who are queer in other ways (i.e., because of their gender expression or sexual orientation). This is most certainly not the case.[79] As someone who has spent a chunk of her life as a relatively "out" male crossdresser, and later as an androgynous bigender boy, I have found that people, on average, were extraordinarily more tolerant of—and comfortable with—my gender status back then than they are now when I tell them I'm a transsexual. And if you ask other transsexuals—even those who were out and proud queers prior to transition—why they didn't choose to transition earlier in their lives, most will tell you that they feared the social ramifications that come with transitioning: being disowned by family and community, losing a job, being considered undesirable in the eyes of others, having one's identified gender constantly questioned by others. Not only is sex reassignment just about the most stigmatized medical procedure that exists in our society, but transsexuals themselves are rarely accepted culturally and legally as legitimate men or women. It is safe to say that lesbians and gay men are far more accepted and respected by the straight mainstream than transsexuals are. Thus, the idea that a trans person would transition in order to "conform to heterosexist gender norms" is nothing more than an illogical and disrespectful farce.

It seems to me that the entire debate in academia over whether transsexuals are radical or conservative with regards to gender is founded on cissexual privilege. Because these scholars have not had to live with the reality of gender dissonance, they are afforded the luxury of intellectualizing away subconscious sex, thus allowing them to project their own interests or biases onto trans people. Not surprisingly, the researchers' academic backgrounds seem to be the primary determinant as to what explanations for transsexuality they will posit. Being that Harry Benjamin (who was trained as an endocrinologist) believed that transsexuality was caused by fetal hormone levels, and Richard Green, Robert Stoller, and John Money (all trained in psychology) looked to relationships with parents and/or events that occurred during one's formative years as its primary cause, it is not surprising that social scientists generally argue that transsexuality is the result of societal gender norms, lesbian and gay scholars claim it is the result of heterosexism, feminists blame it on patriarchy, and poststructuralists simply deconstruct it into nonexistence.

Moving Beyond Cissexist Models of Transsexuality

The last fifty years of sexological and sociological discourses regarding transsexuality have been nothing more than a charade, where the opinions of those who have academic and clinical credentials always trump those of transsexuals themselves; where trans people are treated as nothing more than blank slates for cissexual gender researchers to inscribe their pet theories upon. And while researchers in the humanities often frame their work as being in opposition to that of the gatekeepers, it seems to me that the similarities between both groups far outweigh the differences. Both clinicians and academics are obsessed with meticulously documenting and subcategorizing the transgender population; both display the effemimanic compulsion of focusing primarily on MTF spectrum trans people; and both view transsexuals as anomalies that require explanation and justification rather than viewing us as a part of human diversity that just simply exists.

The needs, desires, and perspectives of transsexuals have become lost in a shameful tug-of-war between those who wish to show that stereotypical gender differences arise naturally from biological predisposition and those who wish to demonstrate that those same gender differences are entirely socially constructed. As a transsexual, my lived experiences are at odds with both strict gender essentialist and social constructionist accounts of gender. And while the idea that gender is a combination of many things—some biological and others sociological—does not make for a catchy sound bite or a sexy "hook" for one's book or thesis, it appears to me to be indisputable. And maybe once most sexologists and sociologists finally come to accept this fact, they will stop exploiting and dissecting the lives of transgender people and others who have exceptional gender inclinations and sex characteristics.

If there is anything to be learned from sexological and sociological accounts of transsexuality, it is that cissexism—i.e., the tendency to hold transsexual genders to a different standard than cissexual ones—runs rampant not only among the general public, but also throughout the medical and psychiatric establishments and in the ivory towers of academia. If sociologists truly wanted to better understand transsexuality, rather than focus exclusively on the behaviors and etiology of transsexuals, they would study the irrational animosity, fear, and disrespect that many cissexuals express toward trans people (and others with exceptional gender and sexual traits). If sexologists were truly interested in transsexuals' mental and physical well-being, they would not try to micromanage our transitions, but rather focus their energies on correcting the huge disparity that exists between cissexual and transsexual access to gender-related healthcare. It is the gatekeepers' failure to adequately advocate on behalf of their trans patients that has allowed U.S. insurance companies (which regularly cover cissexual hormone replacement therapy, genital and breast reconstruction, and procedures to enhance or enable cissexual fertility and sexuality) to get away with denying coverage for similar treatments for transsexuals. And the popular stereotype that transsexuals are "crazy"—that our identified genders are merely the product of overactive imaginations and are not to be taken seriously—is also the result of the same medically and psychiatrically sanctioned double standard: while cissexuals are free to choose from hundreds of different types of surgical body modifications without being pathologized or requiring anyone else's permission, procedures required for transsexuals to lead full and healthy lives are singled out for gatekeeper approval and an accompanying diagnosis of gender identity disorder.

Despite the recent civil rights progress that has accompanied the rise of transgender activism in the 1990s, the gatekeeper model of transsexuality still dominates in the United States. While HBIGDA has slightly liberalized its *Standards of Care* in recent years, it still requires transsexuals to gain psychiatric approval in order to gain access to hormones, obtain surgery, and change their legal sex. This system is inherently cissexist, as it requires trans people to accommodate and appease the gender presumptions of individual therapists (who potentially harbor traditional sexist, oppositional sexist, and/or cissexist biases) in order to have our identified genders recognized. It's time we replace the existing gatekeeper model with one that's centered on the needs of trans people themselves. This begins with the public acknowledgment that all people have the right to self-identify (even if that identity falls outside of the male/female binary), and that one's self-identified gender is necessarily more legitimate than the one that is rather naively assigned to them by others. Further, the process of socially and legally changing one's sex should be entirely uncoupled from medicine and psychiatry: No specific medical procedure should be required for one to have one's identified sex recognized, nor should any medical or psychiatric professional have the authority to prevent someone from living in their identified sex. Those trans people who feel that they need to hormonally or physically transition in order to ease their gender dissonance should be allowed that option if they wish (in the same way that cissexuals ultimately choose for themselves whether or not to undergo hormone replacement therapy, genital or breast reconstruction, fertility and sexuality-related procedures, etc.).

The idea that trans people should decide for themselves whether or not to physically transition—what some have disdainfully referred to as "sex change on demand"—has been opposed by the gatekeeper establishment from the beginning. The most common argument is that the system as it stands acts as a safeguard to prevent people who are not transsexual (e.g., cissexuals who are merely embarrassed or confused about their atypical sexuality or who exhibit "delusional" or "antisocial" behavior) from undergoing potentially irreversible medical procedures.[80] Once again, such practices reveal the cissexist biases of the gatekeepers: Trans people are denied immediate treatment of their gender dissonance in order to protect the well-being of a rather small minority of cissexuals. One can only imagine how furious and frustrated most cissexuals would feel if they had to undergo psychotherapy for three to six months (so that a psychiatrist could rule out the possibility that they were transsexual) before obtaining permission to undergo hormone replacement therapy or gender-related surgeries they required.

The gatekeepers' fear of "sex change on demand" rings particularly hollow in a world where most trans people cannot even afford to take the medically and psychiatrically sanctioned route to transition. Psychotherapy is prohibitively expensive for those who do not have adequate insurance; many trans people rely on underground markets and overseas pharmacies to obtain affordable hormones without a prescription. Many undergo sex reassignment surgeries in countries like Thailand, where it is much less expensive and where there are fewer restrictions than in the United States. Clearly, gatekeeper micromanagement of transitioning has only served to force a significant percentage of trans people (who either cannot afford to follow the HBIGDA standards of care or fail to convince their therapists that they are "true" transsexuals) out of the system.

Those gatekeepers who believe that they alone should have the authority to determine who should and should not be allowed to transition ignore the obvious fact that gender dissonance has always been a "self-diagnosed" condition: There are no visible signs or tests for it; only the trans person can feel and describe it. Once we make the arduous decision to transition—letting go of other people's perceptions of us in favor of being true to ourselves—there is really nothing anyone can do to stop us. For these reasons, medical and mental health professionals should turn their attention away from regulating sex reassignment and toward facilitating the safe access to the means of transitioning. Thankfully, some have already begun working toward this goal, designing programs that provide trans people with affordable access to information, hormones, and the appropriate medical tests to ensure a safe transition.[81] Others in the field of psychiatry have similarly advocated that mental health professionals move away from the gatekeeper model and toward one focused on helping the transsexual manage the emotional stress and obstacles they are faced with when transitioning.[82]

While all of these changes represent a promising start, true equality for transsexuals and transgender people will remain elusive as long as gender variance remains pathologized by the American Psychiatric Association, which publishes the *DSM*. Human beings show a large range of gender and sexual diversity, so there is no legitimate reason for any form of cross-gender behavior or identity to be categorized as a mental disorder.

That said, I also take issue with those who argue for completely demedicalizing transsexuality, or who advocate removing GID from the *DSM* without first ensuring that there are provisions in place to allow people who choose to transition affordable access to transsexual-related medical procedures. Some have suggested creating a medical diagnosis for transsexuality to replace the current psychiatric diagnosis of GID; this makes sense, being that most transsexuals feel that our problem lies not with our minds, but with our bodies.[83] Once these medical provisions are in place, the importance of psychiatrically depathologizing transgenderism cannot be underestimated. After all, it is the popular misconception that gender variance constitutes a mental illness—that transsexual and transgender people are the ones who have the problem—that enables cissexual and cisgender prejudice against us.

8

Dismantling Cissexual Privilege

UNTIL NOW, DISCOURSES ON transsexuality have invariably relied on language and concepts invented by clinicians, researchers, and academics who have made transsexuals the objects of their inquiry. In such a framework, transsexual bodies, identities, perspectives, and experiences are continuously required to be explained and inevitably remain open to interpretation. Corresponding cissexual attributes are simply taken for granted—they are assumed to be "natural" and "normal" and therefore escape reciprocal critique. This places transsexuals at a constant disadvantage, since we have generally been forced to rely on limiting cissexual-centric terminology to make sense of our own lives.

In recent years, the rise of transgender activism has provided a new paradigm for understanding the experiences of the gender-variant population (of which transsexuals are a subset). According to this model, gender-variant people are oppressed by a system that forces everyone to identify and be easily recognizable as either a woman or a man. This perspective has led transgender activists to primarily focus their attention on opposing binary gender norms—

particularly those that place limitations on one's gender expression and appearance—and to celebrate and create cultural space for those who defy, transcend, or fail to identify within the male/female binary. While transgender activism has undoubtedly benefited the transsexual community in many ways, it has also made invisible many of our distinct issues and experiences. To a large extent, this is because transgender rhetoric favors the perspectives of those who identify outside the male/female binary (whereas most transsexuals typically identify within it) and those whose gender expression and appearance does not conform to the binary (whereas transsexuals typically cite the discrepancy between their subconscious sex and physical sex as the major obstacle in their lives).

While I believe that creating space for people who exist outside of the male/female binary remains a cause worth fighting for, those of us who are transsexual must begin to simultaneously develop our own language and concepts that accurately articulate our unique experiences and perspectives and to fill in the many gaps that exist in both gatekeeper and transgender activist language. I contend that this work should begin with a thorough critique of *cissexual privilege*—that is, the double standard that promotes the idea that transsexual genders are distinct from, and less legitimate than, cissexual genders. Before describing how cissexual privilege is practiced and justified, we must address two underacknowledged yet crucial aspects of social gender that enable cissexual privilege to proliferate, yet remain invisible: *gendering* and *cissexual assumption.*

Gendering

Most of us want to believe that the act of distinguishing between women and men is a passive task, that all people naturally fall into one of two mutually exclusive categories—male and female—and that we observe these natural states in an unobtrusive, objective manner. However, this is not the case. Distinguishing between women and men is an active process, and we do it compulsively. If you have any doubt about this, simply observe how quickly you determine other people's genders: It happens instantaneously. Not only that, but we tend to make the call one way or another no matter how far away a person is or how little evidence we have to go by. While we may like to think of ourselves as being passive observers, in reality we are constantly and actively projecting our ideas and assumptions about maleness and femaleness onto every person we meet. And all of us do it, whether we are cissexual or transsexual, straight as an arrow, or as queer as a three-dollar bill.

I call this process of distinguishing between females and males *gendering,* to highlight the fact that we actively and compulsively assign genders to all people based on usually just a few visual and audio cues. Recognizing the ubiquitous nature of this phenomenon calls into question most definitions of "gender" itself. We can argue all we want about what defines a woman or a man—whether it's genes, chromosomes, brain structure, genitals, socialization, or the legal sex on a birth certificate or driver's license—but the truth is, these factors typically play no role whatsoever in how we gender people in everyday circumstances. Typically, we rely primarily on secondary sex characteristics (body shape and size, skin complexion, facial and body hair, voice, breasts, etc.), and to a lesser extent, gender expression and gender roles (the person's dress, mannerisms, etc.). I will refer to the gender we are assigned by other people as our *perceived sex* (or *perceived gender*).

A major reason the act of gendering remains invisible to most people is that, in the vast majority of cases, our assessment of a person's gender tends to be in agreement with that person's gender identity and the gender assignments made by other people. (If the genders we assigned to individuals regularly differed from the assignments made by other people, the guesswork inherent in gendering would become far more obvious to us.) However, as a transsexual, I have been in numerous situations (particularly during my transition) where two or more people simultaneously came to different conclusions regarding my perceived gender—that is, one person assumed that I was female, while another assumed that I was male. Such instances demonstrate the speculative nature of gendering. I have also found that people's experiences and preconceptions around gender dramatically affect the way they gender other people. For example, back when I identified as a male crossdresser, I found that I could "pass" as a woman rather easily in suburban areas, but in cities (where people were presumably more aware of the existence of gender-variant people) I would often be "read" as a crossdressed male. Most cissexuals remain oblivious to the subjective nature of gendering, primarily because they themselves have not regularly had the experience of being *misgendered*—i.e., mistakenly assigned a gender that does not match one's identified gender. Unfortunately, this lack of experience usually leads cissexuals to mistakenly believe that the process of gendering is a matter of pure observation, rather than the act of speculation it is.

Cissexual Assumption

The second process that enables cissexual privilege is *cissexual assumption*. This occurs when a cissexual makes the common, albeit mistaken, assumption that the way they experience their physical and subconscious sexes (i.e., the fact that they do not feel uncomfortable with the sex they were born into, nor do they think of themselves as or wish they could become the other sex) applies to everyone else in the world. In other words, the cissexual indiscriminately projects their cissexuality onto all other people, thus transforming cissexuality into a human attribute that is taken for granted. There is an obvious analogy to heterosexual assumption here: Most cissexuals assume that everyone they meet is also cissexual, just as most heterosexuals assume that everyone they meet is also heterosexual (unless, of course, they are provided with evidence to the contrary).

While cissexual assumption remains invisible to most cissexuals, those of us who are transsexual are excruciatingly aware of it. Prior to our transitions, we find that the cissexual majority simply assumes that we fully identify as members of our assigned sex, thus making it difficult for us to manage our gender difference and to be open about the way we see ourselves. And after our transitions, many of us find that the cissexual majority simply assumes that we have always been members of our identified sex, thus making it impossible for us to be open about our trans status without constantly having to come out to others. Thus, while most cissexuals are unaware that cissexual assumption even exists, those of us who are transsexual recognize it as an active process that erases trans people and their experiences.

Cissexual Gender Entitlement

For most cissexuals, the fact that they feel comfortable inhabiting their own physical sex, and that other people confirm this sense of naturalness by appropriately gendering them, allows them to develop a sense of entitlement regarding their own gender: They feel entitled to call themselves a woman or a man. This is not necessarily a bad thing. However, because many of these same cissexuals also assume that they are infallible in their ability to assign genders to other people, they can develop an overactive sense of *cissexual gender entitlement.* This goes beyond a sense of self-ownership regarding their own gender, and broaches territory in which they consider themselves to be the ultimate arbiters of which people are allowed to call themselves women or men. Once again, most cissexuals are unaware of their gender entitlement, because (1) the processes that enable it (i.e., gendering and cissexual assumption) are invisible to them, and (2) so long as they are cissexual and relatively gender-normative, they have likely not been inconvenienced by the gender entitlement of others. Because gender-entitled cissexuals assume that they have the ability and authority to accurately determine who is a woman and who is a man, they in effect grant a privilege—*cissexual privilege*—to those people whom they appropriately gender. To illustrate this point, imagine that I'm approached by someone who appears male to me (i.e., I gender them male). If they were to introduce themselves as "Mr. Jones," I would probably extend them cissexual privilege—that is, I would respect their male identity and extend to them all of the privileges associated with their identified sex. I might call them "sir," grant them permission into a male-only space, find it appropriate when they tell me they're married to a woman, etc. However, if I were gender-entitled, there might be some instances in which I'd refuse to extend them the privileges associated with their identified sex. For instance, if the person introduced themselves as "Ms. Jones," but I chose to view the gender

I'd initially perceived them as (i.e., male) to be more authentic or legitimate than their female identity, then I would be denying them cissexual privilege. Similarly, if I were to learn that "Mr. Jones" was transsexual and had been born female, and if that knowledge led me to re-gender him as female rather than male, I would again be denying him (in this case) cissexual privilege.

An excellent example of how gender entitlement produces cissexual privilege, and how that privilege can be used to undermine transsexual genders, can be found in the following Germaine Greer quote:

> *No one ever asked women if they recognized sex-change males as belonging to their sex or considered whether being obliged to accept MTF transsexuals as women was at all damaging to their identity or self-esteem.*[1]

The immediate sense that one gets after reading this quote (besides nausea) is Greer's severe sense of gender entitlement. Despite the fact that she knows that transsexual women identify as female, Greer refers to us instead as "sex-change males," demonstrating that she feels entitled to gender us in whatever way she feels is appropriate. Similarly, because of her cissexual assumption (i.e., her belief that cissexuality is "natural" and goes without saying), she doesn't bother defining exactly what she means when she uses the word "women"; in her mind, it's a given that she is referring only to cissexual women. Greer grants these women cissexual privilege when she suggests that they (along with her) are equally entitled to be consulted about whether transsexual women should belong to their sex or not. It is particularly telling that Greer uses the word "asked" in this context. After all, nobody in our society ever asks for permission to belong to one gender or another; rather, we just are who we are and other people make assumptions about our gender accordingly. Thus, when Greer uses the words "asked" and "obliged," she is not talking about whether trans women should be allowed to be female, but whether or not our femaleness should be respected and legitimized to the same extent as cissexual women's femaleness. By applying different standards of legitimacy to people's identified and lived genders based on whether they are cissexual or transsexual, Greer is producing and exercising cissexual privilege.

The Myth of Cissexual Birth Privilege

Since cissexuals are generally unaware that their gender entitlement arises from the acts of gendering and cissexual assumption, they often find themselves having to justify their belief that their gender is more legitimate or "real" than that of a transsexual. The most common myth used to justify this cissexual privilege is the idea that cissexuals inherit the right to call themselves female or male by virtue of being born into that particular sex. In other words, cissexuals view their gender entitlement as a birthright. This is often a deceitful act, as many (if not most) cissexuals in our society tend to look disparagingly upon societies and cultures that still rely on class or caste systems—where one's occupation, social status, economic disposition, political power, etc., is predetermined based on an accident of birth. So while most Western cissexuals frown upon birth privilege as a means to determine these other forms of social class, they hypocritically embrace it when it comes to gender.

Once a cissexual assumes that their gender entitlement is a birth privilege, then it becomes easy for them to dismiss the legitimacy of transsexuals' identified and lived sex. After all, in their eyes, transsexuals are actively trying to claim for themselves a gender that they are not entitled to (having not been born into it). However, as a transsexual, I find several obvious flaws with this "birth privilege" argument. First of all, the sex we are assigned at birth plays almost no role whatsoever in day-to-day human interactions. None of us need to carry our birth certificate around with us to prove what sex we were born into. And since I have been living as a woman, I have never had a single person ask me whether I was born a girl. Indeed, cissexual assumption essentially renders my birth sex irrelevant, as others will automatically assume that I was born female (based solely on the fact that they have gendered me female).

Gender-entitled cissexuals may try to claim that I am actively setting out to "steal" cissexual privilege by transitioning to, and living as, female, but the truth is that I don't have to. In fact, I have found that cissexuals dole out cissexual privilege to complete and total strangers rather indiscriminately. Every time I walk into a store and someone asks, "How can I help you, ma'am?" they are extending me cissexual privilege. Every time I walk into a women's restroom and nobody flinches or questions my presence, they are extending me cissexual privilege. However, because I am a transsexual, the cissexual privilege that I experience is not equal to that of a cissexual because it can be brought into question at any time. It is perhaps best described as *conditional cissexual privilege,* because it can be taken away from me (and often is) as soon as I mention, or someone discovers, that I am transsexual.

Cissexuals may want to believe that their genders are more authentic than mine, but that belief is dishonest and ignorant. The truth is, cissexual women feel entitled to call themselves women because (1) they identify that way, (2) they live their lives as women, and (3) other people relate to them as women. All of these markers apply to my transsexual womanhood. In the realm of social interactions, the only difference between my transsexual gender and their cissexual genders is that my femaleness is generally mischaracterized as second-rate, as illegitimate, as an imitation of theirs. And the major difference between my life history as a woman and theirs is that I have had to fight for my right to be recognized as female, while they have had the privilege of simply taking it for granted.

Trans-Facsimilation and Ungendering

Because cissexuals have a vested interest in preserving their own sense of cissexual gender entitlement and privilege, they often engage in a constant and concerted effort to *artificialize* transsexual genders. A common strategy used to accomplish this goal is *trans-facsimilation*—viewing or portraying transsexual genders as facsimiles of cissexual genders. This strategy not only mischaracterizes transsexual genders as "fake," but insinuates that cissexual genders are the primary, "real" version that the transsexual merely copies.

The tactic of trans-facsimilation is evident in the regularity with which cissexuals use words such as "emulate," "imitate," "mimic," and "impersonate" when describing transsexual gender identities and expression. It can also be seen in the way cissexual media producers tend to depict real or fictional transsexual characters in the act of affecting or practicing gender roles associated with their identified sex. These depictions of transsexuality as mere affectation undermine the very real gender inclinations and experiences that lead transsexuals to live as members of their identified sex in the first place. Further, they ignore the ways in which all people—whether transsexual or cissexual—observe and imitate others with regard to gender. For cissexuals, such imitation mostly occurs during childhood and adolescence, when they may emulate certain gendered behaviors exhibited by a parent or an older sibling of the same sex. For transsexuals, this process often occurs later in life, at the period just before or during one's transition. In both cases, imitation is primarily a form of gender experimentation, with behaviors that the person feels comfortable with being retained over time, while those traits that feel awkward or incongruous with their sense of self eventually falling by the wayside. Once we recognize this, then it becomes apparent that transfacsimilation is a blatant double standard that ensures that acts of cissexual gender imitation will typically be overlooked (thus naturalizing their genders), while acts of transsexual gender imitation will be overemphasized (thus artificializing our genders).

Another way in which transsexual genders are often dismissed as "fakes" is by applying different standards of gendering to transsexuals and cissexuals. This practice is well-illustrated by the following passage from Patrick Califia's book *Sex Changes:*

> *Recently, I had a very educational experience. I found out that one of my long-term women acquaintances is transgendered.... Given how much work I've done to educate myself about transsexuality, I didn't think it would make that much of a difference. But I found myself looking at her in a whole different way. Suddenly her hands looked too big, there was something odd about her nose, and didn't she have an Adam's apple? Wasn't her voice kind of deep for a woman? And wasn't she*

> *awfully bossy, just like a man? And my God, she had a lot of hair on her forearm.*[2]

Califia goes on to say that this incident made him aware of the double standard that exists in the way transsexuals are often viewed. For example, when we presume a person to be cissexual, we generally accept their overall perceived gender as natural and authentic, while disregarding any minor discrepancies in their gender appearance. However, upon discovering or suspecting that a person is transsexual, we often actively (and rather compulsively) search for evidence of their assigned sex in their personality, expressions, and physical bodies. I have experienced this firsthand during the countless occasions when I have come out to people as transsexual. Upon learning of my trans status, most people get this distinctive "look" in their eyes, as if they are suddenly seeing me differently—searching for clues of the boy that I used to be and projecting different meanings onto my body. I call this process *ungendering,* as it is an attempt to undo a trans person's gender by privileging incongruities and discrepancies in their gendered appearance that would normally be overlooked or dismissed if they were presumed to be cissexual. The only purpose that ungendering serves is to privilege cissexual genders, while delegitimizing the genders of transsexuals and other gender-variant people.

Moving Beyond "Bio Boys" and "Genetic Girls"

The first step we must take toward dismantling cissexual privilege is to purge those words and concepts from our vocabularies that foster the idea that cissexual genders are inherently more authentic than those of transsexuals. A good place to start is with the common tendency to refer to cissexuals as "genetic" or "biological" males and females. Despite its frequent occurrence, the use of the word "genetic" seems particularly strange to me, since we are unable to readily see other people's sex chromosomes. In fact, since so few people ever have their chromosomes examined, one could argue that the vast majority of people have a genetic sex that has yet to be determined. In the rare cases where people do have their chromosomes checked out (such as sex testing at the Olympics or in infertility clinics), a person's genetic sex not matching their assigned sex occurs far more often than most people would ever fathom.[3]

The use of the word "biological" (and its abbreviation "bio") is just as impractical as the word "genetic." Whenever I hear someone refer to cissexuals as being "biological" women and men I usually interject that, despite the fact that I am a transsexual, I am not inorganic or nonbiological in any way. If I press people to further define what they mean by "biological," they'll often say that the word refers to people who have a fully functioning reproductive system for their sex. Well, if that's the case, then what about people who are infertile or who have their reproductive organs removed as the result of some medical condition? Are those people not "biological" men and women? People often insist that "biological" refers to someone's genitals, but I would ask them how many people's genitals they have ever seen up close. Ten? Twenty? A hundred? And in the vast majority of instances where we meet somebody who is fully dressed (and therefore their genitals are hidden), how do we know whether to refer to them as "she" or "he"? The truth is, when we see other people and classify them as either female or male, the only biological cues we typically have to go on are secondary sex characteristics, which are themselves the products of sex hormones. That being the case, as someone who has had estrogen in her system for five years now, shouldn't I be considered a "biological" woman?

When you break it down like this, it becomes obvious that the words "biological" and "genetic" are merely stand-ins for the word that people really want to use: "natural." Most cissexuals want to believe that their maleness or femaleness is "natural" in the same way that most heterosexuals want to believe that their sexual orientation is "natural." In fact, if you look at the entire spectrum of social and class issues, you will see a trend of people trying to "naturalize" their privileges in some way—whether it be wealthy people who try to justify the huge gap between rich and poor by appropriating Darwin's theory of natural selection, or white people who make claims that they are smarter or more successful than people of color because of their biology or their genes. When it comes to gender, "natural" is the ultimate trump card because it takes the relevant issues—privilege and prejudice—off the table and frames the very real and legitimate perspectives of sexual minorities as "unnatural" or "artificial," and therefore unworthy of any serious consideration.

This is why I prefer the term *cissexual.* It denotes the only relevant difference between that population and those of us who are transsexual: Cissexuals have only ever experienced their subconscious and physical sexes as being aligned.

Third-Gendering and Third-Sexing

Cissexual people who are in the earliest stages of accepting transsexuality (and who have not fully come to terms with their cissexual privilege) will often come to see trans people as inhabiting our own unique gender category that is separate from "woman" and "man." I call this act *third-gendering* (or *third-sexing*). While some attempts at third-gendering trans people are clearly meant to be derogatory or sensationalistic (such as "she-male" or "he-she"), other less offensive ones occur regularly in discussions about transsexuals (such as "s/he" or "MTF"). While "MTF" may be useful as an adjective, as it describes the direction of my transition, using it as a noun—i.e., literally referring to me as a "male-to-female"—completely negates the fact that I identify and live as a woman. Personally, I believe that popular use of "MTF" or "FTM" over "trans woman" or "trans man" (which are more respectful, easier to say, and less easily confused with one another) reflects either a conscious or unconscious desire on the part of many cissexuals to distinguish transsexual women and men from their cissexual counterparts.

When discussing the act of third-gendering, it is crucial to make a distinction between people who identify themselves as belonging to a third gender and those who actively third-gender other people. As with any gender identity, when people see themselves as belonging to a third gender, that is their way of making sense of themselves and their place in the world, and it should be respected. As someone who has identified as bigender and genderqueer in the past, I believe that it's important for us to recognize and respect other people's gender identities, whatever they are. But it's for this very same reason that I object to people who actively third-gender people against their will or without their consent. I believe that this propensity for third-gendering others is simply a by-product of the assumptive and nonconsensual process of gendering. In other words, we are so compelled to gender people as women and men that when we come across someone who is not easily categorized that way (usually because of exceptional gender inclinations), we tend to isolate and distinguish them from the other two genders. There is a long history of the terms "third gender" and "third sex" being applied to homosexuals, intersex people, and transgender people by those who considered themselves to have "normal" genders. This strongly suggests that the tendency to third-gender people stems from both gender entitlement and oppositional sexism.

Passing-Centrism

Another example where language presupposes that transsexual and cissexual genders are of inherently different worth is the use of the word "pass." While the word "pass" serves a purpose, in that it describes the very real privilege experienced by those transsexuals who receive conditional cissexual privilege when living as their identified sex, it is a highly problematic term in that it implies that the trans person is getting away with something. Upon close examination, it becomes quite obvious that the concept of "passing" is steeped in cissexual privilege, as it's only ever applied to trans people. For instance, if a store clerk were to say, "Thank you, sir," to a cissexual woman, nobody would say that she "passed" as a man or failed to "pass" as a woman; instead, we would say she *is* a woman and was *mistaken* for a man. Further, we never use the word "passing" to describe cissexual men who lift weights every day in order to achieve a more masculine appearance, or cissexual women who put on makeup, skirts, and heels to achieve a more feminine appearance. Yet, because I'm a transsexual woman, if I roll out of bed, throw on a T-shirt and jeans, and walk down the street and am generally recognized by others as female (despite my lack of concern for my appearance), I can still be dismissed as "passing" as a woman.

The crux of the problem is that the words "pass" and "passing" are active verbs. So when we say that a transsexual is "passing," it gives the false impression that they are the only active participant in this scenario (i.e., the transsexual is working hard to achieve a certain gendered appearance and everyone else is passively being duped or not duped by the transsexual's "performance"). However, I would argue that the reverse is true: The public is the primary active participant by virtue of their incessant need to gender every person they see as either female or male. The transsexual can react to this situation in one of two ways: They can either try to live up to public expectations about maleness and femaleness in an attempt to fit in and avoid stigmatization, or they can disregard public expectations and simply be themselves. However, if they choose the latter, the public will still judge them based on whether they appear female or male and, of course, others may still accuse them of "passing," even though they have not actively done anything. Thus, the active role played by those who compulsively distinguish between women and men (and who discriminate between transsexuals and cissexuals) is made invisible by the concept of "passing."

It should be mentioned that this view of "passing" is further supported by the use of the word with regards to other social class issues. For instance, a gay man can "pass" for straight, or a fair-skinned person of color can "pass" for white. Sometimes people work hard to "pass," and other times they don't try at all. Either way, the one thing that remains consistent is that the word "pass" is used to shift the blame away from the majority group's prejudice and toward the minority person's presumed motives and actions (which explains why people who "pass" are often accused of "deception" or "infiltration" if they are ever found out).

It has been my experience that most cissexuals are absolutely obsessed about whether transsexuals "pass" or not. From clinical and academic accounts to TV, movies, and magazine articles, cissexuals spend an exorbitant amount of energy indulging their fascination regarding what transsexuals "do"—the medical procedures, how we modify our behaviors, etc.—in order to "pass" as our identified sex. This *passing-centrism* allows cissexuals to ignore their own cissexual privilege, and also serves to privilege the transsexual's assigned sex over their identified and lived sex, thereby reinforcing the idea that transsexual genders are illegitimate.

Ironically, it has been common for cissexuals to claim that transsexuals are the ones obsessed with "passing." Such accusations dismiss the countless transsexuals who are not concerned with how they are perceived by others and also make invisible the fact that both parties have disparate vested interests when it comes to transsexual "passing." Specifically, while cissexuals have no legitimate reason to be concerned over whether any given transsexual "passes" (other than as a means to exercise cissexual privilege over them), transsexuals understand that being taken seriously in our identified sex has extraordinary ramifications on our quality of life. Living in this extraordinarily cissexist (and oppositionally sexist) world, transsexuals recognize cissexual privilege for what it is: a *privilege*. Being accepted as members of our identified sex makes it infinitely easier for us to gain employment and housing, to be taken seriously in our personal, social, and political endeavors, and to be able to walk down the street without being harassed or assaulted.

Cissexuals (not transsexuals) are the ones who create, foster, and enforce "passing" by their tendency to treat transsexuals in dramatically different ways based solely on the superficial criteria of our appearance. If a transsexual does not "pass," cissexuals often use it as an excuse to deny that person the common decency of having their self-identified gender acknowledged or respected. Sometimes cissexuals even use these situations as if they were an invitation to openly humiliate or abuse transsexuals. And those of us who do "pass" are undoubtedly treated better by cissexuals, although not necessarily with respect. As a transsexual who "passes," I find it quite common for cissexuals, upon discovering my trans status, to praise me using the same condescending tone of voice that people use when praising gay people who don't "flaunt" their homosexuality (i.e., who act straight), or racial minorities who use "proper English" (i.e., who act white). In other words, these are backhanded compliments designed to reinforce cissexual superiority. The most common of these comments, "You look just like a real woman," would clearly be taken as an insult if it were said to a cissexual woman. Another common comment is, "I never would have guessed that you're a transsexual," which essentially praises me for looking *cissexual-like,* once again insinuating that cissexuals are inherently better than transsexuals.

Because the term "passing" creates a double standard between cissexual and transsexual genders and enables cissexual gender entitlement, we should instead adopt language that rightfully recognizes this phenomenon as a by-product of gendering and cissexual assumption. Therefore, I suggest using the term *misgendered* when a cissexual or transsexual person is assigned a gender that does not match the gender they consider themselves to be, and the term *appropriately gendered* when others assign them a gender that matches the way they self-identify. And, as mentioned previously, the term *conditional cissexual privilege* ought to be adopted to describe what has historically been referred to as "passing" privilege.

Taking One's Gender for Granted

An additional problem with the word "pass" is that it is typically only used in reference to a transsexual's identified sex rather than their assigned sex. This gives the impression that transsexuals only begin managing other people's perceptions *after* we transition. Consider that people will talk about the fact that I now "pass" as a woman, but nobody ever asks about how difficult it must have been for me to "pass" as a man before. Personally, I found it infinitely more difficult and stressful to manage my perceived gender back when people presumed I was male than I do now as female. However, once we start thinking in terms of whether a transsexual is being misgendered or appropriately gendered in accordance with their understanding of themselves (as opposed to whether they are "passing" or not in the eyes of others), then we start to gain a more accurate and realistic appreciation for the transsexual experience. In fact, you could say that most transsexuals have the experience of being misgendered throughout their childhoods and sometimes well into their adulthoods. The extent to which this constant misgendering during our formative years shapes our relationship with gender (and our own self-perception) cannot be underestimated.

Having only ever had a trans experience, it took me a long time to realize how differently I experience and process gender compared to the way most cissexuals do. For example, a few months after I had begun living full-time as a woman, a male friend of mine asked me if I had ever accidentally gone into a men's restroom by mistake. At first, the question struck me as bizarre. When I gave him a perplexed look, he tried to clarify himself. He said that he doesn't ever think about what restroom he is entering, never really notices the little "man" symbol on the door, but he always ends up in the right place anyway. So he was wondering whether I had accidentally gone into the men's room *by habit* since my transition. I laughed and told him that there had never been a single instance in my life when I had walked into a public restroom—women's or men's—by habit; my entire life I have been excruciatingly aware of any gendered space that I enter.

Growing up trans—having to manage both the psychological dissonance between my physical and subconscious sex as well as the constant barrage of being misgendered by others—was a harrowing experience and one that caused me to dissociate myself from my own body and emotions. And while physically transitioning and living in my identified sex has allowed me to finally overcome my gender dissonance, I still struggle with an intense hypersensitivity to gender (and more specifically to gendering). Having never had an opportunity to learn to experience my gender as being unquestionable or second-nature (as my friend had), I still sometimes feel an awkward jolt whenever people refer to me as "she" (even though that pronoun is preferable to me). When I look at photos or videos of myself, I still can't help but see the "boy" in my face or hear it in the sound of my voice, even though I haven't had anyone call me "sir" in over five years. I feel assaulted and get extraordinarily upset whenever I'm watching TV or a movie and I'm blindsided by a joke or ignorant comment that dismisses trans people's identified sex or refers to them in their assigned sex. And although I experience gender concordance these days, I still constantly dwell on gender, which, while helpful when writing a book on the subject, can often be unhealthy and exhausting.

My gender hypersensitivity reminds me of what a friend once told me about her relationship with money. She grew up in a family where money was scarce, and where fights regularly stemmed from the financial strain they were under. This irrevocably altered the way my friend relates to money. While most of us who have had a middle-class upbringing see money as simply a means to get the things that we want or need, for my friend it also carries an added emotional element. Even though she is now on more solid ground financially, she still feels undeserving when she receives money and guilty every time she spends it. It still preoccupies her and fills her with anxiety because she doesn't feel like she can ever take it for granted—she understands that it can be taken away from her at any time.

My friend's relationship with money reminds me of my own continuing insecurity regarding gender. Even though I have finally reached a point where I feel comfortable living in my own body, I often feel undeserving and guilty about it. And while everyone else around me seems to feel entitled to their gender to the point where they take it for granted, I always feel like mine can be taken away from me at any minute. And in a sense, it can (and often is) whenever somebody attempts to wield cissexual privilege over me.

Distinguishing Between Transphobia and Cissexual Privilege

The fact that transsexuals have survived a childhood of constantly being misgendered creates major differences in the ways that we and other queers react to public expressions of gender anxiety. For example, a cissexual butch dyke friend of mine shared with me an experience she had of being accused of being a "man" in a women's restroom (presumably because of her masculine style of dress and mannerisms). The woman who made the accusation confronted her in a gender-entitled way by saying, "You don't belong here." My friend, who was obviously disturbed by the incident, responded by pointing to her own breasts and saying, "I *am* a woman and I *do* belong here," which had the effect of making the accuser embarrassed and apologetic. While my friend does not identify as transgender, one could describe this incident as an example of transphobia (she was targeted because her appearance "transgressed" gender norms). And when the accuser apologized, she in effect (belatedly) extended cissexual privilege to my friend. That is to say, the accuser recognized my friend as a legitimate (albeit gender-non-conforming) woman and, as such, acknowledged my friend's right to share that women-only space with her.

I tell this story because it is so radically different from the way some of my trans women friends experience similar situations. When a transsexual woman is accused of being a "man" in the women's room, it's against a backdrop of the transsexual having been misgendered as male all of her life. Thus, rather than feeling like she has been unfairly targeted because her behaviors "transgress" gender norms (as many cissexual queers feel), she will instead feel targeted because of her transsexual status—in other words, she will assume that the accuser is exercising cissexual privilege over her. And the transsexual woman is often correct in assuming this. After all, the accuser became apologetic when my butch dyke friend told her, "I am a woman" (in other words, she was belatedly "read" as a cissexual woman), but when my trans women friends say "I am a woman," they are often still accused of being "men" (in other words, they are "read" as transsexual women and thus denied cissexual privilege).

Recognizing the difference between transphobia (which targets those whose gender expression and appearance differ from the norm) and cissexual privilege (which targets those whose assigned and identified sexes differ) is important, especially when one tries to make sense of contemporary queer/trans politics. For example, some queer women's events and establishments have policies that specifically exclude trans women from attending. Proponents of such policies often claim that they are not transphobic, because they do allow some transgender-identified people to attend (as long as they were "born female"). Thus, rather than calling trans-woman-exclusion policies "transphobic," it is more accurate to say that they are cissexist, as they refuse to accept transsexual women's female identities as being as legitimate as those of cissexual women. (Such policies may also be called *trans-misogynistic,* as they favor FTM spectrum trans people over MTF spectrum folks.) Furthermore, those "female-born" cissexuals (regardless of whether they are transgender-identified) who choose to attend such events can be said to be exercising their cissexual privilege (i.e., they are taking advantage of all of the privileges associated with their female birth sex). Indeed, it is disappointing that most cissexual transgender and queer folks—particularly those who hypocritically accuse transsexuals of trying to attain "passing privilege" by transitioning to our identified sex—have given little to no thought about the countless ways they frequently indulge in their own cissexual privilege.

Once we understand cissexual privilege, it becomes evident that many acts of discrimination that have previously been lumped under the term "transphobia" are probably better described in terms of cissexism. Next, I will reconsider a number of such discriminatory acts, focusing on the ways that they are more specifically designed to undermine the legitimacy of trans people's identified genders rather than targeting trans people for breaking oppositional gender norms.

Trans-Exclusion

Trans-exclusion is perhaps the most straightforward act of prejudice against transsexuals. Simply stated, trans-exclusion occurs when cissexuals exclude transsexuals from any spaces, organizations, or events designated for the trans person's identified gender. Trans-exclusion may also include other instances where the trans person's identified gender is dismissed (for example, when someone insists on calling me a "man," or purposely uses inappropriate pronouns when addressing me). Considering how big of a social faux pas it is in our culture to misgender someone, and how apologetic people generally become upon finding out that they have made that mistake, it is difficult to view trans-exclusion—i.e., the deliberate misgendering of transsexuals—as anything other than an arrogant attempt to belittle and humiliate trans people.

Trans-Objectification

The objectification of transsexual bodies is very much intertwined with the cissexual obsession with "passing." While our physical transitions typically occur over a period of a few years—a mere fraction of our lives—they almost completely dominate cissexual discourses regarding transsexuality. The reason for this is clear: Focusing almost exclusively on our physical transformations keeps transsexuals forever anchored in our assigned sex, thus turning our identified sex into a goal that we are always approaching but never truly achieve. This not only undermines our very real experiences living as members of our identified sex post-transition, but purposely sidesteps the crucial issue of cissexual prejudice against transsexuals (akin to how some heterosexuals focus their interest on what gays, lesbians, and bisexuals do in the bedroom—i.e., how we have sex—in order to avoid contemplating whether their own behaviors and attitudes contribute to same-sex discrimination).

Another common form of *trans-objectification* occurs when cissexuals become hung up on, disturbed by, or obsessed over supposed discrepancies that exist between a transsexual's physical sex and identified gender. Most typically, such attention is focused on a trans person's genitals. Because objectification reduces the transsexual to the status of a "thing," it enables cissexuals to condemn, demonize, fetishize, ridicule, criticize, and exploit us without guilt or remorse.

Trans-Mystification

Another strategy that goes hand in hand with passing-centrism and trans-objectification is *trans-mystification:* to allow oneself to become so caught up in the taboo nature of "sex changes" that one loses sight of the fact that transsexuality is very real, tangible, and often mundane for those of us who experience it firsthand. One can see trans-mystification readily in media depictions of transsexuals, where our assigned sex is often transformed into a hidden secret or plot twist and our lived sex is distorted into an elaborate illusion.

In real life, when I tell people that I am a transsexual, it is common for them to dawdle over me, repeating how they can't believe that I used to be male, as if I had just impressed them with a magic trick. The truth is, there is nothing fascinating about transsexuality. It is simply reality for many of us. I come out to people all the time and there is never any suspenseful music playing in the background when I do. And my femaleness is not some complex production that requires smoke and mirrors for me to pull off; believe it or not, I live my life by just being myself and doing what feels most comfortable to me. Trans-mystification is merely another attempt by cissexuals to play up the "artificiality" of transsexuality, thus creating the false impression that our assigned genders are "natural" and our identified and lived genders are not.

Trans-Interrogation

Passing-centrism, trans-objectification, and trans-mystification delegitimize transsexual identities by focusing on the "how" of transsexuality; *trans-interrogation* focuses on the "why." Why do transsexuals exist? Why are we motivated to change our sex? Is it due to genetics? Hormones? Upbringing? Living in a plastic surgery–obsessed culture? Or maybe it's just a good old-fashioned mental disorder? Such questions represent the intellectualization of objectifying transsexuals. By reducing us to the status of objects of inquiry, cissexuals free themselves of the inconvenience of having to consider us living, breathing beings who cope not only with our own intrinsic inclinations, but with extrinsic cissexist and oppositionally sexist gender discrimination.

While I was working on chapter 7, "Pathological Science," immersing myself in sexological and sociological accounts that attempt to explain why transsexuals exist, it occurred to me that, rather than simply removing the gender identity disorder diagnosis from the *DSM,* we should perhaps consider replacing it with transsexual etiology disorder, to describe the unhealthy obsession many cissexuals have with explaining the origins of transsexuality. Unlike those cissexual researchers who find it fascinating and thought-provoking to ponder and pontificate on my existence, for me the question of why I am transsexual has always been a source of shame and self-loathing. From my preteen years through young adulthood, I was consumed with the question because, quite frankly, I didn't want to be transsexual. Like most people, I assumed that it was better to be cissexual. Eventually, I realized that dwelling on "why" was a pointless endeavor—the fact is that I am transsexual and I exist, and there is no legitimate reason why I should feel inferior to a cissexual because of that.

Once I accepted my own transsexuality, then it became obvious to me that the question "Why do transsexuals exist?" is not a matter of pure curiosity, but rather an act of nonacceptance, as it invariably occurs in the absence of asking the reciprocal question: "Why do cissexuals exist?" The unceasing search to uncover the cause of transsexuality is designed to keep transsexual gender identities in a perpetually questionable state, thereby ensuring that cissexual gender identities continue to be unquestionable.

Trans-Erasure

The only thing more troubling than people who relentlessly wonder why transsexuals exist are people who arrogantly assume that they know the answer to that question. Unfortunately, rather than simply accepting transsexual accounts—which almost invariably describe some sort of intrinsic self-knowledge or subconscious sex—many cissexuals instead choose to project their own assumptions about gender onto us. Often, such attempts center on naive cissexual notions about what a transsexual might socially gain from changing their lived sex: privilege, normalcy, sexual fulfillment, and so on. The idea that we transition first and foremost for ourselves, to be comfortable in our own bodies, is often never seriously considered. This is because transsexuals are generally viewed by cissexuals as nonentities: the processes of trans-objectification, trans-mystification, and trans-interrogation ensure that we are seen not as human beings, but as objects and as spectacles that exist for the benefit or amusement of others. The ease with which transsexual voices are dismissed or ignored by the public is due to the phenomenon of *trans-erasure.*

While all minority voices are silenced to varying extents—usually by being denied access to media and economic and political power—there are several aspects of trans-erasure that make it particularly extensive. First, as with all sexual minorities, oppositional sexism ensures that only a small percentage of trans people ever come out as transsexual. Second, those who come out often do so concurrently with their decision to physically transition, a process that has been historically regulated (and severely limited) by cissexual gatekeepers. Often, those who were granted permission to transition were selected based on the gatekeepers' assessment that they would be gender-normative in their identified sex and would remain silent about their trans status post-transition. This has helped ensure that most transsexuals effectively disappear within the cissexual population both pre- and post-transition.

But perhaps nothing facilitates trans-erasure more than everyday gendering and cissexual assumption. When I come out to people, they often tell me that I am the first transsexual they have ever met. This suggests that most cissexuals never seriously consider the possibility that a certain percentage of the cissexual-appearing people they see every day might actually be transsexual. International statistics indicate that the percentage of "post-operative" transsexuals range from 1 to 3 percent of the population. While there are no rigorous statistics for the number of transsexuals in the U.S., estimates based on the number of sex reassignment surgeries performed suggest that at least one in five hundred people in this country are transsexual (and several times more than that are transgender).[4]

In a world where people are viewed as being either female or male, and where all people are assumed to be cisgender and cissexual, those of us who are transgender and transsexual are effectively erased from public awareness. This allows media producers to depict us however they want, for academics to posit whatever theories they wish about us, and for cissexual doctors, psychologists, and other self-appointed "experts" to speak as proxies on our behalf.

Changing Gender Perception, Not Performance

A thorough understanding of gendering, gender entitlement, and cissexual privilege challenges both the mainstream assumption that cissexual genders are more "natural" and legitimate than transsexual genders, and the recent focus among gender theorists and activists on how all people "do" or "perform" their genders.[5] These performance-centric models of gender can vary quite a bit, but they generally stress the idea that each of us actively creates gender differences by "doing" or "performing" gender in particular ways.

According to this view, femaleness is not a natural state, but one that we reproduce when we call ourselves women—when we act, dress, speak in what are considered feminine ways—and similarly for maleness. Some of the more extreme variations of this theory leave little room for intrinsic gender inclinations, leaning toward the notion that our gender and sexual identities are merely unconscious repetitions of the socialization and gender norms that have been foisted upon us. Because many theorists and activists view gendered performance as the means by which gender privileges, expectations, and restrictions are propagated in our culture, they have argued that the most effective way to counteract oppositional and traditional sexism is to refuse all gender and sexual identities, or to subvert those categories by "doing" gender in nonconventional ways (e.g., drag, androgyny, and so on).

Many gender theorists and activists have embraced performance-centric models, praising these models' potential to free us from oppositional gender norms and to challenge the idea that straight genders are more legitimate than queer ones. But I see several problems with such theories. For one thing, such models display several of the flaws that regularly plague gender theories, which I described in detail at the end of chapter 6, "Intrinsic Inclinations." Further, I believe that the central tenet of performance-centric models of gender—that social gender arises and is propagated by the way individuals "do" or "perform" gender—is problematic. Many of us who have physically transitioned from one sex to the other understand that our perceived gender is typically not a product of our "performance" (i.e., gender expression/gender roles), but rather our physical appearance (in particular, our secondary sex characteristics). This makes sense if you think about it. After all, if you look like a supermodel, you can act as butch as you want to, but other people will inevitably gender you as female. And if you look like a linebacker, you can act as femme as you want, but others will still gender you as male. While the way we "do" gender may influence whether people perceive us as queer or straight, and may tip the scales for those whose appearance is somewhat gender-ambiguous to begin with, the vast majority of us are gendered primarily based on our physical bodies rather than our behaviors.

Personally, I used to have a performance-centric view of gender when I was living as a male, when I used to crossdress and "pass" as a woman in public. The amount of time and effort I had to put into altering my appearance and behaviors to accomplish that feat made it feel like a performance in many ways. But when I eventually did transition, I chose not to put on a performance—I simply acted, dressed, and spoke the way I always had, the way that felt most comfortable to me. After being on female hormones for a few months, I found that people began to consistently gender me as female despite the fact that I was "doing" my gender the same way I always had. What I found most striking was how other people interpreted my same actions and mannerisms differently based on whether they perceived me to be female or male. For example, when ordering drinks at bars, I found that if I looked around the room while waiting for my drink (as I always unconsciously had prior to transitioning), men started hitting on me because they assumed I was signaling my availability (when I was perceived as male, the same action was likely to be interpreted simply as me scoping out the room). And in supermarket checkout lines, when the child in the cart ahead of me started smiling and talking to me, I found that I could interact with them without their mother becoming suspicious or fearful (which is what often happened in similar situations when I was perceived as male).

During the first year of my transition, I experienced hundreds of little moments like that, where other people interpreted my words and actions differently based solely on the change in my perceived sex. And it was not merely my behaviors that were interpreted differently, it was my body as well: the way people approached me, spoke to me, the assumptions they made about me, the lack of deference and respect I often received, the way others often sexualized my body. All of these changes occurred without my having to say or do a thing.

I would argue that social gender is not produced and propagated because of the way we as individuals "perform" or "do" our genders; it lies in the perceptions and interpretations of others. I can modify my own gender all I want, but it won't change the fact that other people will continue to compulsively assign a gender to me and to view me through the distorted lenses of cissexual and heterosexual assumption.

While no gendered expression can subvert the gender system as we know it, we are nevertheless still capable of instituting change in that system. However, such change will not come by managing the way we "do" our own gender, but by dismantling our own gender entitlement. If we truly want to bring an end to all gender-based oppression, then we must begin by taking responsibility for our own perceptions and presumptions. The most radical thing that any of us can do is to stop projecting our beliefs about gender onto other people's behaviors and bodies.

9

Ungendering in Art and Academia

People use books on gender to invisibilize transsexuals.

—Kate Bornstein[1]

Sometimes I think they just don't want to hear the real stories. I get cynical and think, who wants the everyday details of someone's life when you can use people with intersex to fulfill erotic fantasies, narrative requirements, and research programs?

—Thea Hillman[2]

IN PREVIOUS CHAPTERS, I discussed how most depictions of transsexuals are designed to reinforce the idea that female and male are distinct, mutually exclusive, "opposite" sexes. The same can also be said for depictions of other gender-variant people (i.e., those who deviate in some way from societal expectations of femaleness and maleness). In this chapter, I describe a more recent, reciprocal phenomenon—which I call *ungendering*—where gender-variant people are used as a device to bring conventional notions about maleness and femaleness into question. In theory, any person can be ungendered (simply by dwelling on the aspects of their gendered appearance, expressions, and identity that differ from the norm), but this practice seems to most often focus on transsexual and intersex people. While these two groups face very different social and medical issues because of their gender difference, they both tend to be targeted for ungendering because their physical bodies are in some way at odds with their identified and lived genders. Here, I discuss the practice of ungendering as it occurs in cissexual works of fiction (e.g., movies and novels) and in academia. In both cases, ungendering is an exploitive process, involving both the appropriation of gender-variant bodies and experiences while erasing intersex and transsexual voices and perspectives.

Capitalizing on Transsexuality and Intersexuality

A classic example of ungendering can be found in the Emmy Award–nominated HBO movie *Normal,* which depicts a trans woman named Roy who comes out to her family as trans. The movie focuses on how Roy's revelation and her ensuing transition affects her relationship with her wife and children in their small midwestern town. In an interview about the film that appeared on *HBO.com,* writer and director Jane Anderson said that, despite the fact that the subject of transsexuality dominates much of the film, she did not envision *Normal* as a story chronicling the "adventures of a transgender person," but rather as a study of one married-couple's love for one another.[3]

So if the movie is not about transsexuality per se, then why did this non-trans filmmaker go to the trouble of including a transsexual character? Anderson explained that she used transsexuality primarily as a device to challenge the couple's relationship. In fact, she draws a comparison between the way she employs transsexuality and the way other writers have used extra-marital affairs in the past. While Anderson seems to believe that stories that center on extra-marital affairs have become passé (both because the premise has been overused by writers and because many people continue to love the person who has cheated on them), she views transsexuality as "ultimate betrayal" that can occur within a marriage.[4]

So, in other words, one of the characters, Roy, is ungendered in order to throw a monkey wrench into the couple's marriage. And transsexuality is no longer a marginalized identity or a grueling issue that real human beings struggle with; it is merely a literary device—a "metaphor" for the "ultimate catastrophe" that can strike a relationship.

You would think that Anderson—as a woman and a lesbian—would be aware of the troubling way sexual minorities are portrayed (and their voices silenced) by the media, and that she would, at the very least, make a modest attempt to ensure that her character was respectful of the transsexual experience. Unfortunately, this is not the case. When the interviewer asked her if she drew on any sources when researching the movie, Anderson unabashedly answered that she relied solely on her "imagination," that she made it up all herself.[5]

Unencumbered by any need to have her character reflect reality, Anderson was free to turn Roy into a transsexual caricature. She explained in the interview that she purposely set out to make sure that the audience would not take Roy seriously as a woman.[6] Perhaps this is why Anderson makes no attempt to have any of the other characters come to relate to Roy as female or use female pronouns when addressing her. Roy herself doesn't seem to protest this fact or assert her female identity at any point; in fact, she is inordinately meek and docile for someone who is in the process of coming out as transsexual. In a pre-movie interview, Tom Wilkinson, who played Roy in the made-for-cable movie, said, "I wanted to retain the kind of innocence about the whole thing that that *guy* had. *He* doesn't know quite what *he's* getting into." (Emphasis mine.)[7] Thus, like his director, Wilkinson shows no respect for his transsexual character's gender identity. As a result, Roy comes off as excruciatingly mousy and confused, presumably because it never occurred to either Wilkinson or Anderson that a man who wanted to be female could be any other way.

For someone who claims to have little interest in making a film about the "adventures of a transgender person," Anderson sure does fancy her film up in all of the accoutrements of the transsexual transitioning process: The dialogue includes discussions about electrolysis, a play-by-play description of how a vagina is created during MTF sex reassignment surgery, and even talk about what breast size Roy can expect after she goes on hormones. At one point in the movie, close-ups of Roy's hormone prescriptions—Premarin and Spironolactone—precede an early morning family breakfast scene in which Roy, her wife, and her daughter (who has recently had her first period) all start arguing with each other in an apparent hormone-induced frenzy. (Upon watching that scene, I wasn't quite sure if I should be more offended as a woman or as a transsexual.)

In the end, the most damaging aspect of *Normal* is that it gives the impression of being a serious film about transsexuality without ever incorporating the perspectives of real-life transsexuals. There are countless other movies that, on the surface, seem to be more demeaning or insulting toward transsexuals, but I find *Normal* to be more damaging than most. At least the *Ace Ventura*s and *South Park*s of the world don't even bother to pretend that they know what they're talking about when they create transsexual characters. Anderson, on the other hand, did just enough homework about transsexuality to make her film dangerous. She poached and pilfered the transsexual experience without any sense of respect or responsibility for the very people she exploited in the process.

Another writer who knows just enough to be dangerous is Jeffrey Eugenides. His Pulitzer Prize–winning novel *Middlesex* centers on an intersex person named Cal, who is raised female until he discovers his condition during puberty. The book follows Cal as he develops male physical attributes and eventually a male identity. So why did Eugenides set out to write a book about an intersex person? In an interview, he explained that he simply "used a hermaphrodite" (a word most intersex people find stigmatizing) as a metaphor for the confusing changes in identity and sexuality that all people face during adolescence.[8] So, this time, a main character is ungendered to make a larger point about puberty and metamorphosis.

Eugenides says he was initially inspired to write *Middlesex* after reading *Herculine Barbin,* a real-life account of an intersex person who lived during the nineteenth century, published by French philosopher Michel Foucault in 1978. Eugenides was fascinated by the book, but he found that, "as an expression of what it is like to be a hermaphrodite, from the inside, Herculine Barbin's memoir is quite disappointing. She just tends to go into this moaning, talking about how misfortunate she is and . . . it's sad."[9] Rather than be inconvenienced by the overwhelming depression and isolation that often typifies the lives of gender-variant people, Eugenides set out to invent his own new-and-improved intersex story: "I wanted to write about a real person with a real condition. I did a lot of research on the details, but in terms of figuring out what hermaphrodites psychologically went through, I did that from my imagination. That's how I work, I try to identify my narrator and my characters as much as I can instead of going out, observing other intersex people and focus[ing] on the details. Hopefully I make the right assumptions and choices about all these characters, so that someone [who] is interested in intersex reads the book."[10]

Middlesex is chock-full of descriptions of atypical chromosome combinations, genital configurations, and other highly detailed medical references to intersex conditions, yet it remains remarkably untainted by actual intersex perspectives or voices.[11] The book reads like an intersex adventure story, with colorful scenes of Cal's visit with an eccentric, John Money–esque doctor who wishes to perform nonconsensual genital surgery on him, or his befriending other intersex people (as well as transsexuals) when he fulfills the standard gender-variant-person cliché of working as a performer at a sex club. For a character who is supposedly fourteen years old at the time of these events, Cal's narration remains remarkably light, humorous, and generally above the fray at all times, as though it had been whitewashed of all of the shame, self-loathing, and self-consciousness that plagues gender-variant adolescents as their bodies, identities, and behaviors are placed under society's microscope. The way that Eugenides dwells on all of the physical aspects of intersexuality while playing down the emotional trauma and stigma that generally accompanies it gives the book an extraordinarily objectifying and voyeuristic feel to someone who is actually familiar with the subject.

Eugenides and Anderson both claim to use intersexuality and transsexuality merely as metaphors, but this is clearly disingenuous. While *Middlesex* may be an epic novel that follows a Greek American family through several generations, what consistently grabbed people's attention in book reviews and interviews was its intersex protagonist. And while *Normal* may be a film about marriage, it was clearly marketed as a film about transsexuality. The success of *Middlesex* and *Normal* was clearly due in large part to the fact that they offered mainstream audiences a glimpse into what are largely considered the mysterious and exotic lives of gender-variant people. Eugenides and Anderson capitalized on the taboo nature of intersexuality and transsexuality without acknowledging the fact that the stigma associated with these conditions forces real people to the margins of society. These writers took two of the most maligned and misunderstood sexual minorities in existence, hollowed them out, and poured in their own non-intersex, cissexual biases, inclinations, and impressions. In a world where transsexual and intersex works of art never get the chance to be seen on HBO, or are not considered mainstream enough to be nominated for Emmys and Pulitzers, the facade presented in *Normal* and *Middlesex* profoundly shapes and solidifies a naive audience's opinions about transsexuals and intersex people. By replacing gender-variant voices with their own, both Eugenides and Anderson ensure that real transsexual or intersex voices are not heard.

Toying with Gender-Ambiguous Characters

Another form of ungendering in media involves sexually amorphous characters. Perhaps the most famous example of this is Julia Sweeney's character "Pat," who gained popularity on the TV show

Saturday Night Live. Skits involving Pat essentially consisted of one recurring gag: Other characters, disturbed by Pat's indeterminate gender, would ask her/him questions designed to reveal whether he/she was a woman or a man. Pat always replied in a gender-ambiguous fashion that thwarted their efforts. While most of the jokes were made at the expense of the other characters, who expressed ridiculous amounts of concern and frustration over their inability to gauge Pat's sex, the mainstream appeal of the skits was most likely due to the fact that the drooling, whiny, creepy Pat was pretty much a joke him/herself.

Another similar use of an ungendered character can be found in Diane DiMassa's comic strip *Hothead Paisan, Homicidal Lesbian Terrorist.* With its dyke protagonist who confronts expressions of sexism and homophobia with a lethal combination of violence and humor, *Hothead* became a popular vehicle in the '90s for expressing the frustration and anger many queer women felt. At one point in the series, Hothead meets her eventual love interest, Daphne. When they are first dating, Daphne mentions, "I'm just low on friends! Mine took off 'cause they couldn't handle it." After Hothead asks why, Daphne explains, "I'm in the middle of a large-scale transition. Look at me. . . . Do you see?"[12] The fact that this "large-scale transition" is a physical one, and that Daphne follows with, "I'm telling you now so you can do what you gotta do. If you're gonna fly away I'd rather just get it over with," DiMassa is clearly leading the audience to believe that Daphne is transsexual. This is further evident in a later episode when Hothead imagines asking, "So Daphne, what's the story? You gotta dick or pussy or what?"[13] While the fact that Daphne has a feminine name, longish hair, breasts, and identifies as a dyke suggests that she is a trans woman,

DiMassa never clearly spells it out, opting instead to tease the audience by relegating Daphne to a permanently ungendered state.

In 2004, Daphne's ungendered status slammed up against the political reality of actual trans people when a musical based on *Hothead Paisan* was to be performed at the Michigan Womyn's Music Festival. Because many people were led to believe that Daphne was transgender—and more specifically, a trans woman—DiMassa received pressure to denounce the festival's trans-woman-exclusion policy. In response, DiMassa published an open letter on her website in July 2004 stating that she supported the trans-woman-exclusion policy. In an interview with *Bitch* magazine around the same time, she said, "Daphne has become sort of a transgender hero character. But I never used that word. I never said which way she was going. I never said if she was MTF or FTM."[14]

It seems that DiMassa wants to have it both ways here. She wants to toy with the idea of transsexuality without taking responsibility for the fact that real trans people have identities that are regularly dismissed by other people. DiMassa feels entitled to use her gender-variant characters as mere plot devices to provoke other characters and audiences in much the same way that heterosexist TV sitcom writers create walk-on lesbian characters who exist only to challenge the male protagonist's masculinity. Perhaps the most surreal part of the entire incident was DiMassa's defensive reaction to the anger of the trans female community, at one point quipping, "It's just fucking typical that a man-born woman can't get the concept of not being allowed somewhere."[15] Apparently, DiMassa believes that the anger lesbian women feel about being marginalized by the straight, male-dominated mainstream is legitimate, but that the similar anger trans women feel about being dismissed, stereotyped, and exploited by the lesbian community merely represents selfishness on our parts.

I am sure that writers like DiMassa, Eugenides, and Anderson would defend their works by claiming they have artistic license to create characters and stories as they please. To be honest, I would have no problem if their stories contained characters that magically transitioned from one sex to the other. But instead, they chose to base their gender transformations in reality—a reality where transsexual and intersex people are marginalized, where our voices are seldom heard. It is as if these writers feel some kind of sense of ownership about experiences that intersex and transsexual folks—and they alone—struggle with. Transitioning from one sex to another is not simply an interesting anecdote; it is a grueling, tumultuous experience that turns a person's life upside down, that often causes people to lose their family, friends, and jobs. And the discovery that a family member is intersex is not simply some clever plot twist. It is most often a traumatic situation, resulting in the person being endlessly poked and prodded by doctors, an experience that shrouds individuals and their families in shame and secrecy. For writers who have never had to deal with being transsexual or intersex to lay claim to those experiences, to use them for their own purposes, and to profit from them, is nothing short of exploitation.

Fables of the Deconstruction

Arguably, nowhere have people felt more entitled to possess and exploit intersex and transsexual experiences and identities than in academia. The ungendering of gender-variant people has been an ongoing practice among sociologists, poststructuralist theorists, and feminists who wish to demonstrate that our notions of gender are socially constructed. One of the earliest examples of this approach is sociologist Harold Garfinkel's 1967 book *Studies in Ethnomethodology,* which attempted to elucidate how members of society "produce stable, accountable practical activities, *i.e.*, social structures of everyday activities."[16] While Garfinkel could have examined how the average person makes sense of their own gendered experiences, he instead focused on someone who didn't have the privilege of taking their own gender for granted. That person was Agnes, a trans woman who (unbeknownst to Garfinkel) had taken female hormones for a number of years and posed as intersex in the hope of obtaining sex reassignment surgery (during the 1950s in the U.S., such surgeries were regularly carried out on intersex individuals, but not transsexuals).[17] Garfinkel devoted seventy pages to describing Agnes's attempts to reconcile her female identity and feminine behavior with the fact that she had male genitals. The account is extraordinarily objectifying, and not only with regard to Garfinkel's descriptions of Agnes's body (such as, "Her measurements were 38-25-38" and "she was dressed in a tight sweater which marked off her thin shoulders, ample breasts, and narrow waist").[18] He spends page after page relishing the details of how she managed to "pass" as a woman, highlighting her anxiety around the discrepancy between her anatomy and gender identity, and pointing out what he believed were inconsistencies in her personal history and her claims that she always felt like a girl. The entitled way he picks apart Agnes's life, graphically chronicling her fears, secrets, embarrassments, and insecurities, shows no regard for her as a person or for the immense difficulty she must have faced in simply trying to survive and make sense of her life as a gender-variant person living in the 1950s.

Another early example of ungendering can be found in the previously mentioned *Herculine Barbin.* Foucault makes it clear in his introduction to the book that his interest in publishing this nineteenth-century account of an intersex person stemmed solely from the fact that it challenges the modern Western notion that all people have a "true sex." (At one point, he even boasts that "the narrative baffles every possible attempt to make an identification."[19]) It is clear that Foucault had little interest in the desperation and disorientation Herculine felt as she/he grappled with the masculine changes in her/his body and sexuality, as well as other people's reactions to those changes (which apparently led to Herculine's suicide). In reference to Herculine's personal tragedy, Foucault states that he "would be tempted to call the story banal" if it were not for the fact that it provided an example of how society actively imposes a "true sex" onto people.[20] Foucault further dehumanizes Herculine by publishing her/his memoir alongside a dossier that includes medical and legal records, including graphic details of Herculine's body and intersex condition, as well as a sensationalistic fictional account from that time period based on Herculine's story.[21] The needless inclusion of this extra material only adds to the reader's sense that Herculine is nothing more than a specimen for us to freely examine.

The fact that both Foucault and Garfinkel claimed to be making larger points about gender and society (Foucault: that society imposes a "true sex" on *all* of its members; Garfinkel: that we *all* actively manage and produce our gendered sense of self) makes their subject choice seem rather dubious. Wouldn't their cases have been stronger if they'd focused instead on subjects who were not gender-variant—who were not such obvious exceptions to the rule? I would argue that Herculine and Agnes were chosen as subjects not because their conditions offered any unique insight into social gender, but because their gender-variant status facilitated their depiction as specimens. After all, one only has to look at how apologetic people become when they accidentally misgender another person, or how insulting it is generally considered to be to suggest that someone's femaleness or maleness is suspect in any way, to understand that ungendering is an inherently demeaning process. If Foucault and Garfinkel had instead chosen to pick apart the gender identities of young people who were not gender-variant, the process of ungendering would have undoubtedly (and appropriately) seemed intrusive and disrespectful. But because society typically views transsexual and intersex people as illegitimate and unnatural—even inhuman—Agnes and Herculine could be depicted as mere objects of inquiry without any chance of the audience identifying with them or sympathizing with them.

While Foucault and Garfinkel may have seen their subjects as nothing more than interesting case studies, I found both of these writers' accounts—specifically, the way these gender-variant young people were dehumanized and used as pawns to forward academic theories of gender—to be horribly exploitive. Having experienced firsthand what it's like to feel a disconnect between my own physical sex and gender identity, having deeply internalized the shame that's associated with having a body that defies public expectations of what is natural and normal, and having experienced the profound sense of isolation that comes with being a young gender-variant person, I found the lengthy, graphic depictions that Foucault and Garfinkel provide shamelessly voyeuristic. These accounts are akin to offering an explicit play-by-play description of a rape scene for the sole purpose of making some rather generic point about human sexuality.

Unfortunately, the ungendering of transsexual and intersex people does not end with Foucault and Garfinkel. Garfinkel's work has influenced a slew of sociologists, including Suzanne Kessler and Wendy McKenna (mentioned in chapter 7, "Pathological Science"), whose much-celebrated book *Gender: An Ethnomethodological Approach* includes a chapter called "Gender Construction in Everyday Life: Transsexualism," where transsexual gender identities and transitioning strategies are dissected to demonstrate how all people "do" gender.[22] And Foucault's writings—which, ironically, focused on how institutions produce and regulate sexual identities—have formed the foundation of queer theory, a field that has practically institutionalized the practice of ungendering gender-variant persons in an attempt to demonstrate how our culture's notions of binary sex/gender are socially constructed.

One particularly illustrative example of how dehumanizing academic ungendering can be is found in Bernice Hausman's book *Changing Sex* (discussed previously in chapter 7). In the preface, Hausman describes the difficulty she had finding a topic related to identity and feminist theory for her dissertation: "No matter how much I applied myself to the task, most of my thoughts on the issue seemed uninspired, boring, even obvious."[23] But then, lucky for her, she discovered transsexuality! "I inadvertently found texts that dealt with transsexualism. Now *that* was really fascinating. For about six months I read anything and everything I could find about crossdressing and sex change. I attended a national conference for transvestites and transsexuals. . . . The possibilities for understanding the construction of 'gender' through an analysis of transsexualism seemed enormous and there wasn't a lot of critical material out there." (Emphasis hers.)[24] Of course, Hausman chose to use the "Foucauldian" approach of examining "official discourses" (primarily gatekeeper research and transsexual autobiographies), which allowed her to superficially critique transsexuality from a distance, without the inconvenience of having to address the harsh realities and obstacles that actual transsexuals face.

Not all academics who study gender hold gender-variant people in such low regard. However, the very goal of queer theory—denaturalizing and deconstructing the binary sex/gender system—inevitably tempts many scholars to appropriate the bodies and experiences of those people who are most marginalized by that very system. This tendency is thoroughly examined in Viviane Namaste's book *Invisible Lives* (cited in chapter 7), which chronicles the erasure of transsexual and transgender people by public institutions, including academia. Namaste critiques the writings of several prominent queer theorists and shows how their work reduces trans people to "rhetorical tropes and discursive levers."[25] In particular, she argues that trans voices are made invisible by these academics' tendency to focus narrowly on cultural texts (which are almost always of cissexual origin), and the fact that they often conflate and confuse drag, crossdressing, and transsexuality, thereby minimizing the very different perspectives and experiences that distinguish these transgender people from one another. Namaste argues that such queer theorists "have defined the terms of the debate on transgendered people within American cultural studies of the 1990s: terms wherein transvestites and transsexuals function as rhetorical figures within cultural texts; terms wherein the voices, struggles, and joys of real transgendered people in the everyday social world are noticeably absent."[26]

A similar argument is made by Jay Prosser in his book *Second Skins: The Body Narratives of Transsexuality*.[27] In particular,

Prosser focuses on how many queer theorists appropriate transsexuals' gender difference to denaturalize binary gender, yet simultaneously dismiss transsexuals' personal accounts (of strongly identifying as the other sex) and physical experiences (inhabiting their own physically sexed bodies). His critique touches on a certain level of unacknowledged intellectual dishonesty regarding academic ungendering. Cissexual academics eagerly cite aspects of gender-variant lives that support their claims that gender is primarily constructed, while ignoring those aspects that undermine their cases. For example, many academics have focused on the transsexual transition process to argue that gender does not arise "naturally," but that it is learned, practiced, and performed. However, these same academics tend to overlook (or dismiss outright) the fact that most transsexuals experience a lifelong self-knowing that they should be the other sex. This self-knowing exists despite the overwhelming social pressure for a person to identify and behave as a member of their assigned sex, which strongly suggests that there are indeed natural and intrinsic gender inclinations that can precede and/or supersede social conditioning and gender norms.

I also find it disingenuous that academics in gender studies and sociology tend to concentrate rather exclusively on those gender-variant individuals who are most easily ungendered: transsexuals who have just embarked on the transitioning process, intersex people who are in the process of being "treated" by medical institutions, and those transgender people who actively engage in drag, gender bending, and/or who identify outside the male/female binary. While these groups should be given a voice, what regularly goes unreported are the views of transsexuals who are ten or twenty years post-transition, intersex people who have lived fairly gender-normative, heterosexual lives, and transgender people who at one point embraced being "in between" or "outside of" the categories of female or male as part of their coming out experience, but who later came to identify within the male/female binary. These populations of gender-variant people tend to have completely different experiences and opinions around gender. But their stories are never told, most likely because they are at odds with the positions and theories put forward by most academic gender researchers.

While some transsexual and intersex people do identify outside of the gender binary, most of us have experienced a profound understanding of ourselves as being female or male. For us, the greatest struggle in our lives is reconciling the apparent discrepancies that exist between that internal self-understanding and our physical bodies. The fact that our anatomies do not perfectly coincide with the gender we experience ourselves to be results in us regularly having our identities dismissed and our bodies objectified and ridiculed. So when non-intersex, cissexual academics use gender-variant bodies and experiences to unravel the gender binary, they are essentially undermining our efforts to have our self-identifications taken seriously. The truth is that gender deconstructs itself rather easily without having to resort to the exploitation of those who that very system most marginalizes. And because transsexual and intersex people have virtually no voice in academic and political discourses on gender, our perspectives are easily overshadowed, even subsumed, by those who have the academic credentials to position themselves as "authorities" on the subject.

When academics appropriate transsexual and intersex experiences for their essays and theories, and when they clip out specific aspects of our lives and paste them together out of context to make their own creations, they are simply contributing to our erasure. If cissexual academics truly believe that transsexual and intersex people can add new perspectives to existing dialogues about gender, then they should stop reinterpreting our experiences and instead support transsexual and intersex intellectual endeavors and works of art. Instead of exploiting our experiences to further their own careers, they should insist that their universities make a point of hiring transsexual and intersex faculty, and that their publishers put out books by gender-variant writers. And they should finally acknowledge the fact that they have no legitimate claim to use transsexual and intersex identities, struggles, and histories for their own purposes.

I am sure that some readers will object to this call for artists and academics to stop appropriating intersex and transsexual identities and experiences. But at this point in time, when almost no intersex and transsexual voices reach the public, and the few who do are those that non-intersex, cissexual individuals deem worthy, those who do attempt to speak as our proxies, who claim to understand our bodies, our issues, or our identities, necessarily push us further into the margins. Perhaps in the future, when most people are familiar with the work of intersex and transsexual artists and academics, and when the body of work that we have produced is so large that no one non-intersex or cissexual person can drown out our voices, other artists and intellectuals will be able to discuss our existence and our experiences in a respectful, nonexploitive way. But until that time comes, non-intersex, cissexual artists and academics should put their pens down, open up their minds, and simply listen to what we have to say about our own lives.

Trans Women, Femininity, and Feminism

10
Experiential Gender

THERE IS PERHAPS NO BETTER PLACE to begin a discussion about being a trans woman than with the quote that has become practically synonymous with that experience in the public's mind: that we feel like "women trapped inside men's bodies." This saying has become so popular and widespread that it's safe to say these days that it's far more often parodied by cissexuals than used by transsexuals to describe their own experiences. In fact, the regularity with which cissexuals use this saying to mock trans women has always struck me as rather odd, since it was so clearly coined not to encapsulate all of the intricacies and nuances of the trans female experience, but rather as a way of dumbing down our experiences into a sound bite that cissexuals might be better able to comprehend.

Unfortunately, the popularity of the "woman trapped inside a man's body" cliché has become a lightning rod for cissexuals who are disturbed by transsexuality. Some cissexual women, for instance, have accused trans women of being arrogant or presumptuous in claiming that we "feel like women" when, prior to our transitions, we had only ever experienced living in the world as men. Often such criticism is followed with catty remarks such as "How just like a man to say such a thing"—the implication being that our attempts to claim the identity of "woman" are merely (and rather ironically) a by-product of male entitlement.

Speaking for myself, I can honestly say that I never "felt like a woman" before my transition. Even as a preteen struggling with the inexplicable and persistent desire to be female, I understood how problematic that popular cliché was. After all, how can anyone know what it's like to "feel like a woman" or "feel like a man" when we can never really know how anybody else feels on the inside? Most people whose physical and subconscious sexes coincide generally fall rather seamlessly into womanhood or manhood; as a result, they take for granted the identity of woman or man. My gender identity always felt more like a puzzle that I had to put together myself, one in which many of the pieces were missing, where I had no clue as to what the final picture was supposed to be. And the twenty years between my conscious recognition that I wanted to be female and my eventual decision to transition was a time when I painstakingly ruled out the possibilities that my female inclinations were merely a manifestation of my sexuality or a desire to express femininity. And after many years of exploring and experimenting with femininity, masculinity, and androgyny, with crossdressing and role-playing, and with heterosexuality and bisexuality, I realized that for me, being trans had little to do with sexual desire or social gender; it was primarily about the physical experience of being in my own body.

People often assume that transsexuals have some kind of idealized and unrealistic image of what it's like to be the other sex, and that transitioning is our attempt to achieve that fantasy. Nothing could be further from the truth for me. When I decided to transition, I had no idea what it would actually be like to live as a woman, nor did I have any preconceived notions about what type of woman I might actually become. Hell, at the time, I didn't even dare call myself a woman. That word, like the word "man," seemed to have way too much baggage associated with it. At the time, I preferred the word "girl," which seemed more playful and open to interpretation. Or I might say that I identified as female, since the word is more commonly associated with one's anatomy than with any specific gender roles or regulations. But I completely avoided the word "woman" because it seemed to be too weighed down with other people's expectations—expectations that I wasn't sure I was interested in, or capable of, meeting.

My initial avoidance of the label "woman" was fostered even further by my decision to transition in "boy mode," a strategy that many trans women feel is the safest and most effective. Essentially, this meant that I underwent electrolysis and hormone replacement therapy while continuing to live my life as a "man": wearing the same jeans, sneakers, T-shirts, flannel shirts, and sweat-jackets I always wore and acting pretty much the same as I always had. The idea is that you simply go about your life until you reach the point where most people begin to assume that you are female despite your (tom)boyish gender presentation; some trans women refer to this as the point when they lose the ability to "pass" as a man.

At the start of my transition, I had the same assumptions that most people have about gender: I believed that there were obvious, concrete differences between women and men. Thus, I figured that I would have to spend a good deal of time during my transition being "in between" genders—too physically ambiguous for people to classify as either female or male. But that didn't really happen. To my surprise, people almost always made the call one way or another, even though their conclusion as to my gender often differed from person to person. For instance, it was common for me to go into a store and have an employee say, "Can I help you, sir?" Then a few minutes later, as I was leaving, a different employee might say, "Have a good day, ma'am."

After about a month or two of never knowing whether any given person was gendering me as female or male, I experienced a dramatic change. It felt like the world suddenly shifted around me. Almost overnight, I sensed that everything was very different. At first, I suspected that this feeling was coming from within me, perhaps a psychological or emotional change related to my being on female hormones. But then I realized that it wasn't me, but rather the rest of the world, that was acting differently. In public, strangers began standing much closer to me. Women seemed to let their guard down around me. Men, for no apparent reason, would smile at me. Everybody spoke to me differently, interacted with me in different ways. I realized that I had passed through some sort of threshold and suddenly everybody saw me as female.

The weirdest part about this experience was that I was pretty much the exact same person that I had been prior to that. I was acting and dressing the same. And over the four months I'd been on hormones, I had barely changed physically. I still had some stubble growing out of my face (although not nearly as much as before). My breasts were sore and tingling and definitely beginning to grow, but they were hardly noticeable. The only visible changes were the softening of my complexion and a little extra facial fat around my cheeks, and yet I completely lost my ability to "pass" as a man quite suddenly. Granted, my transition went a lot quicker than it does for many trans women, since I started out as a small, long-haired boy who was occasionally "ma'am"ed even before taking hormones. Nevertheless, the speed and extent of my transition, and the fact that it occurred without my having to change my behavior or mannerisms, challenged everything I used to believe to be true about gender.

My initial reaction to this experience was to even further embrace my "genderqueerness"—my sense of otherness. The taken-for-granted assumption that female and male were fixed and reliable states suddenly appeared to me to be the product of a mass hallucination, held together only by the fact that so few people actually had the firsthand experience of transitioning—of seeing how such small differences in one's physical gender can result in such a large difference in the way one is perceived and treated by others. Suddenly, I no longer felt like I was journeying from one gender to the other. I felt more like I was floating in a little dinghy that had been recently released from the dock I had been anchored to my whole life; and now I was being tossed about on an ocean of other people's perceptions of me. And while I was definitely searching for a place where I could feel at home in my own body, I was no longer quite sure what that place might look like or what I might call it when I finally arrived.

From conversations I've had with a number of transsexual friends who transitioned before me, I would say that my attitude at the time—my questioning of (and refusal to identify within) the male/female binary—was a fairly common response to being in the throes of physical and social transition. Transitioning is such an upending, mind-blowing experience that it seems to me to be almost a necessity for one to let go of one's preconceived notions of maleness and femaleness in order to traverse those states of being. Being perceived as female while having an entirely male history and a mostly male body (as I did at the time) made me feel not like an imposter (as some might imagine), but more like an alien. I was just being myself, but other people were relating and reacting to me in ways that were foreign to me. I felt less like a woman or a man than I did a stranger in a strange land.

As with many of my transsexual friends, I found that this sense of otherness steadily subsided with time. And over the course of a year or two, I eventually did come to identify as a woman. Part of this evolution in my self-perception was driven by how different I felt in my body after physically transitioning. This is one of the most difficult aspects of transitioning to describe, as there are so few words in our language to articulate "body feelings" of any sort. I'm sure that this lack in language is related to our cultural tendency to dismiss or discount the way that our bodies feel to us. Indeed, many of us tend to think of ourselves as brains or souls crammed inside of a shell—a shell that is our body. We delude ourselves into believing that the shell itself is not important, not connected to our consciousness, that it's merely a vessel that contains us, or a vehicle that we move about with our minds. But the truth is, our bodies are inseparable from our minds. This becomes evident whenever hunger, thirst, or physical pain grows to the point where we can think of nothing else, or when mental grief or stress manifests itself in physical aches and exhaustion. All of us who have experienced the physical difference between feeling healthy and feeling ill, or perhaps most profoundly, between pre- and post-puberty, have a deep understanding (whether we acknowledge it or not) that our body feelings make a vital and substantial contribution to our senses of self.

You could say that my decision to transition was primarily driven by my choosing to trust my body feelings—in this case, my subconscious sex—over my conscious understanding of gender. So perhaps it's no surprise that the most immediate change in my body feelings that I experienced upon starting hormone therapy was an easing of my gender dissonance—the chronic gender sadness that I had carried around with me for as long as I could remember. I am not sure whether this was a direct effect of having female hormones in my system or a more psychological effect of knowing that my body was finally moving in the right direction. Either way, the relief I felt was beyond measure; for the first time in my life, I slowly began to feel comfortable being in my own skin.

Female hormones have also produced numerous other body feelings that have greatly reshaped my sense of self. There have been profound changes in the way that I experience sensations and emotions, and in my tastes, urges, and responses to stimuli. And the physical changes to my body, which unfolded over a greater span of time, have also influenced the way I experience the world. Granted, when strangers first began gendering me as female (back when I was still identifying as genderqueer), unclothed I probably looked like a slightly feminized male. But after five years of being on female hormones, there is virtually nothing about my body that looks or feels male (with the obvious exception of my genitals, as I have not had bottom surgery). In those intervening years, my skin has become much softer, my center of gravity has totally shifted, my metabolism has changed, clothing fits my body differently, heavy objects seem to have become much heavier, and room temperature seems to have dropped about two or three degrees. The changes in the shape of my body and in my muscle/fat distribution have significantly altered the way I walk, run, dance, hold my body, and move in general. Simply put, my body no longer feels male to me; rather, it feels female.

Of course, body feelings are not the only facet of my being that has contributed to my identity as a woman. As I alluded to earlier, the changes in my social gender—how other people relate to and interact with me—were at least as dramatic as (if not more so than) the physical changes to my body. While being treated as a woman felt foreign to me at first, over time it simply became my everyday life. My identity as a woman grew out of positive experiences, such as feeling comfortable with my own female body. Yet it also arose out of negative ones, such as the regularity with which other people placed unsolicited attention upon my body, whether it was the catcalls and sexual innuendos strangers would sometimes hurl at me or the occasional comments people started to make insinuating that I could stand to lose a little weight (even though I weighed the same as I did before my transition, and nobody saw my weight as a problem back then). My identity as a woman grew out of my frustration over being called a "bitch" any time I stood up for myself, or having others make remarks about my hormone levels any time I became legitimately upset or angry about something. My identity as a woman grew out of my experiences at parties and other social occasions when I would come across a group of men talking and laughing, and witness them suddenly fall silent when I approached. My identity evolved out of a million tiny social exchanges where others made it very clear to me that my status in the world—my class, if you will—was that of a woman and not a man.

Not surprisingly, no aspect of my social transition has been more difficult for me to adjust to than the way I am treated by some (but certainly not all) men. Granted, this was not entirely unexpected. Before my transition, I had often asked my female friends about their experiences living as women in a male-centered world. On an intellectual level, I knew that I would sometimes be dismissed or harassed once I started living as female, but I underestimated just how frustrating and hurtful each one of those instances would be. Words cannot express how condescending and infuriating it feels to have men speak down to me, talk over me, and sometimes even practically put on baby-talk voices when addressing me. Or how intimidating it feels to have strangers make lewd comments about having their way with me as I'm walking alone at night down dark city streets. And while I had numerous run-ins and arguments with strange men back when I was male-bodied, I'd never before experienced the enraged venom in their voices and fury in their faces that I sometimes do now—an extreme wrath that some men seem to reserve specifically for women who they believe threaten their fragile male egos. It became more and more difficult for me to see the point in identifying outside of the male/female binary when I was so regularly being targeted for discrimination and harassment because I was a woman, when I so frequently had to stand up for myself as a woman in order to make sure that other people did not get away with it.

After a couple of years living in the world as female, I eventually came to embrace the identity of "woman." Thinking of myself as a woman simply began to make sense; it resonated with my lived experiences. Before my transition, I was hesitant about calling myself a woman, mostly because I had no desire to live up to the societal expectations and ideals that others often project onto that identity. I used to fear that embracing that identity would be tantamount to cramming myself into some predetermined box, restricting my possibilities and potential. But I now realize that no matter how I act or what I do or say, I remain a woman—both in the eyes of the world and, more importantly, in the way that I experience myself. While I used to view the word "woman" as limiting, I now find it both empowering and limitless.

Together, all of the changes I've experienced since my transition—in my body feelings, in my interactions with other people, and in my growing life history as a woman—have led to me becoming a somewhat different person than I was before. Granted, my personality, habits, opinions, sense of humor, etc., are mostly still the same, but my life itself has taken on a different shape. While I can think back to before my transition and imagine how I looked and acted, I find that my memories of how it felt to be in my body—to be physically male—are becoming increasingly vague with time. It's not dissimilar to how I feel when I think back to high school—recalling all of the things that I thought, said, and did, yet feeling almost as if I were reminiscing about another person. I now look back on my years as an adult male, remembering how I acted and interacted with others, but having some difficulty relating to the person I was back then. My life has very much been reshaped by the experiences of being and feeling physically female and having other people react to me as such.

People often squabble over what defines a person as a woman or a man—whether it should be based on their chromosomes, assigned sex, genitals, or other factors—but such reductionist views deny our indisputably holistic gendered realities. For all of us, gender is first and foremost an individual experience, an amalgamation of our own unique combinations of gender inclinations, social interactions, body feelings, and lived experiences.

While our experiential gender is often shaped or influenced by our perceived gender (the gender others assume us to be), one does not necessarily follow from the other. For example, I had lived and was treated as a man for many years, yet I always felt rather ambivalent about belonging to that class. Sometimes when my female friends would go off on a tirade about men in general, I would join in with them, not because I hated men or enjoyed making generalizations about people, but as a way of expressing the fact that I did not feel like a man. That identity never made sense to me given my constant struggles with gender dissonance, the persistent body feelings I experienced that informed me that there was something not quite right with my being physically male, and my personal history of consciously exploring and expressing my femaleness and femininity both in my imagination and in public. I gravitated toward genderqueer identities for most of the years that I was male-bodied—at different points, viewing myself as a boy who wanted to be a girl, a crossdresser, and bigender—because they resonated with the myriad of gendered experiences that I had had up to that point. They captured the fact that, at the time, I really did feel like I was straddling both maleness and femaleness in some way.

Genderqueer identities no longer resonate with my experiential gender in the same way. This is not to say that I now denounce them altogether, as I know firsthand just how rewarding and empowering it can be to see yourself as being outside, in between, or transcending both femaleness and maleness. It's just that at this point in my life, I don't feel genderqueer anymore. Experiencing the world (and my own body) as female makes the word "woman" feel like a far better fit for me now. Unfortunately, I have met a few genderqueer-identified people who have expressed suspicion or have been dismissive of the idea that someone could "transition" from genderqueer to unapologetically woman or man. Such assertions are clearly the product of gender entitlement, of these individuals projecting their own perspectives and beliefs onto other people's gendered bodies, identities, and experiences. However, the majority of the transgender people I know understand that our experiential gender is potentially fluid and often changes over time as we accumulate new experiences. I have found that transsexuals in particular are often acutely aware of this fact, having experienced the dramatic changes in our body feelings, anatomies, personal relationships, and histories that typically accompany social and physical transitioning.

Personally, I find that the concept of experiential gender not only helps me make sense of my own transition, but it gives me an appreciation of the inherent limits in my ability to understand or speak on behalf of other people's genders. While I may have experienced a wider variety of aspects of social and hormonal gender than most people, these experiences are still far outweighed by the vast multitude of gendered feelings and experiences that I have not experienced. Therefore, it would be both ignorant and arrogant for me to project my limited experience onto other people's gendered lives and bodies.

This is precisely what frustrates me about those cissexuals who are most bothered when trans women say that we feel like women. They assume that we are somehow trying to claim to know how other women feel, when in reality all we are saying is that the identity of woman most resonates with our own experiential gender.

And by insisting that we trans women cannot possibly know what it's like to "feel like a woman," they're the ones being presumptuous, both by arrogantly assuming that other women experience femaleness the way they do and by implying that they know enough about how trans women feel on the inside to claim that we do not legitimately experience ourselves as women. Their claims that they somehow understand "womanhood" better than trans women do by virtue of having been born and socialized female is just as naive and arrogant as my claiming to understand "womanhood" better because, unlike most women, I have had a male experience to compare it to. Any claim that one has superior knowledge about womanhood is fraught with gender entitlement and erases the infinite different ways for people to experience their own femaleness.

There are countless experiences that can shape a woman's gendered experiences: being socialized as a girl (or not), experiencing menstruation and menopause (or not), becoming pregnant and giving birth (or not), becoming a mother (or not), having a career outside of the home (or not), having a husband (or a wife or neither), and so on. Women's lives are also greatly shaped by additional factors such as race, age, ability, sexual orientation, economic class, and so on. While each of these individual experiences are shared by many women—and each is rightfully considered a "women's issue"—it would be foolish for anyone to claim that any one of these was a prerequisite for calling oneself a woman. So long as we refuse to accept that "woman" is a holistic concept, one that includes all people who experience themselves as women, our concept of womanhood will remain a mere reflection of our own personal experiences and biases rather than something based in the truly diverse world that surrounds us.

11
Deconstructive Surgery

BECAUSE I'M AN OUT TRANS WOMAN, there is one question that follows me around wherever I go. Inquiring minds want to know: Have I "gone all the way"? You know, have I had "the surgery"?

And to me, it feels like a no-win inquisition. If I tell the truth—"No, not yet"—then I get to deal with everybody else's emotional baggage, because nothing makes people more paranoid than a real-life female with a phallus. Straight men shake in their boots at the possibility that they might "accidentally" become attracted to me. And those who patrol the gates of women-only spaces are often dead set on discriminating against me, driven by the ridiculous belief that my girly little estrogenized penis is somehow still pulsating with hypermasculine energy.

On the other hand, having the operation has its own stigma attached to it. No medical methodology induces as much fear and anxiety as SRS—sex reassignment surgery. A friend told me that he once saw SRS on the video *Faces of Death,* sandwiched between real-life shark attacks and murder attempts. Some people go so far as to call SRS a form of self-mutilation, conveniently ignoring the fact that more common procedures, such as nose jobs and liposuction, similarly involve the removal of a small amount of nonessential tissue.

Most people are surprised when I tell them that the surgeons don't really cut the penis off. They just turn it inside out and move the nerve endings around to make a functional and realistic-looking clitoris and vagina. At that point, I am invariably asked if I want SRS so that I can have sex with a man. And you should see the blank stares that I get when I reply, "No, but I'm really looking forward to having my wife fuck me with a strap-on dildo."

See, we live in a phallus-obsessed culture, where we're all brought up to believe that everything having to do with gender and sexuality somehow revolves around the penis. That's why so many clueless straight guys come on to dykes with pickup lines like, "Once you've had the real thing, baby, you won't ever go back." Some men actually buy into that phallocentric crap! And it's also why most people can't even talk about transsexual women or SRS without centering the discussion on the penis.

But my desire to have SRS has virtually nothing to do with my penis. This is about me *wanting* to have a clitoris and vagina. But we don't even have the language to describe this desire. It's the ultimate Freudian slip: We naturally assume that all young girls suffer from penis envy, but we can't imagine that any boy could possibly have its polar opposite. It's all in the words we use. When someone is bold or brave, we say they have "balls," while words like "pussy" and "cunt" are only ever spoken as insults. And while everyone seems to understand how the penis works, we treat female genitalia like they're a mysterious black box. Most young women aren't even taught the names of all their own body parts; some people are unaware that the clitoris even exists; and as for the vagina, well, aren't we all taught to see that as simply the hole where the penis is supposed to go?

So it's no wonder that most people assume that I must be mentally ill, because in this culture, wanting to be a woman is something most people find literally unimaginable. And when I do have SRS, my surgically deconstructed genitals will no doubt be seen by some to be an abomination or a blasphemy. Because my cunt will be the ultimate question mark, asking: How powerful can the penis really be if a sane and smart person like me decides she can do without it? And if the world supposedly revolves around the penis, then my SRS will knock it off its axis. And phallic symbols everywhere will come crashing down like nothing more than a house of cards. After all, a cigar is *always* just a cigar. And I am simply me. And I am fed up with other people projecting their penis obsessions onto my body. As far as I'm concerned, if they can't fathom why I might want to trade in my penis for a clitoris and vagina, then they're the ones who have the gender disorder.

12

Bending Over Backwards: Traditional Sexism and Trans-Woman-Exclusion Policies

Prejudice usually can't survive close contact with the people who are supposed to be so despicable, which is why the propagandists for hate always preach separation.

—Patrick Califia[1]

OVER THE LAST SEVERAL YEARS, a major focus of my trans activism and writing has been the issue of trans-woman-inclusion in lesbian and women-only spaces. I first heard of the issue back in 1999, around the time that I was beginning to call myself transgender—about two years before I began my physical transition. At the time, I was voraciously reading everything I could get my hands on related to trans experiences and issues. As I read, I kept stumbling upon past instances of anti-trans-woman discrimination from within the lesbian and feminist communities. These included derogatory anti-trans-woman remarks by influential feminist thinkers such as Mary Daly, Germaine Greer, Andrea Dworkin, Robin Morgan, and of course

Janice Raymond (who, in addition to writing the anti-trans screed *The Transsexual Empire,* tried to convince the National Center for Health Care Technology to deny transsexuals the right to hormones and surgery); stories about transsexual "witch hunts," in which committed lesbian-feminists like Sandy Stone and Beth Elliott were publicly outed, debased, and exiled from the lesbian community solely for being transsexual; and of course, trans-woman-exclusion policies, such as the Michigan Womyn's Music Festival's euphemistically named "womyn-born-womyn-only" policy, which was retroactively instated in the early 1990s after an incident in which a woman named Nancy Burkholder was expelled from the festival when it was discovered that she was trans.[2]

While I found it disappointing that people who identified as lesbians and as feminists would come down so harshly on another sexual minority, I cannot say that I was really surprised. After all, practically every facet of our society seemed to hate or fear trans people back then, and these incidents seemed more like a symptom of society-wide transphobia rather than something unique or specific to the lesbian community. And as I was giving thought to becoming involved in trans activism myself, there seemed to be plenty of other, more practical and relevant issues for me to take on.

But in the years that followed, I experienced a number of changes in my life that would considerably reshape my views on this matter. For one thing, there was my physical transition and the countless social changes I experienced as a result of being perceived as female. But for me, being trans didn't merely involve learning how to navigate my way through the world as a woman. I have the privilege of being appropriately gendered as female, so in my day-to-day life, when I am forced to come out to someone, nine times out of ten it is not as a transsexual, but as a lesbian. It happens every time somebody asks me if I am seeing someone and I reply, "Actually, I have a wife." It happens every time Dani and I dare to hold hands or kiss in public. It happens when Dani is not around, but someone assumes that I am a dyke anyway because of the way that I dress, speak, or carry myself.

After my transition, I began to write not only about being transgender, but about my experiences living in the world as a woman and a dyke after years of being perceived as a straight man. Not surprisingly, most of what I wrote had a definite feminist bent. It seemed impossible for me, as a trans woman, to discuss my journey from male to female without placing it in the context of the differing values our society places on maleness and femaleness, on masculinity and femininity.

Unfortunately, many people tend to artificially separate feminism from transgender activism, as if they are distinct issues that are in no way related. However, I have found that much of the anti-trans discrimination that trans women come across is clearly rooted in traditional sexism. This can be seen in how the media Powers That Be systematically sensationalize, sexualize, and ridicule trans women while allowing trans men to remain largely invisible. It's why the tranny sex and porn industries catering to straight-identified men do not fetishize folks on the FTM spectrum for their XX chromosomes or their socialization as girls. No, they objectify trans women, because our bodies and our persons are female. I have found that many female-assigned genderqueers and FTM spectrum trans people go on and on about the gender binary system, as if trans people are only ever discriminated against for breaking gender norms. That might be how it seems when the gender transgression in question is an expression of masculinity. But as someone on the MTF spectrum, I am not dismissed for merely failing to live up to binary gender norms, but for expressing my own femaleness and femininity. And personally, I don't feel like I'm the victim of "transphobia" as much as I am the victim of trans-misogyny.

This idea—that much of what is commonly called transphobia is merely traditional sexism in disguise—moved to the forefront of my mind as I began to be invited to do spoken word performances at various queer women's events around the San Francisco Bay Area. While I was welcomed very warmly by most of the women who attended these events, I would sometimes come across certain women who would act dismissively toward me, who seemed bothered by me being there, who acted as if they were granting me a special favor by tolerating my presence, who would make offhand and inappropriate comments about my trans status as if to remind me that I was not a real woman like they were. This sense of ownership and entitlement about being a woman or being lesbian seemed hypocritical to me. After all, as soon as we would walk out the door, all of us would face similar discrimination for being women and for being dykes. But what was most frustrating about the way that many of these women dismissed me was the fact that they seemed to have no problems at all with female-bodied folks expressing masculinity and with trans people on the FTM spectrum attending their events. In other words, they didn't have much of a problem with transgender people per se, just so long as they were male- or masculine-identified rather than female- or feminine-identified.

This privileging of trans men over trans women is not merely a bias held by certain individuals, but rather one that is often institutionalized within queer women's culture and organizations. These days, it is not uncommon to see the word "trans" used to welcome trans men (but not trans women) on everything from lesbian events to sex surveys and play parties. And even at the Michigan Womyn's Music Festival, women are no longer defined based on their legal sex, appearance, or self-identification, but on whether or not they were born and raised a girl. And while some performers who identify as transgender and answer to male pronouns are invited to take the festival stage each year, someone like myself—who identifies 100 percent as female—isn't even allowed to stand in the audience.[3]

As with most forms of prejudice, trans-woman-specific discrimination within the queer women's community seems to proliferate even more in the absence of trans women than in our presence; this is no surprise, as bigots are typically too cowardly to dare have their views openly discussed or debated with the very people they despise. While anti-trans-woman sentiments are generally expressed outside of my view, I still hear about them all the time from my trans male and queer female friends, who often tell me about self-identified dykes in their community who openly discuss lusting after trannybois and trans men one minute, then in the next, deride trans women for being "creepy" and "effeminate."

The popular spin given to this preferential treatment of trans men over trans women states that trans men have been raised female and therefore should have a place in women's and lesbian communities, whereas trans women have experienced male privilege and remain physically male on some level, and therefore should be excluded. However, this argument makes little sense when examined more closely. After all, how can someone who identifies as female and currently lives as a woman have less in common with women than a male-identified person who has male physical attributes and currently benefits from male privilege? The premise that trans women should be singled out because we "used to be men" is highly suspect. Rather, I believe that this preference for trans men over trans women simply reflects the society-wide inclination to view masculinity as being strong and natural, and femininity as being weak and artificial. In other words, it is a product of traditional sexism.

My appreciation for the ways in which traditional sexism shapes popular assumptions about trans women started to really take shape during 2003 and 2004, as I became involved in Camp Trans, an organization that works to end the exclusion of trans women from women-only spaces, most notably the Michigan Womyn's Music Festival. In my work on this issue, I learned firsthand how the occasional anti-trans-woman sentiment I would come across in the relatively trans-friendly Bay Area was just the tip of the iceberg. Some of the women who travel from all over the country to attend Michigan think nothing of wearing their suspicion or hatred of trans women on their sleeves, and they will often make extraordinarily ignorant and insensitive comments about trans women in their attempts to justify our exclusion. I am sure these women believe that they are protecting the values of lesbian and women's space by opposing our inclusion at all costs, but in reality the specific points they make generally undermine feminist goals and beliefs rather than support them. After all, at its core, feminism is based on the conviction that women are far more than the sex of the bodies that we are born into, and our identities and abilities are capable of transcending the restrictive nature of the gender socialization we endure during our childhoods. I have yet to meet the person who can explain to me how refusing trans women the right to participate in women's spaces and events is consistent with this most central tenet of feminism.

Indeed, some of the most common arguments used to deny trans women the right to participate in women-only spaces also happen to be the most antifeminist. For example, many argue that trans women should be barred from women's spaces because we supposedly still have "male energy." But by suggesting that trans women possess some mystical "male energy" as a result of having been born and raised male, these women are essentially making the case that men have abilities and aptitudes that women are not capable of.

Another popular excuse for our exclusion is the fact that some trans women have male genitals (as many of us either cannot afford or choose not to have sex reassignment surgery). This "penis" argument not only objectifies trans women by reducing us to our genitals, but propagates the male myth that men's power and domination somehow arise from the phallus. The truth is, our penises are made of flesh and blood, nothing more. And the very idea that the femaleness of my mind, personality, lived experiences, and the rest of my body can somehow be trumped by the mere presence of a penis can only be described as phallocentric.

It's distressing that such phallocentric arguments, along with related arguments that harp on the idea that trans women "physically resemble" or "look like" men in other ways, are so regularly made by lesbian-feminists, considering that they are based in the society-wide privileging of male attributes over female ones. In what is now considered classic research, sociologists Suzanne Kessler and

Wendy McKenna showed that in our culture, when people (both women and men) gender others, we tend to weigh male visual cues as far more significant than female ones, and almost invariably consider the penis as being the single most important gender cue of all (i.e., its presence trumps all other gender cues; the presence of a vagina does not elicit a similar effect).[4] In their words, "There seem to be no cues that are definitely female, while there are many that are definitely male. To be male is to 'have' something and to be female is to 'not have' it."[5] Kessler and McKenna view this privileging of male cues as resulting from male-centrism (similar to how people often favor using the pronoun "he" when speaking generically). Taking this into account, it becomes rather obvious that when cissexual women deny trans women the right to participate in women-only spaces because of their own tendency to privilege any "mannish" or "masculine" traits we may have over our many female attributes, they are fostering and promoting male-centrism.

Of course, trans-woman-exclusion cannot be justified solely on the basis that some of us look or act "mannish" or "masculine"—otherwise, butch women would have to be excluded as well. Indeed, in recent years, as feminism itself has shifted away from gender essentialist theories and toward more social constructionist ones, the basis for trans-woman-exclusion is more frequently our male socialization rather than our male biology. This approach also provides convenient intellectual cover for those who wish to include FTM spectrum folks (who were socialized female) in women's spaces. But once again, such an approach runs counter to the precepts of feminism. After all, feminists regularly insist that women are capable of doing anything men can despite having been raised as girls and encouraged to take a subordinate position to men. Thus, women can (and often do) transcend their female socialization. It remains unclear why these same feminists would paradoxically insist that trans women are unable to similarly transcend our male socialization.

The fact that socialization is a specious argument became obvious to me during an exchange I had with a trans-woman-exclusionist who insisted that my being raised male was the sole reason in her mind for me to be disqualified from entering women-only spaces. So I asked her if she was open to allowing trans women who are anatomically male but who have been socialized female—something that's not all that uncommon for MTF children these days.[6] She admitted to having concerns about their attending. Then, I asked how she would feel about a person who was born female yet raised male against her will, and who, after a lifetime of pretending to be male in order to survive, finally reclaimed her female identity upon reaching adulthood. After being confronted with this scenario, the woman conceded that she would be inclined to let this person enter women-only space, thus demonstrating that her argument about male socialization was really an argument about biology after all. In fact, after being pressed a bit further, she admitted that the scenario of a young girl who was forced against her will into boyhood made her realize how traumatic and dehumanizing male socialization could be for someone who was female-identified. This, of course, is exactly how many trans women experience their own childhoods.

Another popular reason used to justify trans-woman-exclusion is cissexual women's fears that we will somehow make women-only spaces unsafe. For example, it's common for trans-woman-exclusionists to express concerns over the possibility that we might assault other women—an accusation that is entirely unfounded, as there is no credible evidence to suggest that trans women are any more violent or abusive than women as a whole. Even in San Francisco (the U.S. city most likely to have the highest percentage of trans women per capita), there has never been a single police report of a trans woman harassing another woman in a bathroom.[7] Others argue that trans women could potentially trigger those who have survived physical or sexual violence at the hands of men—a suggestion that is offensive not only because it is rooted in the male-centric tendency to view trans women as "men" (which is the result of privileging male attributes over female ones), but because it denies the fact that many trans women are physically violated and sexually assaulted for being women, too. But what I find most dumbfounding about lesbian-feminist arguments that trans women might somehow threaten cissexual women's safety is how eerily similar they are to the arguments some heterosexual women have made in the past in their attempts to exclude lesbians from women's spaces and organizations.[8]

This is why it's so disappointing for me to see members of my own dyke community practically bending over backwards, embracing hypocrisy, in a last-ditch effort to prevent trans women from entering lesbian and women-only spaces. Women who are appalled by the military's "don't ask, don't tell" policy regarding homosexuality seem to find no fault with Michigan for enforcing a similar policy regarding gender. Women who have struggled against patriarchal ideals of what makes a "real" woman think nothing of turning around and using the word "real" against trans women. Women who would be outraged if an all-male panel were to discuss women's or lesbian issues in *Newsweek* or *Time* magazine see nothing wrong with the fact that, in the last few years, several of the largest lesbian and feminist magazines have run articles and roundtable discussions on the issue of Michigan and trans-woman-inclusion without inviting any trans women to participate.[9] It's sad to see women so desperate to prevent trans women from attending Michigan that they will actually try to make the ridiculous case that this "womyn's" festival was never actually meant to be an event for women, but rather for those who were born and raised as girls.

I am sure that a lot of the same people who support Michigan's trans-woman-exclusion policy, or who sit on the fence on this issue, would have a very different opinion if it were their own inclusion that was being debated. Can you imagine how angry these very same women would be if the largest annual women-only event in the world was run by straight women who decided to exclude queer women from attending? Can you imagine how insulted they would feel if they were told that they were not allowed to enter women-only space because they were not "real" women, or that their attraction to women might threaten the safety of other women? Can you imagine how condescending they would find it if straight women talked to them about being queer-positive one minute, then turned around and purchased a $400 ticket to a "queer-free" women's event the next?

As much as I am bothered by the long history of trans women being expelled from the lesbian community during the '70s, '80s, and early '90s, I am willing to chalk that up to the fact that the transgender movement hadn't fully come into its own yet, and there were few people who were able to articulate a clear message for transgender rights and inclusion at the time. But now, in 2007, there is no legitimate excuse for trans-woman-exclusion in lesbian and women-only spaces. Most LGB groups have long since added Ts to the ends of their acronyms. And while there was a time when trans-inclusion debates only took place on the outskirts of the queer community, they now take place in workplaces and courthouses all across the United States. In the last twenty years, nine states (Minnesota, Rhode Island, New Mexico, California, Maine, Illinois, Hawaii, Washington, and New Jersey) and scores of cities and counties across the country have extended their nondiscrimination laws to explicitly include transgender people.[10] It's downright embarrassing that so many folks within the queer women's community, who generally pride themselves on their progressive politics, have managed to fall behind Peoria, Illinois, and El Paso, Texas, in recognizing and respecting trans people's gender identities.

But trans-woman-exclusion in lesbian and women-only spaces is not merely a trans rights issue—if it were, I would consider it to be important, but I probably would not have devoted so much of my time and energy to it. The main reason why trans-woman-exclusion evokes such passion and frustration in me is precisely because it is both anti-trans and antifeminist. And as a feminist, it gravely disturbs me that other self-described feminists are so willing to overlook or purposefully ignore how inherently sexist trans-woman-exclusion policies and politics are: They favor trans men over trans women, they rampantly objectify trans female bodies, and they privilege trans women's appearances, socialization, and the sex others assigned to us at birth over our persons, our minds, and our identities.

And what saddens me even more than the irrational trans-misogynistic fear and hatred displayed by the vocal minority who most adamantly oppose our inclusion is the apathy of the silent majority of queer women and feminists who enable that prejudice: those who continue to attend women's events that exclude trans women; those who excuse or choose not to confront antifeminist/anti-trans-woman comments and actions made by members of their own community; those who tacitly give credence to antifeminist/anti-trans-woman rhetoric by referring to the issue of trans-woman-exclusion as a "controversy" or a "debate." I would submit to them that there has never been a legitimate debate regarding this issue, as the overwhelming majority of dialogues and discourses on this subject have taken place among cissexual women in the absence of any trans women.

Perhaps the most naive and condescending refrain apologists for the trans-woman-exclusionists make is that these apologists are working hard to change these women-only organizations and spaces from within. This is a seriously flawed notion. If you look back at history, there has not been a single instance where people have overcome a deeply entrenched prejudice without first being forced to interact with the people they detest. Mere words cannot dispel bigoted stereotypes and fears; only personal experiences can. The queer rights movement would not have made the progress that it has if activists merely relied on queer-positive straight people to lobby on our behalf, to speak as our proxies. Social progress was only made through both the frontline work of outspoken activists shouting, "We're here, we're queer, get used to it!" and that of committed straight allies who absolutely refused to tolerate anti-queer remarks and discrimination from members of their own communities. Similarly, I entreat all feminists and all queer women to recognize that the divisive issue of trans-woman-exclusion will continue to be with us as long as we fail to directly confront and repudiate antifeminist/anti-trans-woman policies and rhetoric wherever they exist.

13
Self-Deception

In 2002, teenager Gwen Araujo was brutally murdered by four men who bludgeoned her to death because she was born male, because she was a transgender woman. But this is not another piece about the horrors of hate crimes or another desperate rant about violence, ignorance, or prejudice. No, this piece is about the myth of deception.

A year and a half after her death, three of Gwen's murderers stood on trial together. The evidence demonstrated that they had plotted her murder a week in advance. And normally, premeditation ensures a first-degree murder sentence, but not in this case. The trial ended with a hung jury, a victory for the defense lawyers, who insisted that the murder was merely manslaughter because the defendants were somehow victims of Gwen's "sexual deceit." Two of the killers had been intimate with her, and their lawyers argued that when they later discovered that she had male genitals, they were driven to commit a "crime of passion."[1]

Deception. It's the noose that the narcissistic drape around the necks of transgender women. Lesbian-feminist Janice Raymond used the word "deception" over and over again in *The Transsexual Empire* as a way to dismiss transsexual women's femaleness, so that she could call them men and accuse them of transitioning in order to "penetrate . . . women's space" and "rape women's bodies."[2] And scientists who study animal mating behavior often use the word "deception" to explain why the males of many species engage in courtship rituals with feminine males—creatures the researchers dismiss as "female mimics" to deny any possibility that the masculine males willingly choose to partner with feminine males.[3]

Behind every accusation of deception lies an unchallenged assumption—in this case, that no male in his right mind could ever be attracted to someone who was feminine, yet physically male. This premise underlies Jay Leno's infamous question to Hugh Grant: "What were you thinking?"[4] It's why Grant and fellow celebrity Eddie Murphy are still able to star in films for Disney while the trans prostitutes they allegedly sought out are reduced to cinematic novelties: tasteless jokes in teen comedies, bad Lou Reed anecdotes in art films produced by Andy Warhol wannabes, or as examples of urban decay in police dramas set on sordid and seedy city streets.

Transgender women are portrayed as deceivers so that rabid heterosexuals can turn a blind eye to the transsexual porn ads that litter the back of men's magazines like *Hustler* and *Penthouse,* so that mainstream moviegoers can watch *The Crying Game* and act surprised to find out that the woman who performs in the drag bar happens to have a penis. "Deception" is the scarlet letter that trans people are made to wear so that everybody else can claim innocence.

This is why the police, lawyers, and press who worked on the Gwen Araujo case ignored the multiple sources who insisted that

Gwen's killers knew she was transgender to begin with.[5] It's why nobody ever questioned how next-to-impossible it would be for two of Gwen's killers to have had anal sex with her without ever coming across her genitals. Nobody was willing to even consider the possibility that Gwen's murderers knowingly had sex with her. Why challenge our culture's myopic view of male sexuality when it's so easy to blame it all on one deceiving tranny? And why question the psychotic paranoia with which many men defend their masculinity when it's so convenient to trash one young trans person's gender identity? The truth is that the myth of transsexual deception is merely a ruse, a smoke screen designed to hide societal complicity in this tragedy.

Most people want to believe that Gwen's murder was an isolated incident, an egregious act committed by a handful of young men who were provoked into doing the unthinkable. That way they need not confront the fact that half of the hung jury was more willing to identify with male homophobic hysteria than with an innocent transgender teenager. They need not examine how the news coverage and commentary, articles, editorials, and analyses invariably chose to view this crime through the murderers' eyes, or through a grieving mother's tears, for fear of what might happen if they dared to imagine themselves as Gwen, a young trans woman they so desperately wanted to believe was nothing like them.

Everyone chose to tiptoe around the subject because they were too afraid to put themselves in Gwen Araujo's shoes, if only for a moment, to ask what the world looked like from her view: To imagine how frustrated you might be if you were unable to explore your own sexuality without having other people turn your body into a lightning rod for their own insecurities. To imagine how unjust it would feel to be dismissed as a fraud despite being the only nineteen-year-old in your known universe with the guts to truly be yourself. To imagine how frail masculinity would seem to you if you had seen a pack of young men in their twenties exude pure fear over one feminine transgender teen. To imagine how flat-out foolish those boys must have seemed as they confronted you with the question, "Are you a woman or a man?" And to picture the blank stares on their faces when you replied, "Isn't it obvious?" To imagine how hollow accusations of deception would sound to you if you understood that the real question that needed to be asked was "Who's deceiving whom?"

As I said, this piece is not about hate crimes, violence, ignorance, or prejudice. It's about self-deception. It's about the assumptions that people like me live with on a daily basis. Because like Gwen, I was born male. I am a transgender woman. And if we were to meet and if I didn't immediately share that information with you, would that be an act of deception? Could you accuse me of telling a lie if you were to see what you wanted to see with your own eyes and I decided to simply keep quiet? And if I were to presume things about you that were not true, could I accuse you of misleading me too? Or would such careless accusations of deception merely be expressions of callous pride, a stubborn refusal to acknowledge our own mistaken assumptions?

The untold story behind Gwen's much-publicized death is that she is only the tip of the iceberg. Gwen's murder took place in the San Francisco Bay Area, where there are thousands of people who identify as transgender. Keep that in mind every time you walk down the street or flirt with a stranger. A certain percentage of the people you meet either appear to be a sex different from the one they were assigned at birth or identify as a gender different from the one you assume they are. And if this makes you feel uneasy, it is only because you are choosing not to live in reality.

It is time to move beyond pseudoliberal sound bites about how we all need to accept people who differ from us. Mere tolerance is insufficient. If we are to learn any lesson from Gwen Araujo's death, it's that we each need to take personal responsibility for our own presumptions. We should stop buying into the myth of deception, because the truth is that every day, each of us is guilty of committing countless acts of assumption.

14
Trans-Sexualization

I NEVER FULLY APPRECIATED what it meant to be sexualized when I was male-bodied. Back then, I would sometimes overhear men shouting lewd comments at women, or deliberately turning their heads to ogle women as they walked by. At the time, I assumed that the men who committed such acts were simply expressing a form of sexual interest, albeit in a rude and adolescent manner. While other men may have experienced a similar attraction to the woman in question, I thought, most were apparently respectful enough not to vocalize such thoughts publicly. In this sense, catcalls reminded me of those bad teen sex comedies—undoubtedly crude and obnoxious, but relatively harmless. In retrospect, I now realize that this interpretation was largely enabled by the fact that I had not been on the receiving end of such acts before.

My perspective changed radically almost immediately after I began hormone therapy. In fact, one of the first indications I had that others were beginning to gender me as female was the occasional sexual innuendo that I received from strange men as I walked down city streets. My previous assumption—that such comments were expressions of sexual desire—suddenly seemed unlikely to me. At the time (only two months into my transition), I barely even looked like a woman and had no figure whatsoever. Nor did the comments have anything to do with my being dressed in a particularly feminine or revealing fashion, as I was still dressing in boy-mode, wearing flannel shirts over T-shirts over sports bras to hide the fact that I was developing breasts. In addition, many of these comments were unarguably mean-spirited and insulting, and no attempt was made to disguise them as flirting. I was clearly being overtly sexualized by these strangers, and not because I was deemed attractive, but simply because I appeared to be a woman. And the purpose of such blatantly vulgar remarks was not to express attraction or potentially garner my interest, but rather to exert a modicum of control over me: to make me feel uncomfortable, intimidated, angry, or fearful, to force me to look away or to cross the street to avoid their harassment.

These days, I recognize the huge difference between sexual desire and sexualization. Sexual desirability is something that we all hope to have to some extent. When other people express their sexual desire for us, it can be extremely empowering, so long as such expressions are reserved for the appropriate time and place—i.e., from the right person and when we have signaled our openness or willingness to reciprocate. Sexualization, on the other hand, has the opposite effect: Rather than empowering the person, it's used to leverage power over them. This can be seen all the time in the media, where women often appear not as fully formed human beings with their own thoughts, feelings, and opinions, but as purely sexual objects used to sell cars, beer, and other commodities. Some might naively argue that these women have power—specifically, the power to lure men—but it's a power that only serves heterosexual male interests. After all, how much power is there in being a carrot on a stick dangled in front of someone? Such depictions exist in sharp contrast to media expressions of sexuality that center on real-life women's sexual desires and perspectives, such as *The Vagina Monologues* or a Margaret Cho show.

The fact that sexualization is an attempt to dehumanize and disempower women is even more evident in remarks we get on the street, which invariably occur when women are presumed vulnerable (when we are alone or outnumbered) and often go unchallenged solely because the men who make such comments are physically stronger than the women they harass. Perhaps it's only one in fifty or one in a hundred men who stoop to the level of catcalls (or worse), but over time they take their toll and achieve their intended effect: They make us feel like we are targets. Indeed, the sexualization that occurs in both media imagery and public harassment reinforces a power dynamic between the sexes in which men are invariably viewed as predators and women as prey. This predator/prey mind-set makes it virtually impossible for us to imagine that a woman has the potential to be a sexual aggressor (evident in the common disbelief about, and inability to articulate, instances of woman-on-woman sexual violence or female fetishism) or that a man can be a sexual object (as seen by the tendency for people to view young boys who are seduced by adult women as being "lucky," as opposed to being victims of statutory rape).[1] In fact, the only instances in which adult men seem to have the potential to become sexual objects is when they are sexualized or coerced into sexual acts by male aggressors.

Understanding this predator/prey dichotomy is crucial for us to make sense of the way transsexual women are sexualized in our society. Even though many people insist that trans women remain male despite our transitions, we are hardly ever sexualized as "men." Sure, there have been a handful of movies that depict fictional MTF transsexuals violently preying on women, but such characters are almost always portrayed as "deviant" or "deranged" males rather than as actual trans women. For example, the characters in the movies *Dressed to Kill* (1980) and *The Silence of the Lambs* (1991) neither live as nor physically transition to female, and their supposed transsexuality is treated simply as a psychosis that drives them to commit violence. In the vast majority of cases, however, the sexualization of trans women casts us in the role of sexual object rather than sexual aggressor. For example, the tranny sex and porn industries, which primarily cater to straight-identified men, overwhelmingly feature trans women as their sexual objects. In contrast, trans men are not objectified by straight-identified men to nearly the same extent; trans male porn (what little of it there is) attracts a predominantly gay male and queer female audience.[2]

In my own experience, I have found that the way I'm sexualized as a trans woman is similar to how I'm sexualized when I'm presumed to be a cissexual woman (i.e., I'm sexually objectified rather than seen as an aggressor). Invariably, though, the former is more invasive and debasing. For example, when I am assumed to be cissexual, the sexualizing comments I receive almost always come from random strangers in public. However, if I meet a man in a more social situation (e.g., at a party or a bar), he rarely stoops to blatantly crass, sexualizing comments, even when he is flirting with me. However, in social settings where I am known to be transsexual (e.g., at events where I perform spoken word poetry), men do often blatantly sexualize me: I have had men immediately engage me in conversations about how much they enjoy "she-male" porn, flat-out tell me "I'm turned on by 'girls like you,'" and explicitly describe the sex acts they have had with other trans women in the past. And numerous times I have received unsolicited emails, presumably from men who found my website during a search using the keyword "transsexual," in which they describe their sexual fantasies about trans women in gory detail, or ask me graphic questions about my body and sexual activities. These emails are always centered on my transsexual femaleness; I do not receive similar emails from people who presume that I am a cissexual female.

Some might suggest that the reason why I experience more hardcore sexualization as a trans woman has to do with the fact that transsexuals are rather rare, thus leading others to view us as exotic. While rareness may contribute to this phenomenon, I don't believe that it's a sufficient explanation. After all, there are plenty of types of women who are relatively rare, but they are not all sexualized in the same manner that trans women are. Perhaps a better explanation lies in the responses I receive when I make it clear to these men that I am troubled by the explicit nature of their comments. While it's a given that any "respectable" woman would be offended if a strange man immediately began sharing his sexual thoughts and fantasies with her (in fact, many catcallers seem to enjoy provoking these very feelings of insult or embarrassment in the women they harass), I find that the men who sexualize me as a trans woman are often dumbfounded and angered by my unwillingness to engage them on a sexually explicit level. I have even had a man accuse me of misleading him, as if the only legitimate reason for me to be out as a transsexual was to signal my sexual availability or to solicit sexual attention from men. This assumption—that I am somehow "asking for it"—is eerily similar to the attitudes some men have toward women who they believe are dressed or behaving in a sexually provocative fashion.

Once again, this sort of thinking stems directly from the predator/prey power dynamic, where a woman can never truly be seen as a sexual aggressor, only a sexual object. Thus, women who do take sexual initiative are not considered to be preying on men per se, but rather opening themselves up to or inviting male sexual aggression. Of course, what constitutes "inviting" male sexualization is typically defined by male presumptions. For example, women who are raped by men are often mischaracterized as instigating their own sexual violation by virtue of the clothing they wore, their past sexual histories, or their willingness to meet privately with a man. In fact, any action carried out by a woman that can be misconstrued as enabling others to view her as a sexual object is presumed to invite male sexual advances. In this context, I would argue that trans women are hypersexualized in our culture because we are viewed as enabling our own sexual objectification (by virtue of the fact that we physically transition from male to female) in much the same way that a woman who wears a low-cut dress is presumed to facilitate her own objectification.

The idea that trans women deliberately transform ourselves into women to invite male sexualization and sexual advances is perhaps the most popular assumption made about trans women. According to this myth, trans women do not "prey" on men so much as we "lure" them, by turning ourselves into sexual objects that no red-blooded man can resist. Framing the matter this way not only relieves men of any responsibility for their own sexual actions, but also prevents them from being cast in the role of sexual object or prey—an inherently subordinate position. Further, this tactic insinuates that trans women's physical transitions are centered on the desires of men, in much the same way that people presume that women who wear highly feminine or revealing outfits do so not for themselves, but in order to attract male attention. This point is crucial: If trans women were seen as changing our sex primarily because we *wanted* to be female (as is generally the case), then MTF transitioning would become both a self-empowering act and one that potentially empowers femaleness itself. However, the assumption that we change our sex in order to attract men essentially sexualizes our motives for transitioning, a move that disempowers trans women and femaleness while reinforcing the idea that heterosexual male desire is central. This sexualization of trans women's motives not only belittles our own female identities, but also implies that women as a whole have no value beyond their ability to be sexualized by men.

This tendency to focus on heterosexual male desire also dominates mainstream discourse on the MTF transitioning process itself. For instance, in the media, it seems that the most commonly described effect of MTF hormone therapy is that it causes trans women to develop breasts or "curves." While this is certainly true, trans women themselves do not always see this specific change as the most important result of hormone therapy. Most of us tend to cite the more psychological and emotional effects of estrogen, or the fact that it facilitates our being perceived by others as female in a more general way, as being the primary positive outcome of hormone therapy. Similarly, most people assume that trans women undergo bottom surgery not because we want to have a clitoris and vagina, or that we wish to align our physical bodies with our own subconscious self-image, but instead because we wish to be penetrated by a man. Of course, many trans women (like their cissexual counterparts) are attracted to men and wish to have sex with them, but it's demeaning to suggest that any woman's physical femaleness (whether trans or cis) exists only to experience male penetration.

Of course, attempts to focus on male desire when considering MTF transsexuality are undermined by the fact that many trans women are either lesbian or bisexual. This inconsistency is often downplayed in the media, which tends to either make trans women who have female partners invisible or asexualize them. For example, the media may depict their relationships as entirely platonic, or holdovers from a marriage that has ceased being heterosexual. Indeed, as a dyke-identified trans woman, the most common question I'm asked when I do trans outreach presentations is, "Why did you change your sex if you are attracted to women?" Essentially, what these people are asking me is why on earth would I choose to be a woman if not to attract and appease the desires of heterosexual men? Similar questions surround the existence of trans women who choose not to undergo bottom surgery or who are not interested in cultivating a highly feminine image. In all of these cases, public confusion stems from the implicit assumption that we transition in order to become the objects of heterosexual male desire. If people were to assume instead that we transition primarily for ourselves (as is indeed the case), then it would become easy to understand why some trans women might not want to put on makeup, dresses, and heels every day, or why they would choose not to undergo an expensive form of genital surgery that could potentially result in a loss of sensation or other medical complications.

The popular assumption that trans women deliberately transform ourselves into sexual objects also explains why we are so frequently depicted in the media as sex workers.[3] The fact that trans female sex workers have reached the status of "stock characters" is of particular interest, as such depictions are at complete odds with other cissexual presumptions about transsexuality. Media representations of trans people that do not involve sex work typically go out of their way to stress the fact that transsexuality is an extraordinarily rare phenomenon, and to promote the idea that transsexuals are sexually undesirable. So it is unclear why, being as rare and undesirable as we supposedly are, we seem to make up such a significant percentage of sex workers on TV and in the movies. This inconsistency implicitly suggests that trans women must somehow specifically seek out jobs as sex workers, presumably because we so desperately wish to be sexually objectified by men.

In fact, many trans women are sex workers, but generally not because they wish to be sexual objects. Like their cissexual counterparts, many trans women turn to such work because few other viable economic options are available to them. For example, in San Francisco, perhaps the most trans-friendly city in the nation, approximately 75 percent of transgender people cannot find full-time work, 57 percent have experienced employment discrimination on the job, and 96 percent live below the city's median income.[4] In other words, any realistic portrayal of transgender sex workers would necessarily have to address the issue of poverty that comes at the hands of anti-trans prejudice. This, of course, rarely happens on TV or in movies, where depictions of trans female sex workers are almost always brief and superfluous. Thus, media stereotypes of trans female sex workers not only promote the misconception that trans women transition so they can be sexualized, but they also deny the cissexual prejudice that drives many actual trans women into sex work in the first place.

While there has been extensive feminist analysis examining the ways in which women are sexualized in the media, such work has typically ignored media depictions of trans women. In fact, some feminists even seem to accept at face value media stereotypes of trans women as hyperfeminine and wishing to be sexualized—a rather illogical position given their own critiques of how images of women and other sexual minorities are typically distorted and mischaracterized by a predominantly straight-male-centric media. However, it's a mistake for cissexual women to view depictions of trans women as having little to do with themselves, as they are so obviously meant to dismiss both transsexuality *and* femaleness. After all, in a world where women are regularly reduced to objects of male desire, it's no accident that trans women—the only people in our society who actively choose to become women and who actively fight for their right to be recognized as female—are almost universally depicted in a purely sexualized manner.

Unfortunately, the narrow context of the predator/prey power dynamic has shaped not only media and pop culture depictions of trans women, but psychiatric depictions as well. The long-standing assumption that only men can be sexual aggressors (arising from phallocentric models of libido formation that have been forwarded by many influential psychoanalysts) has led psychiatrists to define a long list of "paraphilias" and "perversions" that regularly "afflict" men, but which are described as "rare" or "nonexistent" in women. In reality, many of these practices do occur in women and have been described by researchers in other fields, but have been overlooked or hand-waved away in psychiatry because they are presumed to require a "male agent" (i.e., a legitimate sexual aggressor).[5] Similarly, in psychiatric discourses regarding transsexuality—in which trans women are labeled and conceptualized as "male transsexuals" and trans men as "female transsexuals"—the tendency has been to play down FTM spectrum gender and sexual diversity, while focusing heavily on MTF spectrum transgenderism, due in part to the latter group's presumed "male agency."[6] However, it is not simply that MTF spectrum trans people are studied more because they are (or used to be) male. Because psychiatrists who buy into the predator/prey dichotomy tend to view expressions of femininity as serving the sole purpose of attracting and appeasing male sexual desire, and view the desire to be female as synonymous with the desire to be sexually objectified, they have consistently tried to frame MTF transgenderism as being driven primarily or exclusively by sexual impulses.

This psychiatric sexualization of MTF transgenderism is most evident in the historic tendency to divvy up all MTF spectrum trans people into two classes: transvestites and transsexuals. While the transvestite/transsexual dichotomy fails to account for the broad spectrum of MTF transgenderism, it has predominated because it mirrors the predator/prey dichotomy that many psychiatrists implicitly buy into. Until very recently, to be considered a MTF transsexual, one had to express a desire to be female, be sexually attracted to men, be feminine in gender expression, wish to have a vagina rather than a penis, and appear unquestionably female post-transition. In other words, psychiatrists required transsexual women to be willing and able to become desirable sexual objects in the eyes of heterosexual men. For many decades, those MTF spectrum trans people who failed to meet any one of these criteria (i.e., who were unwilling to meet all of the prerequisites of a sexual object) were denied their requests to physically transition and were often presumed to be "merely" transvestites.

Unlike MTF transsexuals, who were typically perceived as sexual objects, transvestites were viewed as men, and thus sexual aggressors. Their desire to dress as women was viewed not as a self-empowering or even neutral act of gender expression, but rather as a fetish for wearing feminine clothing. This sexualization of feminine gender expression has been codified in the psychiatric diagnosis transvestic fetishism, which is so vaguely written as to suggest that all heterosexual men who crossdress are driven by this "sexual paraphilia."[7] The bizarre assumptions built into the transvestic fetishism diagnosis—especially its specific exclusion of nonheterosexual men who crossdress—suggest that it has been created for the sole purpose of reinforcing the predator/prey dichotomy. In a sense, Transvestic Fetishism misconstrues feminine gender expression in heterosexual males as a somewhat "normal" (albeit misdirected) example of male sexual aggressors who sexually objectify femininity. Homosexual males are presumably exempt because women are not their sexual object choice (as that would undermine the labeling of their crossdressing as a fetish) and/or their expressions of femininity are presumed to primarily facilitate their own sexual objectification by other men.

Over the years, the MTF transsexual/transvestite dichotomy has increasingly been called into question, as it has become apparent that many (but certainly not all) self-identified male crossdressers eventually come to see themselves as transsexuals and choose to physically transition to female.[8] This occurs despite the fact that they often remain primarily attracted to women and/or that their gender expression may not be viewed by others as sufficiently feminine. Now, if we were to attempt to account for this phenomenon in the simplest way and with the least number of assumptions, we might suggest that some crossdressers (like their transsexual female counterparts) also have a female subconscious sex. However, in a world where women are regularly assumed to be "naturally" feminine and attracted to men, MTF spectrum trans people who do not meet those expectations may have a more difficult time considering the possibility that becoming female and living as a woman is a realistic option for them. So they may initially gravitate toward a crossdresser identity because it seems to be the only viable alternative for them. This was most certainly true in my case. For me, it was only after I fully explored crossdressing (eventually finding it to be insufficient to ease my gender dissonance), and had the opportunity to meet several trans women who did not fit the classic transsexual archetype, that I realized that it was actually possible for me to physically transition and live as a somewhat nonconforming woman with regard to gender and sexuality.

While a subconscious sex that is independent of sexual orientation and gender expression (as I have previously described in chapter 6, "Intrinsic Inclinations") may be the simplest and soundest model to explain why some male crossdressers eventually come to see themselves as trans women, it has not sat well with certain psychiatrists. This is presumably because the existence of nonheterosexual and nonfeminine trans women entirely undermines the predator/prey logic that these researchers take as a given. In the late 1980s, in an apparent attempt to reconcile this issue, psychologist Ray Blanchard put forward a different (and more confounding) model to explain MTF transgenderism.[9] His theory creates a new dichotomy between what he calls *autogynephilic* and *homosexual* transsexuals, which recapitulates the predator/prey dichotomy. While Blanchard's controversial theory is built upon a number of incorrect and unfounded assumptions, and there are many methodological flaws in the data he offers to support it, it has garnered some acceptance in the psychiatric literature and gained mainstream attention with the publication of psychologist J. Michael Bailey's book *The Man Who Would Be Queen*.[10]

According to Blanchard's model, "homosexual" transsexuals are trans women who are feminine and exclusively attracted to men (the confusing nomenclature arises from Blanchard's and other psychiatrists' practice of viewing trans women as "males"). They fulfill the requirements for the role of sexual object by virtue of their willingness to accommodate heterosexual male desire: "Homosexual gender dysphorics are directly aroused by the objective features of the male physique, especially the sight and feel of male genitalia."[11] The implication here (stated even more explicitly in Bailey's book) is that "homosexual" transsexuals are feminine gay men who transition to female because that's the only way they can attract heterosexual men.[12]

Blanchard goes on to claim that all "nonhomosexual" MTF transsexuals suffer from autogynephilia, a paraphilia that Blanchard invented to support his contention that "all gender-dysphoric males [*sic*] who are not sexually aroused by men . . . are instead sexually aroused by the thought or image of themselves as women."[13] Thus, autogynephilics fulfill the requirements for being sexual aggressors: They are assumed to be "males" who sexually objectify femaleness and femininity. From Blanchard's perspective, the only problem is that their "normal" heterosexual sex drive is misdirected toward themselves (i.e., they are attracted to the images of themselves as women, rather than, or in addition to, images of other women). Autogynephilia, like transvestic fetishism before it, exempts those who are deemed "homosexual," as they would necessarily undermine the predator/prey dichotomy upon which these theories are built. So instead of assuming that there is a unified basis for transsexuality (i.e., a subconscious sex that is at odds with one's physical sex), Blanchard proposes two separate causes of MTF transsexuality in order to accommodate his sexualization of MTF gender identity and expression.[14]

Blanchard has argued that his model is simpler than other psychiatric theories of MTF transgenderism because it subsumes male crossdressers and "nonhomosexual" trans women into one category: "Transvestites, on this view, would be understood as autogynephiles whose only—or most prominent—symptom is sexual arousal in association with crossdressing and who have not (or not yet) become gender dysphoric."[15] This is problematic, however, as some crossdressers and trans women say they have never experienced sexual arousal in the manner Blanchard describes. Perhaps even more common in the MTF community are people who describe being sexually aroused by their own cross-gender expression during their early stages of gender experimentation, but who over time experience a reduction or a complete loss of arousal in response to such feminine self-expressions.[16] This is particularly true for many trans women, for whom previous sexual fantasies related to wearing women's clothes or having a female body may become rather banal or pointless after one has physically transitioned to female and lived as a woman day in and day out. This fact is a serious blow to Blanchard's model, as it suggests that sexual arousal is not what drives these trans women to change their sex, and that the temporary sexual phase they experienced when they were crossdressing was more related to their overcoming the highly sexualizing cultural symbolism commonly associated with femaleness and femininity. Blanchard tries to get around this caveat by claiming that autogynephilia is not only a paraphilia, but a sexual orientation, and that trans women who no longer experience sexual arousal in response to images of themselves as women have formed a sort of "pair-bond" with their female selves.[17] (Perhaps he sees this as analogous to how long-term married couples may stay together despite a reduction in their sexual interest in one another.)

Blanchard's categorization of autogynephilia as a sexual orientation reveals a startling naiveté regarding his understanding of human sexuality. In focusing exclusively on "sexual object choice," he neglects to consider the role that *our own bodies* play both in our sexual fantasies and in our realities. Our sexual experiences, whether masturbatory or with partners, typically involve various combinations of sexual attraction and desire for others, as well as sexual sensations and responses to mental, visual, tactile, and other stimuli that arise from our own physically sexed bodies. Since cissexuals are able to take their own physically sexed bodies for granted, they often focus exclusively on that aspect of sexuality which they cannot take for granted—namely, their potential sexual partners. In contrast, pre- and non-transition trans people are unable to take their own physical sex for granted, and thus their sexual fantasies often revolve around physically becoming or being their preferred sex. Every trans person I've spoke with about this—whether MTF or FTM spectrum, homosexual, bisexual, or heterosexual—has said that their sexual fantasies almost always involve (on some level) their being in the appropriately sexed body.

When one takes this necessary difference in trans and cis perspectives into consideration, it becomes obvious that Blanchard's "autogynephiles," who have fantasies that center on thoughts of their own physical femaleness rather than on the "physique of the partner," are not significantly different from cissexual women who sometimes have fantasies of being fondled or penetrated by faceless men, or cissexual men who imagine receiving blow jobs from faceless women. In fact, given the prominence of the penis in straight male porn, men's locker room conversations, and public restroom stall artistry, one could easily make the case that male heterosexuality is driven to a large extent by *autophallophilia*—being aroused by the image or thought of oneself as having a penis. Of course, it is unlikely that Blanchard would even consider this possibility, both because it places trans people and cissexuals on equal footing and because it implies that a man can sexually objectify his own male body, an act that is fundamentally incompatible with predator/prey logic. In fact, the restrictive nature of the predator/prey dichotomy ensures that only MTF spectrum trans people can ever be accused of sexually objectifying their own preferred gender. Cissexual women may be aroused by wearing sexy feminine articles of clothing and FTM spectrum trans folks may be turned on by the thought of having a penis, but because these groups are considered female (in the eyes of many psychiatrists, at any rate), they are not deemed to be legitimate sexual aggressors. And while cissexual men are regularly characterized as sexual aggressors, any sexually charged feelings they may have related to their own maleness or masculinity will be ignored because of our societal reluctance to consider men as sexual objects.

Many people, both within and outside the field of psychiatry, seem so compulsively driven to sexualize MTF gender identities and expressions that they fail to ask a far more relevant and pressing question: How does the ubiquitous and assumed predator/prey dichotomy shape the way MTF spectrum trans people come to view themselves? Given the immense amount of research (much of it carried out by psychologists) into how representations of women in the media and popular culture strongly influence girls' and women's sexualities, behaviors, and body images, it is remarkable that few (if any) in the field have attempted to apply such work to the MTF community. After all, despite being socialized male, those of us on the MTF spectrum have been exposed to many of the same explicitly sexualizing cultural messages about womanhood and femininity as those socialized female, and we are just as susceptible of constructing our own sexualities and self-images around those very same cultural ideals.

I would argue that MTF spectrum trans sexualities make far more sense once we recognize them as being on the receiving end of cultural messages that sexualize femaleness and femininity, rather than being the perpetrators of such sexualization themselves. Those who fit the so-called "true" transsexual archetype (i.e., Blanchard's "homosexual" group) typically identify as female from an early age and transition relatively early in life. Because they identify as female for much of their lives, they are likely to absorb much of the same cultural encouragement that non-trans heterosexual girls do, such as becoming focused on being conventionally attractive and attracting boys. On the other hand, MTF spectrum trans people who become aware of their cross-gender desires after they have already consciously accepted the fact that they are "boys" (i.e., Blanchard's "autogynephilics") tend to have greater difficulty reconciling their female or feminine inclinations with societal messages that insist that men and women are "opposite" sexes, and that girls are inferior to boys. Rather than feeling entitled to call themselves female or to act outwardly feminine, they often develop intense feelings of shame and self-loathing regarding their cross-gender inclinations. To cope, they may develop sexual thoughts and fantasies that associate their desire to be female/feminine with subordination, humiliation, and sexual objectification. If anything, these fantasies share more in common with the exhibitionistic, submissive, and rape fantasies experienced by many women rather than the sexually aggressive and objectifying fantasies commonly associated with men.

Because the relentless sexualization of MTF spectrum trans people has become one of the most common tactics used to delegitimize our gender identities and expressions, many in our community have tried to disavow their sexual predilections. I believe that this approach is inadequate because it fosters a continuing shame regarding our sex and fantasy lives, and because it leaves a void which is too easily filled by the ideas of so-called experts (like Blanchard and Bailey) who are all too eager to put their own cissexist, oppositionally sexist, and traditionally sexist spins on our sexual thoughts and behaviors. Personally, I prefer to be open about my sexual history while also placing it in the appropriate political context. After all, if society is going to insist that all MTF spectrum trans people are "perverts" and "sexual deviants," then they should be made to answer for the fact that it is their misogynistic, predator/prey-obsessed, oppositionally sexist gender prejudices and practices that make it inevitable that we will be judged this way in the first place.

15
Submissive Streak

WHEN I WAS A CHILD, I was sexually assaulted, but not by any particular person. It was my culture that had his way with me. And when he was through, he carved his name in my side so that I'd always have something to remember him by. It's the scar that marks the spot where my self-esteem was ripped right out of me. And now all that's left is a submissive streak that's as wide and as deep as the Grand Canyon.

And maybe I was born transgender—my brain preprogrammed to see myself as female despite the male body I was given at birth—but like every child, I turned to the rest of the world to figure out who I was and what I was worth. And like a good little boy, I picked up on all of the not-so-subliminal messages that surrounded me. TV shows where Father knows best and a woman's place is in the home; fairy tales where helpless girls await their handsome princes; cartoon supermen who always save the damsel in distress; plus schoolyard taunts like "sissy" and "fairy" and "pussy" all taught me to see "feminine" as a synonym for "weakness." And nobody needed to tell me that I should hate myself for wanting to be what was so obviously the lesser sex.

When I hit puberty, my newly found attraction to women spilled into my dreams of becoming a girl. For me, sexuality became a strange combination of jealousy, self-loathing, and lust. Because when you isolate an impressionable transgender teen and bombard her with billboard ads baring bikini-clad women and boys' locker room trash talk about this girl's tits and that girl's ass, then she will learn to turn her gender identity into a fetish.

So without ever having seen pulp fiction or hardcore porn, my thirteen-year-old brain started concocting scenarios straight out of BDSM handbooks. Most of my fantasies began with my abduction: I'd turn to putty in the hands of some twisted man who would turn me into a woman as part of his evil plan. It's called forced feminization, and it's not really about sex. It is about turning the humiliation you feel into pleasure, transforming the loss of male privilege into the best fuck ever.

While I never really believed the cliché about women being good for only one thing, I found that that sentiment kept creeping into my fantasies. In my late teens, I would imagine myself being sold into sex slavery and having strange men take advantage of me. It wasn't so much that I was attracted to men, but that movies and magazines made it seem that being feminine meant allowing yourself to be dominated by men. In my mind, I've been pinned down by bodies so large that they dwarfed me, felt the ghost pains that accompanied the unwanted groping of body parts that did not yet belong to me, experienced the helplessness of having some faceless guy stick his cock into the cunt that I hated myself for wishing that I had. And with each make-believe thrust, I felt simultaneous ecstasy and shame. My rape fantasies were bastard Catholic sacraments, as I absolved myself of guilt by combining my desire to be female with self-inflicted penance and punishment.

In my twenties, I discovered role-playing relationships: placing personal ads in the "wild side" sections of weekly papers, conducting phone interviews with potential tops who got off on the idea of dominating a small and "passable" crossdresser. For them, I wore skimpy outfits and four-inch heels, not because I thought it made me more of a woman, but because I spent so much of my life guarded and making myself invisible that it was a thrill to be so exhibitionistic and vulnerable. I pretended to be their secretaries or call girls, roles that had as much to do with class as they did with gender and sex. We were creating fantasy worlds out of real-life meanings and symbols, turning ourselves into caricatures of a culture that denies its own infatuation with hierarchies and pecking orders.

Sometimes the line between fantasy and reality would blur, like the time I had a top who refused to stop for safe words.[1] When I finally thwarted his advances, he guilt-tripped me with fucked-up lines about how I had led him on and how it was all my fault for being such a tease. When I got home, I sat in the shower for almost an hour, but I still felt dirty and diseased. And I didn't dare tell a soul because, on a subconscious level, I couldn't shake the feeling that I had deserved what happened to me.

At some point, all of us who identify as female have to come face-to-face with our own internalized misogyny. And when people ask me what has been the hardest part of being a transsexual, expecting me to say that it was coming out to my family or the growing pains of going through a second puberty, I tell them that the hardest part, by far, has been unlearning lessons that were etched into my psyche before I ever set foot in kindergarten. The hardest part has been learning how to take myself seriously when the entire world is constantly telling me that femininity is always inferior to masculinity.

These days, I am an outspoken feminist and transgender activist. And most days, I dress like a tomboy in striped shirts, jeans, and Chuck Taylors. To most people, I probably seem pretty self-confident, but that's only because they can't see my submissive streak. It's like a scar I keep hidden up my sleeve, a scar that still sometimes opens up and bleeds. Like a shark bite, it literally tore me apart when it was first happening to me. But these days, my submissive streak is just another reminder of how I survived.

16
Love Rant

IT STARTED AS A CONVERSATION with a friend. Okay, it was more of a rant. I was going off about that stupid, crass, recurring scene that I have seen in at least thirty-nine different mainstream movies by now. You know, the one where the guy falls for a girl who turns out not to be "all girl" genital-wise. And the audience always obediently identifies with the guy, empathically laughing at his embarrassment or groaning along with his disgust. And nobody ever thinks twice about the tranny—who she is or how she feels about the incident—because she is just a prop, like the banana peel that only exists for the silent film star to slip upon. And I ended my diatribe by lambasting all of those arrogant and ignorant people who only ever see trans women in terms of how we might affect their own sexual orientation.

My straight-male-identified friend, who had been listening patiently to my entire tirade, asked me: "Well, tell me, how would you feel if you became interested in a woman, but then discovered that she was a transsexual?"

Now, my friend knows that I am happily married and monogamous, so it was a given that this was largely a hypothetical question. Nevertheless, he seemed surprised when I replied that I would not be bothered one bit. And it's not that I would merely "tolerate" a relationship with a trans woman. On the contrary, I would consider it an honor. Truth be told, over the last three years, about half of the women who have piqued my interest, who I would consider approaching if I were actively dating, just so happened to be trans women.

Now, as soon as I mentioned this, my friend said, "Oh, I had no idea that you had a 'tranny fetish.'" So I sarcastically thanked him for insinuating that the only reason why a person might find someone like myself attractive is if they suffered from a sort of "sexual perversion." After reprimanding him, I went on to say that there are a number of personality traits that I find attractive in women: passion, creativity, sense of humor, and self-confidence. And it has been my experience that trans women tend to have these qualities in full force. While some male "admirers" of trans women tend to fetishize us for our femininity or our imagined sexual submissiveness, I find trans women hot because we are anything but docile or demure. In order to survive as a trans woman, you must be, by definition, impervious, unflinching, and tenacious. In a culture in which femaleness and femininity are on the receiving end of a seemingly endless smear campaign, there is no act more brave—especially for someone assigned a male sex a birth—than embracing one's femme self.

And unlike those male tranny-chasers who say that they like "T-girls" because we are supposedly "the best of both worlds," I am attracted to trans women because we are *all* woman! My femaleness is so intense that it has overpowered the trillions of lame-ass Y chromosomes that sheepishly hide inside the cells of my body.

And my femininity is so relentless that it has survived over thirty years of male socialization and twenty years of testosterone poisoning. Some kinky-identified thrill-seekers may envision trans women as androgyne fuck fantasies, but that's only because they are too self-absorbed to appreciate how completely fucking female we are.

At this point in the conversation, my friend tried to play what he probably thought was his trump card. He asked me, "Well, what if you found out that the trans woman you were attracted to still had a penis?"

I laughed and replied that I am attracted to people, not to disembodied body parts. And I would be a selfish, ignorant, and unsatisfying lover if I believed that my partner's genitals existed primarily for my pleasure rather than her own. All that you ever need to know about genitals is that they are made up of flesh, blood, and millions of tiny, restless nerve endings—anything else that you read into them is mere hallucination, a product of your own overactive imagination. To paraphrase that famous saying, the opposite of attraction is not repulsion, it's indifference. Therefore, any person who would freak out over their female lover's seemingly inconsistent genitals is probably a little more interested in penises than they'd ever care to admit. (And by the way, this also applies to those "womyn-born-womyn"-identified lesbians who seem to emulate stereotypical straight male attitudes when it comes to this particular issue.)

My friend, still seemingly perplexed, asked me, "So if it's not about genitals, what is it about trans women's bodies that you find most attractive?"

I paused for a second to consider the question. Then I replied that it is almost always their eyes. When I look into them, I see both endless strength and inconsolable sadness. I see someone who has overcome humiliation and abuses that would flatten the average person. I see a woman who was made to feel shame for her desires and yet had the courage to pursue them anyway. I see a woman who was forced against her will into boyhood, who held on to a dream that everybody in her life desperately tried to beat out of her, who refused to listen to the endless stream of people who told her that who she was and what she wanted was impossible.

When I look into trans women's eyes, I see a profound appreciation for how fucking empowering it can be to be female, an appreciation that seems lost on many cissexual women who sadly take their female identities and anatomies for granted, or who perpetually seek to cast themselves as victims rather than instigators. In trans women's eyes, I see a wisdom that can only come from having to fight for your right to be recognized as female, a raw strength that only comes from unabashedly asserting your right to be feminine in an inhospitable world. In a trans woman's eyes, I see someone who understands that, in a culture that's seemingly fueled on male homophobic hysteria, choosing to be female and openly expressing one's femininity is not a sign of frivolousness, weakness, or passivity, it is a fucking badge of courage. Everybody loves to say that drag queens are "fabulous," but nobody seems to get the fact that trans women are fucking badass!

It was at that point in the conversation that I realized that perhaps I find trans women attractive because I see a little bit of myself in them. In their eyes, I see a part of myself that nobody else ever seems to see, the part that those who haven't had a trans female experience never seem to understand. And perhaps it's narcissistic to be attracted to someone who reminds me a bit of myself. But after spending most of my life feeling ashamed of who I was and what I desired, I'd like to think that maybe my attraction to trans women is a sign that I am finally beginning to learn to love myself.

17

Crossdressing: Demystifying Femininity and Rethinking "Male Privilege"

THE WORD "CROSSDRESSING," in its most generic sense, refers to wearing clothing associated with the other sex. Both female- and male-bodied people crossdress, and they may choose to do so for a variety of reasons: as part of a drag or theatrical performance, in a sexual context, to have others perceive them as the other sex, and/or as an expression of a deeply felt cross-gender identity. While crossdressing (the verb) is a general phenomenon, the word "crossdresser" (and its psychiatric synonym "transvestite") is often used specifically to refer to certain MTF spectrum people who channel their feminine expression into occasional (and typically private) spurts during which they immerse themselves in "women's" clothing and gender roles, sometimes even taking on an alter ego entirely separate from their male lives. In contrast, pre- and non-transitioning FTM spectrum folks more typically live openly and continuously as butch or masculine women (rather than as feminine women who occasionally dress fully as men).

MTF spectrum crossdressers (who will be referred to simply as "crossdressers" for rest of this essay) are relentlessly mischaracterized and disrespected by the public at large, as well as in specific fields such as psychiatry and gender studies, where their practices are coldly dissected and critiqued by those who are not crossdressers themselves. This lack of personal experience allows these clinicians and academics to naively and conveniently assign motives to crossdressers. Some of the more common of these assumptions are that crossdressing is a form of appropriating or objectifying womanhood; that it is an expression of latent homosexuality, exhibitionism, autogynephilia, or some other form of "sexually deviant" behavior; or that some males take refuge in femininity because they are unable or unwilling to live up to masculine ideals.

As someone who identified as a crossdresser for twelve years, and who has shared many intimate conversations with other crossdressers during that time, I offer this essay as a (hopefully) more enlightened and thoughtful perspective on the MTF crossdressing experience. The explanations I offer here stem directly from my personal experiences as a crossdresser—one who has since gone on to identify and live as a woman—so it is likely that what I have to say will not resonate with all crossdressers, particularly those who happily embrace that identity throughout their lives without transitioning. My purpose here is not to insinuate that all crossdressers are transsexuals-in-waiting, nor is it to project my individual experience onto other people's very different gendered experiences. This should simply be seen as my personal take on this very complex and misunderstood identity.

Effemimania and Feminine Expression

If you ask crossdressers their opinions about why this is a predominantly "male" phenomenon, most will mention the gross disparity between what is considered acceptable and unacceptable cross-gender expression between the sexes. While a hundred years ago, much of society considered it deviant for women to wear pants or other traditionally "male" articles of clothing, today women can wear such items without anyone making a fuss. In fact, a female-bodied person pretty much has to be dressed in full male-specific attire to even be considered crossdressed, whereas a male-bodied person may be considered a crossdresser if they wear a single female-specific article of clothing (such as a dress or a skirt). Thus, the liberalization of dressing norms that women have experienced over the last century has not been reciprocated to nearly the same extent for men.

While all crossdressers are cognizant of this double standard, some mistakenly view it as a form of "reverse" sexism—i.e., that men are specifically denied a "right" regarding attire that women take for granted. I would argue instead that this double standard stems directly from traditional sexism. After all, these days it's not so much a legal barrier that prevents most crossdressers from incorporating "women's" clothes into their daily wardrobes as it is a class barrier. Because femininity is seen as inferior to masculinity, any man who appears "effeminate" or feminized in any way will drastically lose status and respect in our society, much more so than those women who act boyish or butch. But it's not just that males who act feminine lose the advantages of male privilege; rather, they come under far more public scrutiny and disdain. This is because, in a male-centered world, women who express masculinity may be seen as breaking oppositional sexist norms, but they are not a perceived challenge to traditional sexism (i.e., their "wanting to be like men" is consistent with the idea that maleness is more valued than femaleness). In contrast, males who express femininity challenge both oppositional and traditional sexist norms (i.e., someone who is willing to give up maleness/masculinity for femaleness/femininity directly threatens the notion of male superiority as well as the idea that women and men should be "opposites").

In my own experiences, I have found that this obsession and anxiety over male expressions of femininity (which I called *effemimania* in chapter 7, "Pathological Science") extends far beyond critiquing men who wear "women's" clothing. In the years just before my transition, when I was living as a male who was open and comfortable with my own feminine inclinations, I regularly experienced gender anxiety from other people over the most trivial things. On more than one occasion, I was questioned about the fact that I had a bright red umbrella ("Is it your girlfriend's?" or "Are you just borrowing it?"). I was also interrogated regarding my tendency to color-coordinate my T-shirts and sneakers ("Is it just a coincidence or do you make them match on purpose?" or "Why would you do that?"). Another time, a friend asked me to hold her purse for a minute and then ostracized me for strapping it onto my shoulder ("I asked you to hold it, not to *wear* it!"). And I was regularly subjected to strange looks and comments for using words like "cute," "adorable," or "pretty" in a nonsarcastic way. I have hundreds of anecdotes like these—of people commenting, critiquing, and expressing concern over even the slightest manifestations of my femininity, given that I was male-bodied.

Unfortunately, I have found that many women fail to appreciate effemimania as a very real and pervasive form of traditional sexism, one that oppressively restricts and undermines feminine gender expression in male-bodied people. During a question and answer session at a gender-themed event I participated in, a trans woman brought up the intense ridicule a man can face for the simple act of wearing a pink tie. The audience, who was made up predominantly of people who were socialized female, laughed at this remark in what seemed to me to be a highly unsympathetic way, as though they believed that the hypothetical man in question suffered from some irrational form of male paranoia. This sort of thinking not only makes invisible the role that women often play in employing and propagating effemimania (in fact, all of the effemimanic remarks I described in the previous paragraph were made by women), but entirely dismisses the severity of this form of sexism. In my five years of living as a woman—one who very rarely wears makeup, who regularly dresses like a tomboy, who often goes long periods of time without shaving her legs or armpits, who sometimes curses like a sailor, who is sometimes very physically active, and who is unafraid to take on supposedly masculine tasks such as using tools, lifting heavy boxes, etc.—I have not experienced a single gender-anxious comment or critique regarding my masculine gender expression that has even come close to the level of intensity or condescension that I regularly received for my feminine expressions back when I was perceived as male.

Effemimania is not merely a phenomenon that affects adults, but rather one that begins early in childhood; this is highlighted by a recent study carried out by Emily Kane, who examined parental responses to gender nonconformity in their preschool children.[1]

Kane found that the parents she studied often encouraged gender nonconformity in their female children and few offered negative responses when they engaged in stereotypically masculine activities. On the other hand, while the parents sometimes reacted positively when their male children engaged in certain stereotypically feminine activities—specifically those related to domestic skills, nurturing, and empathy—other activities related to what Kane called "icons of femininity," such as wearing pink or girl-specific clothing, wanting to wear nail polish, and expressing interest in dance, ballet, or Barbie dolls, were generally greeted with negative reactions by both fathers and mothers, and in parents of varying race, economic class, and sexual orientation.

Many of the consequences of this society-wide effemimania are chronicled in Stephen J. Ducat's book *The Wimp Factor: Gender Gaps, Holy Wars, and the Politics of Anxious Masculinity*. Ducat describes the ways in which male development and thought processes are shaped by effemimania and cites studies that show that feminine boys are viewed far more negatively, and brought in for psychotherapy far more often, than masculine girls.[2] As Ducat explains, "I don't think that it underestimates the damage done to girls and women under the regime of patriarchal gender norms to say that males suffer certain constraints and conflicts from which females, with a few notable exceptions, are largely exempt. Specifically, boys from early on learn that cross-gender behavior is a taboo often enforced with predictable ferocity by family, peers, and the larger society. For example, unlike girls, boys who do play with toys of the other sex often try to hide it from others."[3]

This very much resonates with my own experiences as a young boy. Some of my earliest childhood memories (around the ages of five and six) are of censoring of my own thoughts, behaviors, and desires because I was worried that they would lead me to be perceived by others as feminine. I vividly remember anxiously describing anything having to do with girls as being "yucky" or "dumb," not because of any actual strong negative feelings that I had, but because I was aware that I was expected to have such an attitude toward anything feminine. In first grade, when a female friend invited me to her birthday party, I hid the invitation because I was embarrassed to have been invited to a girl's party.

This feeling, that a boy must hide female or feminine gender inclinations, helps explain why many MTF spectrum children and teenagers channel those inclinations into very specific and private occasions, unlike their FTM spectrum counterparts, who typically express their masculine interests and mannerisms in an open and regular way. In other words, effemimania drives many MTF spectrum children and teens to develop strict divisions between "boy-mode" (i.e., public) and "girl-mode" (i.e., private). Such distinctions often persist well into adulthood and are typically considered to be a hallmark of the crossdresser identity. However, it would be an oversimplification to claim that crossdressing is simply a form of hiding one's feminine side or remaining closeted. After all, many crossdressers continue to maintain their split male/female personas long after they come out publicly as crossdressers. To fully understand the boy-mode/girl-mode dichotomy and the fascination surrounding women's clothing that typifies the MTF crossdressing experience, we must first take into account how the marginalization of women in our society affects those who are raised male.

Enforced Ignorance and the Mystification of Femininity

When we talk about marginalization, we refer to the way that "those perceived as lacking desirable traits or deviating from the group norms tend to be excluded by wider society."[4] One of the most lucid descriptions of marginalization that I've read comes from bell hooks's book *Feminist Theory: From Margin to Center,* in which she focuses on how most prominent feminists of the 1960s and 1970s tended to ignore the viewpoints and concerns of economically and racially marginalized women such as herself. This was because, being predominantly white and middle-class, these feminists existed in the center with regard to race and class, so they had little awareness or understanding of lives and perspectives on the margins. However, the reverse is not true: People at the margins must understand life at the center in order to survive. As hooks explains: "Living as we did—on the edge—we developed a particular way of seeing reality. We looked both from the outside in and from the inside out. We focused our attention on the center as well as on the margin. We understood both."[5]

While hooks is referring here to her experiences growing up as a person of color in white America, her observations about margins and centers can readily be applied to other class issues. For example, those who are marginalized for being lesbian tend to have a thorough understanding of the assumptions and experiences of the heterosexual center—after all, they grow up in a predominantly heterosexual world and constantly have to navigate other people's heterosexual assumptions. In contrast, most heterosexuals understand very little about lesbians and lesbian culture, as such knowledge has been systematically shut out of dominant society. Similarly, while I understand cissexual culture (as I was raised as, and generally assumed to be, cissexual), most cissexuals tend to have an extraordinarily limited understanding of transsexuality.

It is important to note that the lack of understanding that those at the center have of those at the margin is not solely due to their lack of exposure (such as the fact that they've never been to a lesbian bar or to a transsexual support group). Rather, ignorance about marginalized people is often *enforced* from within the center. For example, if a straight woman decided to go to a lesbian bar (where she might have the opportunity to learn more about lesbian people and perspectives), she risks having her straight friends and family members assume that she is lesbian. In other words, she risks being marginalized herself. Similarly, if a straight man were to buy a book on transsexuality (say, for example, this book), others might suspect that he is a closeted transsexual or a tranny-chaser. The constant threat of being ostracized, which is directed toward people who show even the slightest interest in marginalized cultures and perspectives, creates within the center an *enforced ignorance* regarding those at the margins.

It is safe to say that, despite the fact that we make up more than half of the population, women are marginalized in our male-centered society. This can be seen not only in women's underrepresentation in political, economic, and media positions of power, but in the way that virtually anything associated with femaleness or femininity is typically relegated to a separate category. In the media, stories produced by men, and that feature male protagonists, are seen as universal, while those created by women and featuring female protagonists are often relegated to their own genre (women's literature, chick flicks, etc.). When talking about sports, it's a given that one is referring to male leagues unless the sport name is preceded by the word "women's." Until very recently, most medical research that examined general health concerns had been conducted on men, and still today women's specific health issues are typically removed from general medicine and placed in their own category, such as ob-gyn or women's reproductive health.

Because our society centers on maleness, most men are able to get by in life without ever understanding or appreciating women's experiences or perspectives. In contrast, women need to be able to appreciate both female and male perspectives in order to successfully navigate society. In fact, in many ways, women in our culture are even *encouraged* to understand aspects of maleness better in order to fulfill the role they are often expected to play as family caregiver for male partners and children. One example of this is how women's magazines feature articles with titles like "The Sex He Craves," which offer advice about what men supposedly want, while most magazines geared toward men are entirely devoid of any information designed to shed light on women's perspectives or desires.

Because of enforced ignorance, those who are socialized male typically end up mystifying femaleness—meaning that they develop a sensationalized and taboo curiosity about womanhood that is similar to that which many heterosexuals develop toward homosexuality, or that cissexuals develop toward transsexuality. Girls and women suddenly become perplexing creatures who males are entirely unable to identify with or relate to. While one might be tempted to say that the reverse is also true (after all, both sexes complain about not being able to understand the other sex), it has been my experience that most women are able and willing to put themselves in men's shoes temporarily. For example, I have been struck by how women often wince when seeing images of men who are kicked in the groin or upon hearing stories of men who sustain injuries to their genitals, despite not ever having had male genitals themselves. In contrast, I have never once seen a man have a similar reaction upon hearing about reciprocal accounts of women (like stories about female genital mutilation). Similarly, while most women seem to understand how men "get off" via their penises, men seem curiously unable to imagine what it might be like to be on the receiving end of female sexual stimulation. This is evident in comments I've heard men make: that if they had breasts or female genitals they would fondle themselves all the time, as though the only pleasure they could relate to was the sensation of touching female body parts from the outside.

The mystification of women focuses not only on female bodies, but on feminine gender expression as well. It's common for men to describe feminine women as being "enchanting" and "mysterious," and as having the ability to "cast a spell" over them. In other words, they relegate femininity to the realm of the supernatural—by definition, not natural and impossible to understand. Perhaps no aspect of femininity is more mystified than women's clothing, which often emphasizes women's sexuality, and which is designed in color, texture, and style to be vastly different from "men's" clothing (right down to the shirt and pants buttons, which are conveniently on the "opposite" side).

While enforced ignorance and the subsequent mystification of femaleness/femininity is a pervasive phenomenon, it clearly affects different individuals to different extents. Stephen Ducat makes a strong case that those boys who are most fiercely taught to disavow femininity within themselves are the ones who tend to have the most outwardly misogynistic attitudes overall.[6] This makes sense when one considers the fact that enforced ignorance and mystification act to dehumanize those who are female and feminine, thus enabling certain men to sexually objectify, harass, and outright abuse members of those groups without experiencing any feelings of empathy or remorse. On the other hand, those boys who are given the freedom to express their full range of gendered expression, and/or who are encouraged to listen, respect, and relate to the women in their lives, may avoid the intense enforced ignorance that other males face. Additionally, like any form of childhood socialization, enforced ignorance may be overcome later in life as one gains a greater understanding of women or as one grows more comfortable with feminine expression both within oneself and in others.

Crossdresser Development

Now that we understand enforced ignorance and the mystification of femaleness/femininity in those who are socialized as male, we can ask what specific effect this has on crossdresser development. The first thing that needs to be said is that those who embrace the crossdresser identity are likely to be a heterogeneous group, encompassing a spectrum of individuals who have a feminine gender expression and/or a female subconscious sex, and who experience those inclinations at varying intensities. This would explain why some crossdressers never transition, while others eventually do, and why some view crossdressing as a way to express a feminine side of their personalities, while others see it as an opportunity to experience themselves as female as much as a male-bodied person possibly can. The idea that crossdressing is often driven by intrinsic inclinations (rather than simply being a phase, hobby, or kink that individuals stumble upon) is supported by the fact that virtually all self-identified crossdressers report that their desire to dress and act feminine/female persists throughout their lives.

The fact that males are socialized to view femaleness and femininity as enigmatic and taboo helps explain the very different manifestations of gender expression of MTF and FTM spectrum people. It also offers an explanation as to why some MTF spectrum folks learn to channel their femininity/femaleness into crossdressing, while others openly express their femininity/femaleness from a very early age. As mentioned in previous chapters, most psychiatric explanations for this dichotomy in the MTF spectrum population have centered on presumed differences in sexual orientation and arousal. However, recognizing how effemimania, enforced ignorance, and mystification work together to shape MTF spectrum transgender identities offers a nonsexual explanation for this phenomenon, one based on *gender constancy*. While children typically learn to distinguish between females and males, and to describe themselves as either a girl or a boy around the age of two or three, they do not develop gender constancy—the understanding that one's sex is fixed and does not change over time and in different situations—until they're between the ages of four and seven.[7] Interestingly, most trans women who fall under the category of "primary" transsexuals report knowing that they were or wanted to be female as early as three or four years old (that is, before gender constancy set in). In contrast, most "secondary" MTF transsexuals and crossdressers report discovering their cross-gender inclinations at a later age, often during puberty (after they had developed gender constancy).

Taking this into consideration, I would argue that children assigned a male sex who recognize their own female or feminine inclinations prior to gender constancy are more likely to see them as legitimate aspects of their person. Because they feel entitled to, and comfortable with, expressing and exploring their female/feminine inclinations, those identities never become mystified. This would explain why "primary" MTF transsexuals generally express a desire to be female and feminine throughout childhood, and generally transition early in life (during their teens or twenties).

On the other hand, those male children who become aware of their female or feminine inclinations after developing gender constancy have to somehow make sense of those feelings in the wake of having already mystified femaleness and femininity. Thus, they may gravitate toward crossdressing as a way to compartmentalize their female/feminine inclinations, both in response to effemimania and because they are unable (initially, at least) to view their own female/feminine tendencies as legitimate and coming from within themselves. In this context, crossdressing can be a way of exploring and potentially reclaiming gender expressions and identities that one has previously disavowed, that one does not feel entitled to. It is a practice that, over time, demystifies femaleness and femininity for those who have been socialized to believe that these qualities are unnatural and unknowable to them.

Demystifying Femininity and Unlearning Masculinity

The idea that crossdressing can be a continual process of demystification very much resonates with my personal experiences. I consciously recognized my own desire to be female when I was eleven. As much as I wanted to be female, I was taught to believe that this was not a realistic possibility for me. For this reason, I began to channel my female inclinations into fantasies or role-playing, in which I'd imagine I'd turned into a girl somehow. The fact that these fantasies always began with me being a boy (rather than simply imagining myself as a girl from the start) is indicative of how illegitimate I felt my own desires to be female were. I was convinced that I could never attain actual femaleness; in my mind, the best that I could hope for was merely pretending to be female or being "turned into" a girl.

After a year or two of imagining myself becoming a girl (typically a rather tomboyish one who went off on adventures and such), I started experimenting with conventional femininity. This was due both to me wanting to explore my own feminine inclinations and to the fact that (like most people) I was taught to believe that femininity was an intrinsic part of being female. My growing fascination with femininity was also very much intertwined with my growing attraction to women. As a teenager who was dealing with sexual attraction for the first time, I found it hard not to conflate my desire to be female with my sexual attraction for women. And in this respect, feminine accoutrements—whether clothing, cosmetics, or other accessories—became highly symbolic of both.

In chapter 14, "Trans-Sexualization," I explained that trans people who have not transitioned, and who therefore are unable to take their own physical sex for granted, often experience sexual arousal in association with their own cross-gendered thoughts and expressions. While this is true for virtually all trans people, there are a couple of factors specific to crossdressers that intensify this phenomenon. First, testosterone, which significantly boosts one's sex drive across the board, undoubtedly plays some role in amplifying cross-gendered sexual arousal for those who are hormonally male. Second, we live in a culture in which women are frequently viewed as sexual objects, and much of women's clothing emphasizes and exaggerates women's sexuality. For crossdressers, there is no way of getting around the cultural eroticism that surrounds "women's" clothing. Many crossdressers, particularly early in their crossdressing, become particularly interested in the most highly sexual articles of feminine clothing precisely because of the symbolism associated with them. Unfortunately, I have heard women criticize, even ridicule, this tendency among crossdressers, sometimes even suggesting that a crossdresser who covers *their own body* in hyperfeminine or hypersexual articles of clothing somehow sexualizes womanhood as a whole. Such criticism seems to purposefully ignore the fact that many teenage girls similarly tend to dress in sexually provocative or revealing ways when they hit puberty and begin to explore the cultural meanings associated with adult female sexuality. Both teenage girls and crossdressers are exposed to many of the same cultural messages about femininity and female sexuality (albeit from rather different vantage points) and thus both are drawn to experiment with hyperfeminine and hypersexual clothing as a way of literally "trying on" the symbolic meanings associated with adult female sexuality. And most crossdressers, like most cissexual women, eventually move beyond their "teenage girl phase" (as some crossdressers refer to it) and come to recognize sexually provocative clothing as but one of the many options available to them, but not necessarily one that they wish to indulge in every day.

I know that it's common for outsiders to focus on the more sexual aspects of MTF crossdressing (just as they focus on the more sexual aspects of femaleness in general). However, I personally found that, if anything, the social, emotional, and psychological effects of being crossdressed were far more profound than the sexual ones. The truth is that gendered clothing is extraordinarily symbolic of the sex of the body that presumably lies underneath; this is why wearing the clothing associated with the other sex is an almost invariant feature of cross-gender expression and identity across cultures and throughout history. Prior to my transition, dressing up in "women's" clothing was the closest I ever got to actually being a woman, to having my body be aligned with how I imagined it. For me, the fact that "women's" clothing was symbolic of being female far outweighed any sexuality-related symbolism it may have had.

As with many MTF spectrum folks, my crossdressing passed through a series of stages. Each was a demystification process that I began by experimenting with some aspect of femaleness/femininity that seemed unknowable and fascinating to me. Over time, my exploration and experimentation of that aspect of femaleness/femininity led to it becoming demystified; what had previously seemed out of my reach eventually became something that I was capable of, that was within my realm of possibility. The main motivating force behind my exploration of crossdressing was to make sense of my ever-present desire to be female. While this may distinguish me from other crossdressers (e.g., those who are motivated by feminine rather than female inclinations), I believe that the stages I passed through (which are described below) are shared by many crossdressers.

The first stage of crossdressing I passed through was the "clothing phase." It began with trying on individual articles of clothing one at a time (this was after a several-year period where I made due with blankets, curtains, shoelaces, and such while "pretending" to be a girl). Sometimes I would put on a pair of heels, stockings, or a dress, or dabble with cosmetics or shave my legs. Each was its own mini-transformation, where a part of my body would begin to resemble that of a woman in certain ways. After a while, I began to put it all together, to dress completely as a woman from head to toe. I looked rather ridiculous when I first began to do this, but over the course of many years, I slowly figured out what worked for me and what did not. Eventually, I reached the point where I could fairly consistently appear female to myself when I looked in mirror. This "mirror moment" was always the highlight of any crossdressing session for me, as I found it strangely comforting to be able to see my female reflection staring back at me.

As the name suggests, my clothing phase was primarily about becoming familiar with, and eventually demystifying, "women's" clothing. I eventually even stopped thinking about them as "women's" clothes; after all, they were all *my* clothes, as I was the one who purchased and wore them. Similarly, I also stopped thinking of myself as being "crossdressed," and instead began referring to myself as simply being "dressed." Toward the end of this stage, I was no longer very excited by the idea of wearing "women's" clothes just for the sake of it. However, while they had lost their mystified properties, I still understood them as having the transformative property of facilitating my appearance as female. It is this latter role that "women's" clothing played in the next stage of my crossdressing, when I began to venture out in public.

The "public phase" began with my earliest attempts to go out into the world as a woman. My very first experience involved walking around a shopping mall for about fifteen minutes, followed by purchasing a milkshake at a fast-food drive-through window. The fact that nobody seemed to give me a second glance, and that the cashier said, "Thank you, ma'am," as she handed me my change, completely blew me away. Like the mirror moments, these experiences of having my femaleness acknowledged in some small way were profound and moving. Over time, I continued to go out dressed in public more and more, typically doing rather mundane things such as going to museums or shopping. I always made sure that there were lots of people around and that I could easily "get away" in the event that something bad happened. Admittedly, the early sense of excitement associated with being dressed as female in public was enhanced by the inherent sense of danger that unfortunately plagues any public crossdressing experience. The fear, of course, was not merely that I would be noticed or "read" as a crossdresser (which happened on countless occasions during the many years that I publicly crossdressed), but that I might be targeted for violence if I was ever "found out" by the wrong person.

It was during my public phase that I first began going to crossdresser support and social group meetings (this was in Kansas in 1994, before the word "transgender" came into vogue). They were my first opportunity to speak openly about my crossdressing and to meet others who shared that experience. It also provided me with the chance to learn some of the techniques that other crossdressers used to make their female appearance more convincing. I was fortunate enough to have an amazing crossdresser named Deborah take me under her wing. Among other things, she showed me how to use cosmetics to effectively cover my beard shadow, an invaluable skill for any crossdresser who wishes to be gendered by others as female. It's common for people to dismiss crossdressers for what is perceived to be their exaggerated use of makeup. However, the truth of the matter is that crossdressers (unlike cissexual women) typically have beard shadows, which are perhaps the dominant visual cue we rely on when gendering people as male. While I would have preferred to have the privilege of forgoing makeup if I wished, my beard shadow made it virtually impossible for me to be regularly gendered as female without it.

Complaints about how crossdressers overuse cosmetics are often related to more general critiques that claim that crossdressers exaggerate stereotypically feminine dress and behaviors, thus turning themselves into caricatures of women. Often, these sentiments are rooted in the oppositional sexist assumption that cissexual women are entitled to express and explore femininity while those assigned male are not. Even those critiques that are not downright oppositional sexist are still cissexual-woman-centric, in that they view MTF crossdressing solely in terms of how it portrays cissexual women, rather than viewing it from an MTF spectrum perspective. Back when I crossdressed, I very much enjoyed dressing and acting in a highly feminine manner, but not because I thought that women really *were* or *should be* that way. If I indulged in an exaggerated form of femininity, it was only because I never really had the chance to explore that side of myself growing up as a boy. I spent virtually every day of my life wearing T-shirts, jeans, sneakers, and no makeup. So for me, crossdressing represented a rare opportunity to fully indulge my femininity.

The other factor at the time that motivated me to try to achieve stereotypical femininity was that I wanted others to gender me as female. Back when I was crossdressing—when I was still physically male—that never would have been possible had I gone out sans makeup or wearing unisex clothing. To a large extent, I purposely chose the clothing and cosmetics I wore when I crossdressed based on their ability to hide or play down my male physique and facial features. In fact, the public stage of my crossdressing was really the one time in my life when I did go out of my way to emulate how some women looked, walked, talked, moved, and so on. I found that this increased the likelihood that I would be gendered female, which was my overall goal, and which also ensured my safety.

One question that many queer-identified friends asked me back when I was crossdressing was why it was so important for me to "pass" as a woman. Their concern seemed to stem from the common use of the term "pass" in lesbian and gay communities as a synonym for "hide" (i.e., a gay male who "passes" for straight is typically assumed to be hiding or playing down his queerness). This use of the word "pass" is completely different from its use in the transgender community, where it typically refers to whether one is appropriately gendered as the sex one identifies or presents oneself as. From my perspective as a crossdresser, what gay people call "passing" (i.e., hiding) was what I did every day when I lived as male. In contrast, when I dressed and "passed" (in the transgender sense) as a woman, it was a rare moment of being "out" for me, of having others see and acknowledge a part of me that I normally kept hidden.

Eventually, having other people gender me as female became demystified. While I still enjoyed it (as I did with the mirror moments), it was no longer enough in and of itself to ease the gender dissonance that I felt. It was at this point that I moved into the "interactive stage," when I began to go out with other people while I was crossdressed. While I had come out to a number of friends as a crossdresser during my public stage, I now began cultivating relationships with people who primarily or solely knew me when I was in girl-mode. More often than not, these were people who I met via personal ads and who were aware that I was a crossdresser from the start. Over an extremely intense two-year period of my life, I sort of lived a dual life, where I was in boy-mode most of the time, but about one or two times per week I would go out and interact with others (often on dates) as a woman.

Some of the people I saw during this period were men who might be described as admirers of MTF spectrum people. With them, I primarily engaged in role-playing relationships in which we would create sexually charged scenarios based on exaggerations of gender stereotypes. While many people assume that male "tranny-chasers" are closeted homosexuals who are turned on by the "guy" (or the "penis") under the dress, all of the men who I role-played with were primarily attracted to women and, in particular, to femininity. In conversations I had with them, each said that what attracted them to MTF spectrum people was the extreme femininity that many of us (including myself at the time) sometimes displayed. For me, these role-playing experiences were important in helping me demystify the connection between femininity and sexuality. As with previous phases of my crossdressing, acting out my submissive feminine fantasies felt exciting and empowering early on. But over time, once they had become demystified, I found that they began to lose both their erotic and experiential potential.

What played an even greater role in demystifying femaleness and femininity for me were the relationships I cultivated with women around this same time. Most of these women were bisexual or bi-curious, and our relationships involved me being in girl-mode some or most of the times we got together. While I was quite feminine when I was with them and crossdressed, I did not engage in the exaggerated femininity that I had during my role-playing experiences with men. In retrospect, what was most important for me about these experiences with women was that they allowed me to begin to integrate my personality (i.e., the person I was when in boy-mode) with my femme self. In a sense, this represented a merging of boy-mode and girl-mode for me, a sort of mending of the fracture in my psyche that had developed in response to the effemimania and enforced ignorance I'd experienced as a child.

After about two years of being in the interactive phase, of being in relationships with other people while I was in girl-mode, something unexpected happened: I lost interest in crossdressing. This was extraordinarily disconcerting to me at first, as being a crossdresser was such a huge part of my identity at the time. I remember lying in bed one morning and thinking, *I wonder where I should take my crossdressing next?* as if I simply needed to find some new aspect of femaleness or femininity to experiment with, some new crossdressing stage to pioneer, in order to regain interest in it. However, by this point, I had explored femininity and female gender roles as much as possible within the context of being a crossdresser. Fortunately for me, this was when Dani (who was my girlfriend at the time) introduced me to Kate Bornstein's and Leslie Feinberg's writings. Their books allowed me to start viewing myself as bigender rather than as a crossdresser. I began to see my expressions of femaleness and femininity not merely as something that existed outside of myself that I could emulate or imagine but never truly experience, but rather as an intrinsic and legitimate part of my person, as something that came from within me.

Thinking of myself as bigender also helped me make sense of another new development in my life: that people were beginning to pick up on my femininity even when I was in boy-mode. Strangers began to assume that I was gay, and on rare occasions even gendered me as female. These changes, which occurred despite the fact that I was dressing the same and had not consciously altered my behavior, took me by surprise. I eventually realized that over those many years of crossdressing I must have unlearned many of the rote masculine mannerisms that I'd acquired during my adolescence and early adulthood—behaviors that had served as a self-defense mechanism that allowed me to escape effemimanic derision. In other words, during the years that I crossdressed, it wasn't so much that I learned how to be female (as I was no longer employing any of the contrived and stereotyped feminine mannerisms I practiced back when I was crossdressing), but that I had in effect unlearned maleness.

If it were not for my years as a crossdresser, I doubt that I would have been able to demystify femaleness and unlearn maleness to the point that I could live for several years as a feminine bigender boy—an identity that preceded my decision to transition. While I certainly do not believe that crossdressing is merely a phase that eventually leads to becoming a transsexual woman, I do believe that many crossdressers experience similar phases of demystifying femaleness/femininity and unlearning maleness/masculinity over the course of their lives. While crossdressing may seem highly contrived to many outsiders, from an MTF perspective, it is an invaluable way to reconcile our female/feminine inclinations with our male/masculine bodies and socialization. It provides a way to allow parts of ourselves that we have been made to feel shame about, that we have learned to hide or repress, to show through and become integrated with the rest of our personalities.

Rethinking "Male Privilege"

I think it's appropriate to end this chapter with a discussion of "male privilege" with respect to MTF spectrum folks. I have decided to frame "male privilege" in quotation marks here not to suggest that it doesn't exist or to claim that MTF spectrum folks don't experience it to some extent, but to challenge the way in which it is often put forward in dialogues and debates—as though it were the "one and only" gender privilege.[8] The concept of "male privilege" emerged out of the incorrect assumption that sexism functions as a unilateral form of oppression. According to this model, men unilaterally oppress women, and thus they reap *all* of the benefits, while women bear *all* of the hardships. This, however, is a gross oversimplification of sexism for numerous reasons. First, the concept of unilateral sexism denies other important factors, such as racism, classism, ableism, etc., that contribute to discrimination. After all, it's difficult to make the case that a rich white woman is more oppressed than a poor black man in our culture. Second, it ignores oppositional sexism, which favors those with typical gender inclinations over those with exceptional ones, regardless of sex. For example, if you happen to be attracted to men, then your life will certainly be easier in many respects if you happen to be female rather than male. And if you happen to be feminine, you will surely be less marginalized for your gender expressions if you are a woman rather than a man.

While some cissexual women assume that men have a monopoly on gender privilege, this is not the case. Many trans men have written at length about both the male privileges they gained post-transition, as well as the numerous ways their lives became more difficult, complex, or even dangerous once they were regularly perceived as male.[9] Their comments have been echoed by Norah Vincent, a cissexual woman who spent over a year and a half socially "passing" as a man as a part of an investigative journalism project.[10] These perspectives, which all come from people who were born and socialized female, help demonstrate how oppositional sexism ensures that both maleness and femaleness come with their own very different sets of privileges, restrictions, expectations, and assumptions.

The concept of "male privilege" not only ignores oppositional sexism; it assumes that women are the sole targets of traditional sexism. While those who live full-time as women surely bear the brunt of traditional sexism, female- and feminine-inclined male-bodied people are also clearly targeted by this form of sexism, as is evident in our culture's rampant effemimania.

As a trans woman, I have, on many occasions, had cissexual women claim that I shouldn't be given the same rights as them to label myself a "woman" or to enter women-only spaces because I have experienced "male privilege" in the past. This claim always strikes me as odd. After all, unlike them, I have actually experienced having others treat me as both male and female at different points in my life. One could easily make the case that transsexuals are uniquely positioned to give firsthand accounts of what exactly "male privilege" *is* or *isn't*. As I have discussed at various points throughout this book, there are many male privileges that I received prior to my transition: I was generally taken more seriously, given more space, and harassed far less. Perhaps there are additional male privileges that exist but which were regularly denied to me because I was a rather unmasculine (and at times, downright feminine) guy. In any case, as a female- and feminine-identified person, I find that the male privileges I have lost since transitioning, while significant, do not compare to the privileges that I have gained from finally having my subconscious and physical sexes aligned and from being able to live openly as female.

It infuriates me when cissexual women use "male privilege" as an excuse to dismiss MTF spectrum folks, as it belies their reluctance to examine their own birth privilege (having been born into a physical sex that matches their subconscious sex), their socialization privilege (being socialized into a gender consistent with their subconscious sex), and their cissexual privilege (having others consider their femaleness legitimate and unquestionable). Some women bristle when I suggest that they may have experienced socialization privilege, as they assume that I am negating the many ways in which childhood socialization can be restrictive and disempowering for cissexual female children and adolescents. My intention in bringing up the notion of socialization privilege is not to dismiss the obstacles faced by cissexual girls, but to highlight the very different, yet significant, gender disadvantages faced by MTF spectrum children. For example, when I ask my cissexual female friends if they would have preferred it if their parents had decided to raise them male rather than female, most of them immediately answer "no." Posing the question in this way allows them to recognize that the potential male privileges they might have gained if raised male would not be worth the price of having to deny or repress their femaleness and femininity. Male privileges, while very real, are little consolation when you feel like you have to hide your femaleness/femininity from your family and friends; when you've endured being the only female/feminine-inclined person in often-misogynistic male-only spaces such as men's locker rooms; when you cannot safely share your femaleness/femininity with others, but instead must clandestinely explore it on your own in isolation; when you are unable to simply *be* female/feminine without having others accuse you of "emulating" women or of merely being "effeminate."

I am not trying to make the case here that MTF spectrum folks are "more oppressed" than cissexual women, as playing the more-oppressed-than-thou card serves no purpose other than narcissism. But I do hope to encourage cissexual women to take a moment to put themselves in our shoes, to consider how patronizing and condescending dismissive quips about "male privilege" would sound to you if you had been forced against your will into boyhood. As someone who spent my childhood desperately wishing that I could be a girl rather than boy, and who as an adult considers it a privilege to finally have the opportunity to live in the world as a woman rather than a man, I find those attempts to undermine trans women's femaleness by decrying "male privilege" hollow and crass.

Having said all that, I will be the first to admit that many MTF spectrum folks seem to be rather oblivious to the impact that traditional sexism has on their lives—both with respect to the male privileges they gain because of it as well as the special social stigma they receive for their feminine transgender expression and/or for choosing to transition to female. Personally, it was only after I began living full-time as a woman, experiencing firsthand all of the inferior and negative assumptions that others projected onto me because of my femaleness, that I began to make a connection between traditional sexism and the discrimination that I faced because of the specific direction of my transition and transgender expression. Only then did I realize how inadequate the transgender movement's mantra—that we are discriminated against for "transgressing binary gender norms"—is for those of us on the MTF spectrum who primarily grapple with effemimania and trans-misogyny.

MTF spectrum folks need feminism in order to make sense out of our lives and to work toward ending our continuing marginalization. Unfortunately, many cissexual feminists seem to fear that MTF spectrum inclusion within feminism might dilute, distract, or undercut a movement that has historically centered itself on the struggles and issues of cissexual women. Typically, such fears arise from the assumption that we cannot work together because we supposedly have different goals, or that we are unable to relate to one another's experiences. I believe that is a red herring. After all, many lesbian women, who typically do not have to deal with the issue of unwanted pregnancy, work hard for and are committed to protecting the availability of birth control and a woman's right to choose. Similarly, a woman doesn't necessarily have to be a survivor of sexual or physical assault herself to do crucial work in a domestic violence shelter or a rape crisis center. What truly unites feminists is not a shared history (as we each bring a unique set of life experiences to the table), but our shared commitment to fighting against the devaluation of femaleness and femininity in our society and the double standards that are placed onto both sexes. In this respect, cissexual female and MTF spectrum feminists *do* have a lot in common.

It's not just that MTF spectrum folks need feminism, but that feminism needs to embrace MTF experiences and perspectives. The fact that the lion's share of the anti-trans sentiment specifically targets those of us on the MTF spectrum indicates that we are marked, not for failing to conform to gender norms per se but because we "choose" to be female and/or feminine. For feminism to ignore the society-wide effemimania and trans-misogyny we face is to allow one of the most pervasive forms of traditional sexism to go unchecked. Indeed, for feminists to continue to dismiss effemimania solely because it targets those who are male-bodied is particularly shortsighted. After all, as previously mentioned, much of the sexist behavior exhibited by cissexual men arises directly out of their being forced to disavow and mystify femininity from an early age. In this respect, MTF spectrum folks can provide feminism with crucial insight into the workings of effemimania and offer strategies to potentially challenge it. Additionally, those of us who transition to female can provide firsthand accounts of the very different ways that women and men are treated in the world—a perspective that is especially relevant today given how common it is for people to naively claim that we as a society have transcended sexism and moved into a "postfeminist" era.

But perhaps most of all, what MTF spectrum trans people can offer feminism is a very different and far more empowering perspective on femininity. Over the years, many feminists have argued that femininity undermines women, or that it's purposefully designed to subordinate women to men. Such a view no doubt stems from the experiences of those women who have felt that the expectation of femininity has been forced upon them against their will. But those of us on the MTF spectrum who have had the reciprocal experience—of inexplicably being inclined or compelled to express femininity that we were taught to avoid or repress—cannot so easily dismiss femininity as an artifice whose sole purpose is to devalue and disempower women. Because we come to embrace our own femininity *for ourselves* rather than to appease others, we are able to appreciate the many ways in which femininity can be freeing and empowering for those who gravitate toward it on their own. Many of us reject all of the inferior meanings and connotations that others project onto femininity—that it is weak, artificial, frivolous, demure, and passive—because for us, there has been no act more bold and daring than embracing our own femininity. In a world that is awash in antifeminine sentiment, we understand that embracing and empowering femininity can potentially be one of the most transformative and revolutionary acts imaginable.

18
Barrette Manifesto

HEY GIRLS, DID YOU HEAR the news? It's just been scientifically proven that barrettes are dangerous! So are bracelets and bric-a-brac. It's a fact. And don't be fooled by thick-necked macho men who pretend that "girl stuff" is boring or frivolous, because that's just an act. Because as soon as you ask that guy to hold your purse for a minute, he will start to squirm, as if your handbag were full of worms, as he holds it as far away from his rugged body as possible. Because "girl stuff" is made with the gender equivalent of Kryptonite!

That's right, just watch fathers in Sanrio stores standing like petrified trees, like deer caught in Hello Kitty's headlights. Or teenage boys buying their girlfriends flowers, acting as disinterested as possible as they ask the florist for a dozen "whatever"s. That's why they always buy roses, that's why engagement rings are always diamonds. These things are not romantic, they are just clichés—the only types of flowers and jewelry that most men will admit to knowing the names of. And god forbid you were to ask your husband to pick you up a box of tampons. (And men, it's true, the cashier really does think you're buying them for yourselves.)

"Girl stuff" is dangerous, and I should know because I'm a secret double agent. See, I lived as a boy for most of my life and I have insider information straight out of men's locker rooms and college dorms. Hell, I even went to a bachelor party once, so I know this stuff firsthand. And I have a battle plan for absolute sexual equality, but you have to trust me on this. See, feminists have made it okay for girls to explore what used to be an exclusively boy world. But true equality won't come until boys learn to embrace girl stuff as well.

So here's the deal: If you want your boyfriend to treat you with respect, then tell him that you won't sleep with him until he starts putting barrettes in his hair. And I'm not talking about secret bedroom kinky shit. Make him wear them to work! The next time he buys a pair of shoes, make sure they're Mary Janes (and don't forget the white lacy anklets to go with them). Because as soon as he realizes the pure bliss of wearing a frilly, pink, poofy party dress, maybe he'll finally relax a bit and loosen up that uptight male swagger. And maybe once he lets his guard down, he'll look around and realize that the world doesn't revolve around him.

You may think this is funny, but it's no joke. "Girl stuff" is dangerous, so let's use it to our advantage. We truly can change the world! Because if construction workers were man enough to wear skirts and heels, they wouldn't whistle at women who walk by. And if misogynistic rockers and rappers were man enough to cry while watching tearjerkers, they wouldn't need to masturbate all over the mic. And if presidents and generals were man enough to wear lip gloss and mascara, they wouldn't have to prove their penis size by going to war all the time. Because male pride is not really about pride. It's about fear—the fear of being seen as feminine. And that's why "girl stuff" is so dangerous. And as long as most men remain deathly afraid of it, they'll continue to take it out on the rest of us.

19

Putting the Feminine Back into Feminism

I REMEMBER BACK IN COLLEGE—when I was admittedly rather naive with regard to gender politics—someone asked a friend of mine whether she considered herself a feminist. I was surprised to hear her answer "No." After all, she certainly seemed like a feminist to me. She was independent, intelligent, career-minded, pro–women's reproductive rights. She regularly stood up for herself and was keenly aware of the disparity between how certain professors treated her and how they treated her male counterparts. When she was asked why she didn't identify as a feminist, her reply was, "I like being a girl." She went on to explain that she enjoyed, and even felt empowered by, being feminine. And in her experience, those who openly embraced the label "feminist" often displayed a condescending attitude toward her femininity.

Granted, this idea—that feminism and femininity are in opposition to one another—has often been fostered by those who wish to undermine feminism. For several decades now, feminism's opponents have attempted to dissuade women from the movement by repeating two (seemingly contradictory) sound bites: that feminists are "man-haters" (read: "homosexual") while simultaneously "wanting to be men" (read: "masculine"). While one cannot underestimate the negative effect that this antifeminist propaganda has had in turning feminine and heterosexual women away from feminism, we would be doing ourselves a great disservice if we didn't also acknowledge the fact that many feminists themselves have forwarded the idea that femininity is artificial and incompatible with feminism.[1] This anti-femininity tendency may represent the feminist movement's single greatest tactical error. It's high time we rectify this mistake by purposefully putting the feminine back into feminism.

Origins of Femininity

Before we can engage in an in-depth discussion about femininity, we must first accurately define the word. In its broadest sense, femininity refers to the behaviors, mannerisms, interests, and ways of presenting oneself that are typically associated with those who are female. Thus, the first thing we must acknowledge is that femininity is a collection of heterogeneous traits. This is an important point to make, as femininity is often assumed to be a monolithic entity—i.e., a "package deal" of gender expressions, traits, and qualities that are inevitably bundled together. The fact that individual feminine traits are separable is evident in the fact that some women are verbally effusive and emotive (qualities that are commonly considered feminine), but not particularly feminine in their manner of dress. Reciprocally, some women who dress very femininely are not very effusive or emotive. Still other women exhibit both or neither of these qualities. In must also be mentioned that these and other feminine traits are not unique to women, as individual men can (and often do) exhibit them.

The fact that feminine traits are not female-specific, and that they are separable from one another, is far too often brushed aside when people try to answer the question that unfortunately drives most discussions about femininity: namely, what produces feminine expressions in people? Those who wish to naturalize femininity will often describe feminine traits as though they were bundled in a single biological program that is initiated only in genetic females. Such claims gloss over the many people who have exceptional gender expressions (i.e., feminine traits in males and masculine traits in females) in order to fully subsume femininity within femaleness. On the other hand, those who wish to *artificialize* femininity often characterize it as though it were a unified social program designed to shape women's personalities and sexualities via a combination of social norms, constructs, and conditioning. The assumption that femininity is one entity makes it easier for those who favor such social explanations to "prove" that femininity is artificial. After all, one needs only to make the case that certain specific aspects of femininity are clearly "man-made" and vary from culture to culture in order to extrapolate that *all* aspects of femininity are social in origin. Similarly, by showing that certain aspects of femininity are socially imposed on girls and women, one can claim that femininity *as a whole* is unnatural, or it would not have to be enforced at all. What should be clear by now is that the presumption that femininity is a singular program tends to foster an overly simplistic, all-or-none dichotomy between biological and social explanations for gender differences.

Once we let go of the concept of monolithic femininity—and with it, the either/or ideology that plagues nature-versus-nurture debates about gender—it becomes rather apparent that individual feminine traits arise from different combinations of biology and socialization. For instance, during my transition, when I first began to be perceived as female on a regular basis, I was surprised by how often male strangers told me to smile—"Cheer up, things can't be all that bad," they'd say. Needless to say, I found these remarks condescending, as nobody dared to tell me that I should smile for them back when I was perceived as male. However, despite my determination not to conform to the suggestions of patronizing strangers, I nevertheless found that, over time, I stopped hearing such comments. Obviously, something had changed. Maybe on an unconscious level, I learned to smile more without realizing it. Or maybe it had to do with another defense mechanism that I've learned since living as a woman: making eye contact with strangers less often than I did when I was male, which significantly reduced occurrences of strange men harassing me. These behaviors, which are often considered feminine because women primarily exhibit them, seem to originate as an unconscious response to negotiating one's way through the world as a woman. In other words, they appear to be primarily or exclusively social in origin.

Other aspects of femininity that are clearly social in origin include what I call "feminine fashions"—i.e., qualities that have only recently become associated with, or symbolic of, femininity. For example, these days it's common for people to view being thin as a feminine trait. While femininity and thinness have become almost synonymous in contemporary Western culture, women who were more full-figured were considered the feminine ideal in past eras. Similarly, today most of us grow up believing that pink is undoubtedly the most feminine of colors. In the early 1900s, however, it was more common for people to associate pink with boys and blue with girls.[2]

While some feminine traits are predominantly social in origin, others appear to be greatly influenced by biology. One feminine biological trait is being in tune with one's emotions. Virtually all transsexuals transitioning in the MTF direction report an increased intensity in the way that they experience emotions once they begin taking estrogen; those in the FTM direction report the reverse effect upon taking testosterone. Thus, emotional intensity definitely has a biological basis, as it is greatly influenced by adult hormone levels.

Of course, feminine traits that arise from our adult hormonal makeup are relatively easy to categorize as biological, as one can experience the corresponding changes firsthand via hormone therapy. In contrast, other feminine traits that may have biological inputs are more difficult to discern. Two possible examples of this include feminine aesthetic preferences and ways of expressing oneself. Evidence that these tendencies may be hardwired to some extent comes from the fact that they typically appear very early in childhood and often in contradiction to one's socialization (both for children whose parents attempt to raise them in a unisex or gender-neutral fashion, and for boys whose families actively and aggressively steer them away from feminine expression). This indicates that some aspects of feminine verbal and aesthetic expression precede and/or supersede gender socialization. Further, the fact that some feminine male children will often continue to express these exceptional traits well into adulthood despite a lifetime of social conditioning to the contrary shows that these traits cannot be adequately explained by social mechanisms. While feminine verbal and aesthetic expression can surely be influenced or exaggerated by social forces, I would argue that these traits are also driven by intrinsic and deep-seated inclinations that are likely to be the result of biology.

Given the way that gender essentialists have distorted biology to justify sexist behaviors and norms, I can understand why some feminists would be hesitant to admit that biology has any role in producing or contributing to behavioral gender differences. However, the idea that gender differences arise solely from socialization and social norms is highly problematic, in that it assumes that our minds are blank slates with absolutely no intrinsic or instinctual gendered or sexual tendencies. This harkens back to views forwarded by extreme behaviorists like B. F. Skinner, who argued that human beings are merely products of their social conditioning. Such views have since been thoroughly refuted by other work in the fields of psychology and biology. Such behaviorist models are unable to explain how any gender system comes into being in the first place, and how (once it is established) anyone can come to transcend or challenge it. As with those models that assume that gender arises directly and expediently from sex chromosomes or hormones, behaviorist models of gender fail to accurately account for the vast gender and sexual diversity in the world.

While I believe that certain aspects of femininity have biological inputs, it would be foolish for any person to presume that they can fully tease apart the social from the biological: to assume that they can know precisely what biological pathways lie at the root of feminine and masculine behaviors, or to claim to know why or how they evolved. Given the overwhelming number of social variables involved, any researcher who claims to approach human gender expression from a purely biological perspective practices speculation rather than science. Furthermore, I reject the sophomoric biological models of gender that are often proposed in pop psychology and pop science, which often naively portray genes, hormones, and neurons as though they were switches that are simply turned "on" in one gender and "off" in the other. In reality, these aspects of biology are complexly regulated and greatly influenced by an individual's unique genetic and environmental background. This is particularly true of the brain, where neural structure, connections, and activity are constantly being altered and modified in response to new experiences. Biology inevitably produces a broad spectrum of potential combinations of behavioral tendencies in people, making that spectrum compatible with the vast natural diversity we see in human gender expression.

Sexist Interpretations of Femininity

Throughout the rest of this chapter, when I refer to "femininity" or "feminine traits," it should be understood that I'm talking about a heterogeneous, non-female-specific collection of traits that each have a unique biological and/or social origin. In fact, the only quality that all feminine traits share is that they all tend to be associated with women (albeit not exclusive to them). This point becomes highly relevant once we begin to consider how people interpret feminine traits. Indeed, the ongoing and hotly contested debates over whether femininity and masculinity are biological or social in origin have, in my view, served primarily as a distraction from a far more pertinent issue—namely, what meanings, symbolism, and connotations do we assign to different gender expressions? While I disagree with the notion that gender expression itself is entirely social in origin, I do believe that the way we perceive and assign values to feminine and masculine behaviors is primarily, if not exclusively, a social affair. In our male-centered culture, two forces most often shape our interpretations of femininity (as well as masculinity): oppositional and traditional sexism.

Oppositional sexism functions to legitimize feminine expressions in women and to delegitimize feminine expressions in men (and vice versa for masculinity). So while all people are capable of expressing feminine traits, oppositional sexism ensures that such expressions will appear natural when produced by women and unnatural when produced by men. In addition to creating the perception that female femininity is "real" and "right" while male femininity is "fake" and "wrong," oppositional sexism may also influence the "doing" of gender expression. Exceptional gender expressions are regularly dismissed, even stigmatized, in our culture, which may lead some people to hide or curb their own gender-variant behavior, further exaggerating the assumed, apparent differences between the two sexes. In these ways, oppositional sexism creates the assumption that feminine traits—which occur in members of both sexes—are inexorably linked to female biology, and therefore, to one another.

Traditional sexism functions to make femaleness and femininity appear subordinate to maleness and masculinity. This is accomplished in a number of ways. For example, female and feminine attributes are regularly assigned negative connotations and meanings in our society. An example of this is the way that being in touch with and expressing one's emotions is regularly derided in our society. While this trait has virtually nothing to do with one's ability to reason or to think logically, in the public mind, being "emotional" has become synonymous with being "irrational." Another example is that certain pursuits and interests that are considered feminine, such as gossiping or decorating, are often characterized as "frivolous," while masculine preoccupations—even those that serve solely recreational functions, such as sports—generally escape such trivialization.

In addition to placing inferior meanings on feminine traits, traditional sexism also creates the impression that certain aspects of femininity exist for the pleasure or benefit of men. Take, for example, the concern for, or desire to help, others. While those who have this quality of empathy or altruism often express it toward all types of beings (i.e., children and adults, strangers and friends, animals and humans), it's often recast in women as a maternal, "nurturing" quality that is meant to be directed primarily toward one's family. Thus, this thoroughly human trait has been twisted into the expectation that it's women's "natural" duty to take care of their male partners and children, and to carry out the bulk of family and domestic chores.

Another example of this phenomenon is the way that feminine self-presentation is often framed as though it solely exists to entice or attract men. This assumption denies any possibility that those who are feminine might wish to adorn themselves for their own benefit or pleasure. After all, feminine self-presentation tends to highly correlate with a more general desire to surround oneself with beautiful or aesthetically pleasing objects and materials—whether in decorating one's home or adorning one's body. The idea that this trait exists primarily to pique men's interest seems unlikely to me, as most straight men I know seem rather disinterested in the way their homes are decorated, and often are completely oblivious when their female partners don new outfits or hairstyles. It's safe to say that most heterosexual men are far more interested in women's physical bodies than they are in the clothing and accessories that cover them. The idea that feminine self-presentation exists primarily to attract heterosexual men is further undermined by the fact that femme dykes dress in a feminine manner despite their disinterest in attracting men. And some gay men also dress very femininely despite the fact that the gay male community has a history of idolizing and fetishizing hypermasculine images and bodies rather than feminine ones. As someone who's not interested in attracting men, I often enjoy dressing femininely; I simply feel more alive and self-empowered when I do. Whenever people (male or otherwise) assume that women who dress in a feminine manner do so in order to elicit male attention, it always sounds like a slightly toned-down version of that arrogant claim that women who dress provocatively are somehow asking to be raped. Clearly, it's the idea that feminine self-presentation exists for men's benefit that is oppressive to women, not the acts of self-presentation themselves.

The issue of feminine self-presentation also brings up another way in which feminine traits are undermined: They are often cast as being dependent on masculinity and maleness. This sentiment seems to be projected onto virtually all aspects of femaleness and femininity. It can be seen in the way men are often cast as the "protectors" of women, either because they are typically physically stronger or because women are seen as being "emotionally frail." The stereotypic and mythic image of the damsel in distress who requires a masculine man to save her seems to impart an air of helplessness, fragility, and passivity onto virtually all aspects of femininity and female sexuality. Such connotations seem to heavily inform both the materiality and symbolism of certain feminine fashions. They also help foster a predator/prey mentality regarding sexuality, where femininity becomes conflated with being sexually receptive and passive, while masculinity is synonymous with penetration and sexual aggressiveness. This, of course, denies the reality that women are often sexual initiators and that both parties are invariably active during the act of sex.

Indeed, the fact that helplessness, fragility, and passivity are merely meanings projected onto female bodies and feminine expressions (rather than qualities that are "built into" femaleness and femininity) becomes obvious when we imagine what would happen if, instead of centering our beliefs about heterosexual sex around the idea that the man "penetrates" the woman, we were to say that the woman's vagina "consumes" the man's penis. This would create a very different set of connotations, as the woman would become the active initiator and the man would be the passive and receptive party. One can easily see how this could lead to men and masculinity being seen as dependent on, and existing for the benefit of, femaleness and femininity. Similarly, if we thought about the feminine traits of being verbally effusive and emotive not as signs of insecurity or dependence, but as bold acts of self-expression, then the masculine ideal of the "strong and silent type" might suddenly seem timid and insecure by comparison.

The mistaken belief that femininity is inherently helpless, fragile, dependent, irrational, frivolous, and so on, gives rise to the commonplace assumption that those who express femininity are not to be taken seriously and cannot be seen as legitimate authority figures. While such assumptions regularly undermine feminine people of both sexes, they often have a greater net effect on women, because traditional sexism targets female bodies as well as feminine expression, and because traditional and oppositional sexism act together to put women in a double bind: If a woman acts feminine, she will be delegitimized by traditional sexism, and if she acts masculine, she will be delegitimized by oppositional sexism.

Feminist Interpretations of Femininity

Now, I will address different ways in which contemporary feminists have reacted to the sexist devaluing of femininity in society. For the purposes of this discussion, I will focus on two broad trends in feminism, which I call *unilateral feminism* and *deconstructive feminism*. By focusing on only these two general trends, it is not my intention to erase the significant differences that distinguished the individual branches of feminism that together gave rise to these trends, nor is it to ignore other branches of feminism that fall outside of these trends. Rather, my main purpose for this categorization scheme is to illustrate two major tendencies in feminist perspectives on femininity.

Several of the most influential branches of feminism that arose during the 1960s and 1970s may be described as falling under the umbrella of *unilateral feminism,* in that they viewed sexism as a straightforward matter of women being oppressed at the hands of men. One of the canonical writings of unilateral feminism is Betty Friedan's *The Feminine Mystique,* which focuses on the malaise that affected many middle-class women during the 1950s and 1960s as they gave up careers to become housewives and to raise families.[3] Friedan co-opts Sigmund Freud's phrase "feminine mystique" to describe the popular belief at the time that women could only be happy if they fully immersed themselves in femininity. Friedan discusses femininity in relation to what she calls the "housewife trap"—the expectation that middle-class women should become full-time homemakers, a role she believed stifled women's emotional and intellectual growth. To make her case that femininity is a trap (rather than something many women naturally gravitate toward), Friedan spends much of the book discussing the ways in which companies, advertisers, the media, psychiatry, and others actively manipulate women into buying into feminine trappings. *The Feminine Mystique* was a rather narrowly focused book, in that it only dealt with issues that affected middle-class American women, and with those aspects of femininity that are associated with the "housewife trap." But it helped reinforce a notion that would appear repeatedly throughout unilateral feminism—that femininity (or at least certain aspects of it) is an artificial, man-made ploy designed to hold women back from reaching their full potential.

Looking back at unilateral feminist writings, one finds that sexism is often described as arising from a patriarchal system that kept women oppressed via two interrelated tactics: (1) placing belittling meanings and assumptions onto women's bodies, and (2) coercing women into femininity, a program that was seen as inherently stifling and which fostered (or was the product of) women's subservience and subjugation to men. Thus, unilateral feminists viewed the oppositional sexism faced by women as part of traditional sexism. Because masculinity was viewed primarily as a position of privilege, oppositional sexism against male-bodied people remained obscured. Indeed, the very idea that a man might find masculine expectations restrictive seemed as nonsensical to many unilateral feminists as a rich person complaining about being oppressed by their own wealth.

The unilateral feminist notion that women were coerced into femininity was further facilitated by the growing use of the sex/gender distinction, which differentiated between one's sex (which arose from biology) and gender (which arose from one's environment, socialization, and psychology).[4] This gave unilateral feminists the theoretical means to challenge the traditionally sexist messages projected onto women's biology and bodies while ignoring or disavowing the negative messages associated with femininity. In fact, it's clear that many influential unilateral feminists believed that qualities such as helplessness, deference, and passivity were essentially "built into" feminine expressions and practices.[5] In other words, these feminists not only failed to challenge sexist interpretations of femininity, but often accepted those interpretations at face value.

While unilateral feminists almost universally agreed that some or all aspects of femininity enabled sexism, they differed in the proposed solutions for countering it. For example, liberal feminists (such as Friedan) worked within the existing system to try to gain equal access to previously male-dominated areas (particularly professional and leadership positions), often promoting a "women can do anything men can do" philosophy. Implicit in this strategy is the assumption that certain masculine-associated qualities and interests were natural and desirable for women to strive for, whereas the reciprocal feminine qualities were not. Radical feminists argued that women's oppression would only end by entirely rejecting both masculine and feminine gender roles—which were seen as being inexorably tied to men's "oppressor" and women's "oppressed" statuses—and instead adopting a more "natural" androgynous disposition. Cultural feminists took a more essentialist position, arguing that men and women were inherently different, and had distinctive innate traits; for example, men were inherently destructive and oppressive, while women were creative and nurturing. While cultural feminists certainly embraced some feminine traits—even characterizing them as superior to their masculine counterparts' traits—they were careful to portray such traits as arising from a woman's "natural" womanliness rather than from "artifactual, man-made femininity."[6]

The notion that sexism can only be overcome if women work to become more masculine, more androgynous, or more "naturally womanly" all artificialize femininity by assuming that one's gender expression is easily malleable, and can be reshaped according to one's politics. Such one-size-fits-all approaches falsely presume that femininity is monolithic, ignoring how significant differences in class, culture, and biological predisposition give rise to a vast diversity of feminine expressions and perspectives.[7] Because many unilateral feminists refused to accept this diversity in female gender expression, they often developed rather belittling views of women who were unabashedly feminine, characterizing them as having their minds colonized, being "ego repressed," and not being a "whole person."[8] Some unilateral feminists called femininity a "slave status," equating it with masochism, comparing it with Stockholm syndrome, and believing that it existed only to "communicate a woman's acceptance of her subordinate status."[9] Women who engaged in feminine beauty practices were perhaps the biggest target of such criticism, as they were accused of donning "symbols of oppression," being manipulated by "thought control," alienating themselves from their own bodies, and taking part in "self-imposed passivity."[10]

Of course, one of the biggest caveats in the unilateral feminist argument that femininity is artificial and only exists to oppress women is the fact that some people who are assigned and socialized male also express femininity. Perhaps sensing that feminine gay men and MTF spectrum trans people brought unilateral feminists' anti-femininity theses into question, many unilateral feminists developed vehemently disdainful attitudes toward these groups. Interestingly (and not coincidentally), the unilateral feminists who have been most outspoken in deriding feminine gay men and trans women also tend to have the most openly hostile attitudes toward femininity in general. For example, Mary Daly, who referred to feminine women as "painted birds" and portrayed feminist women such as herself as being "attacked by the mutants of her own kind, the man-made women," was similarly resentful of transsexual women (whom she called "Frankenstein's Monsters") and drag queens (whom she compared to whites playing "blackface").[11] Germaine Greer, who has referred to conventionally feminine women as "feminine parasites," has written multiple trans-misogynistic screeds, one of which assails trans woman Jan Morris for her "obsession with femininity."[12] And Sheila Jeffreys, who believes that femininity "is the behavior required of the subordinate class of women in order to show their deference to the ruling class of men," has argued that MTF transsexuality and gay male femininity arise exclusively from sexual masochism.[13] Thus, the anti-gay-male, anti-trans-woman sentiment that persists today among many unilateral feminists has its roots in their traditionally sexist views of femininity.

Many of the unilateral feminist positions that I've discussed so far have been challenged with the rise of *deconstructive feminism* in the 1980s and 1990s. Deconstructive feminists, while varied in their backgrounds and approaches, share the belief that the category "woman" is socially constructed and therefore doesn't exist independent of the societal norms and discourses that bring it into being. Therefore, instead of working to end sexism by highlighting the ways that women are "oppressed" by men (as unilateral feminists had), deconstructive feminists set out to deconstruct our very notions of "woman" and "man," exposing the assumptions and expectations that enable sexism. They describe "man" and "woman" as being situated within a binary gender system that permeates every nook and cranny of our society, infusing itself into our language, traditions, behaviors, and the very way we think about ourselves and others. This binary gender system assumes that men are masculine and aggressive and attracted to women, who are feminine and passive. If one fails to adhere to these assumptions in any way—for instance, if you are an aggressive woman or a feminine man—then you automatically become unintelligible within this system and are therefore marginalized.

Deconstructive feminism differs from unilateral feminism in a number of important ways. First, unlike unilateral feminism, which focuses almost exclusively on traditional sexism, deconstructive feminism focuses primarily on oppositional sexism. In a sense, deconstructive feminism subsumes traditional sexism into oppositional sexism, as it typically depicts the "othering" of "woman" as an inevitable by-product of that identity being binary-paired to "man." Because this relationship privileges oppositional sexism over traditional sexism, deconstructive feminists have been influential in both feminist and queer theory. Deconstructive feminists also differ from unilateral feminists in that they do not subscribe to the sex/gender distinction, but instead argue that our notions about "sex" are just as socially constructed as our notions of "gender."

While deconstructive feminism differs from unilateral feminism in many ways, it shares its predecessor's tendency to artificialize gender expression. This is often accomplished via *gender performativity,* a concept developed by Judith Butler to describe the way in which built-in expectations about maleness and femaleness, straightness and queerness, are constantly imposed on all of us. Butler uses the term "performativity" to highlight how feminine and masculine norms must constantly be cited. She uses the example of the child who becomes "girled" by others at birth: She is given a female name, referred to with female pronouns, given girl toys, and will, throughout her life, have her "girlness" cited by others in society.[14] Butler argues that this sort of reiteration "produces" gender, making it appear "natural." However, many other deconstructive feminists have interpreted Butler's writings to mean that one's gender is merely a "performance." According to this latter view, if gender itself is merely a "performance," then one can challenge sexism by simply "performing" one's gender in ways that call the binary gender system into question; the most often cited example of this is a drag queen whose "performance" supposedly reveals the way in which femaleness and femininity are merely a "performance."[15]

While unilateral feminists typically view femininity in exclusively negative terms, deconstructive feminists believe that femininity is context-dependent: It can be "good" (when it is used to subvert the binary gender system) or "bad" (when used to naturalize that system).[16] In other words, deconstructive feminism only empowers and embraces queer expressions of femininity, while straight expressions of femininity are typically portrayed as reinforcing a sexist binary gender system. Thus, both deconstructive and unilateral feminism share the belief that (1) femininity is not a natural form of expression, but rather one that is socially imposed; (2) most women are "duped" into believing that their femininity arises intrinsically rather than due to extrinsic forces such as socialization or social constructs; (3) people who are "in the know" recognize that gender expression is artificial and easily malleable, and thus they can purposefully adopt a more radical, antisexist gender expression (e.g., androgyny, drag, etc.); and (4) because feminine women choose not to adopt these supposedly radical, antisexist gender expressions, they may be seen as enabling sexism and thus collaborating in their own oppression.

The Ramifications of Artificializing Femininity

So why has the artificializing of femininity become a preoccupation for many feminists over the last several decades? I believe that it has to do with the fact that many of the women who have most strongly gravitated toward feminism are those who have found traditional feminine gender roles constraining or unnatural. In many cases, this is due to their own inclinations toward exceptional forms of gender expression. Because their personal experiences with femininity felt uncomfortable and contrived in comparison with their experiences with androgyny, masculinity, or other gender expressions (which they found more liberating and empowering), they mistakenly projected their own experience and perspective onto all other women. While not necessarily done maliciously, this extrapolation was nevertheless an act of gender entitlement, one that denied that any diversity in gender expression might exist among women arising out of their very different class, cultural, or biological backgrounds and predispositions. By arrogantly assuming that no woman could be legitimately drawn toward feminine expression, these feminists permanently relegated femininity to the status of "false consciousness."

The feminist assumption that "femininity is artificial" is narcissistic, as it invariably casts nonfeminine women as having "superior knowledge" while dismissing feminine women as either "dupes" (who are too ignorant to recognize they have been conned) or "fakes" (who purposely engage in "unnatural" behaviors in order to uphold sexist societal norms). This tendency to dismiss feminine women is eerily similar to the behavior of some lesbian-feminists in the 1970s who arrogantly claimed that they were more righteous feminists than heterosexual women because the latter group was "fucking with the oppressor."[17] It is an extraordinarily convenient tactic to artificialize, and even demean, an inclination (such as femininity or heterosexuality) when you personally are not inclined toward it. Indeed, this is exactly what straight bigots do when they dismiss queer forms of gender and sexual expression as "unnatural." When we feminists stoop to the level of policing gender and start inventing etiologies to explain why some women adopt "unnatural" feminine forms of expression, there's little to distinguish us from the sexist forces we claim to be fighting against in the first place.

While femininity is in many ways influenced, shaped, and enforced by society, to say that it is entirely "artificial" or merely a "performance" is patronizing toward those for whom femininity simply *feels right*. Indeed, one would have to have a rather grim view of the female population to believe that a majority of us could so easily be "brainwashed" or "coerced" into enthusiastically adopting an entirely contrived or wholly artificial set of gender expressions. In fact, it seems incomprehensible that so many women could so actively gravitate toward femininity unless there was something about it that resonated with them on a profound level. This becomes even more obvious when considering feminine folks who exhibit no desire whatsoever to fit into straight society, such as femme dykes (who proudly express their femininity despite being historically marginalized within the lesbian movement because of it) and "nelly queens" (who remain fiercely feminine despite the gay male obsession with praising butchness and deriding "effeminacy").[18]

The idea that "femininity is artificial" is also blatantly misogynistic. While a handful of theorists in the field of gender studies have more recently begun to focus on how masculinity is constructed, the lion's share of feminist attention, deconstruction, and denigration has been directed squarely at femininity. There is an obvious reason for this. Just as woman is man's "other," so too is femininity masculinity's "other." Under such circumstances, negative connotations like "artificial," "contrived," and "frivolous" become built into our understanding of femininity—indeed, this is precisely what allows masculinity to always come off as "natural," "practical," and "uncomplicated." Those feminists who single out women's dress shoes, clothing, and hairstyles to artificialize necessarily leave unchallenged the notion that their masculine counterparts are "natural" and "practical." This is the same male-centered approach that allows the appearances and behaviors of men who wish to charm or impress others to seem "authentic" while the reciprocal traits expressed by women are dismissed as "feminine wiles." Femininity is portrayed as a trick or ruse so that masculinity invariably seems sincere by comparison. For this reason, there are few intellectual tasks easier than artificializing feminine gender expression, because male-centricism purposefully sets up femininity as masculinity's "straw man" or its scapegoat.

As feminists, it's time for us to acknowledge that this scapegoating of femininity has become the Achilles' heel of the feminist movement. While past feminists have gone to great lengths to empower femaleness and to tear away all of the negative connotations that have plagued women's bodies and biology, they have allowed the negative connotations associated with femininity to persist relatively unabated. Nothing illustrates this better than the fact that, while most reasonable people see women and men as equals, few (if any) dare to claim that femininity is masculinity's equal. Indeed, much of what has historically been called misogyny—a hatred of women—has clearly gone underground, disguising itself as the less reprehensible derision of femininity. This new version of misogyny, which focuses more on maligning femininity than femaleness, can be found everywhere. It can be seen in our political discourse, where advocates for the environment, gun control, and welfare are undermined via "guilt by association" with feminine imagery as seen in phrases such as "tree huggers," "soft on crime," and pro-"dependency"—where male politicians who exhibit anything other than a two-dimensional facade of hypermasculinity are invariably dismissed by political cartoonists who depict them donning dresses.[19]

This new misogyny still very much undermines women, and it accomplishes this in several ways. First, the majority of feminine people are women, so by default they make up the largest class of those who are targeted by antifeminine sentiment. Second, our concept of femininity doesn't merely affect how we "do" our own gender expression—it is also an expectation or assumption that we project onto other people's bodies and behaviors. Therefore, while an individual woman may purposefully eschew femininity in her appearance and actions, she cannot escape the fact that other people will project feminine assumptions and expectations upon her simply because they associate femininity with femaleness. In her book *Why So Slow? The Advancement of Women*, Virginia Valian makes a strong case that what has come to be known as the "glass ceiling"—the fact that women, regardless of their skills and merits, tend not to advance as far in their careers as similarly qualified men—is best explained by the fact that all people project feminine assumptions and expectations onto women and masculine ones onto men.[20] This, of course, favors men, since masculinity is by default seen as "strong," "natural," and "aggressive" while femininity is seen as "weak," "contrived," and "passive." Therefore, until feminists work to empower femininity and pry it away from the insipid, inferior meanings that plague it—weakness, helplessness, fragility, passivity, frivolity, and artificiality—those meanings will continue to haunt every person who is female and/or feminine.

Feminists' past privileging of femaleness over femininity has also enabled misogynistic acts that target men who have feminine traits to remain unnoticed and unarticulated. For example, when a gay man ridicules another gay man for being too "flamboyant" or "effeminate," he may be accused of harboring "internalized homophobia"—a nonsensical turn of phrase to describe someone who is openly gay and has no problems with masculine gay men. Isn't this form of antifeminine discrimination better described as misogyny? Similarly, straight women who regularly pair up with macho guys who treat them poorly, yet won't consider dating a "nice guy," might be described as harboring "internalized misogyny." Again, isn't this better described as a form of externalized misogyny directed at men who display qualities that are considered feminine?

Some feminists (particularly unilateral feminists) will no doubt have a negative knee-jerk reaction to my suggestion that we extend our understanding of misogyny to encompass effemimania—our societal obsession with critiquing and belittling feminine traits in males. However, as I have argued in past chapters, effemimania affects everybody, including women. Effemimania encourages those who are socialized male to mystify femininity and to dehumanize those who are considered feminine, and thus forms the foundation of virtually all male expressions of misogyny. Effemimania also ensures that any male's manhood or masculinity can be brought into question at any moment for even the slightest perceived expression of, or association with, femininity. I would argue that today, the biggest bottleneck in the movement toward gender equity is not so much women's lack of access to what has been traditionally considered the "masculine realm," but rather men's insistence on defining themselves in opposition to women (i.e., their unwillingness to venture into the "feminine realm").

Until now, the typical feminist response to men who fear being associated with the "feminine realm" can be paraphrased as "*Get over it!*" Such an attitude is ignorant, as it fails to take into account the fact that male femininity is perceived very differently from female femininity. If femininity in women is already seen as "artificial" and "contrived," then oppositional sexism ensures that femininity in men appears exponentially "artificial" and "contrived." While a handful of feminists have recognized this fact—that male feminine expression tends to evoke levels of contempt and disgust that far exceed that which is normally reserved for female masculinity or femininity—most have unfortunately chosen to ignore or dismiss misogyny when it targets those who are male-bodied.[21] By doing so, these feminists have become enablers for one of the most prevalent and malignant forms of traditional sexism.

The greatest barrier preventing us from fully challenging sexism is the pervasive antifeminine sentiment that runs wild in both the straight and queer communities, targeting people of all genders and sexualities. The only realistic way to address this issue is to work toward empowering femininity itself. We must rightly recognize that feminine expression is strong, daring, and brave—that it is powerful—and not in an enchanting, enticing, or supernatural sort of way, but in a tangible, practical way that facilitates openness, creativity, and honest expression. We must move beyond seeing femininity as helpless and dependent, or merely as masculinity's sidekick, and instead acknowledge that feminine expression exists of its own accord and brings its own rewards to those who naturally gravitate toward it. By embracing femininity, feminism will finally be able to reach out to the vast majority of feminine women who have felt alienated by the movement in the past. The movement would also be able to reach those who are not female (whether male and/or transgender) who regularly face effemimania or trans-misogyny, but who have not been able to seek refuge or have a voice in the feminist movements of the past. Indeed, a feminist movement that encompasses both those who are female and those who are feminine has the potential to become a majority, one with the strength in numbers to finally challenge and overturn both traditional and oppositional sexism.

20

The Future of Queer/Trans Activism

THE MAJORITY OF MY EXPERIENCES as a trans activist and spoken word artist have taken place in what is increasingly becoming known as the "queer/trans" community. It is a subgroup within the greater LGBTIQ community that is composed mostly of folks in their twenties and thirties who are more likely to refer to themselves as "dykes," "queer," and/or "trans" than "lesbian" or "gay." While diverse in a number of ways, this subpopulation tends to predominantly inhabit urban and academic settings, and is skewed toward those who are white and/or from middle-class backgrounds. In many ways, the queer/trans community is best described as a sort of marriage of the transgender movement's call to "shatter the gender binary" and the lesbian community's pro-sex, pro-kink backlash to 1980s-era Andrea Dworkinism. Its politics are generally anti-assimilationist, particularly with regard to gender and sexual expression. This apparent limitlessness and lack of boundaries lead many to believe that "queer/trans" represents the vanguard of today's gender and sexual revolution. However, over the last four years in which I've been a part of this community, I've become increasingly troubled by a trend that, while not applicable to all queer/trans folks, seems to be becoming a dominant belief in this community, one that threatens to restrict its gender and sexual diversity. I call this trend *subversivism.*

Subversivism is the practice of extolling certain gender and sexual expressions and identities simply because they are unconventional or nonconforming. In the parlance of subversivism, these atypical genders and sexualities are "good" because they "transgress" or "subvert" oppressive binary gender norms.[1] The justification for the practice of subversivism has evolved out of a particular reading (although some would call it a misreading) of the work of various influential queer theorists over the last decade and a half. To briefly summarize this popularized account: All forms of sexism arise from the binary gender system. Since this binary gender system is everywhere—in our thoughts, language, traditions, behaviors, etc.—the only way we can overturn it is to actively undermine the system from within. Thus, in order to challenge sexism, people must "perform" their genders in ways that bend, break, and blur all of the imaginary distinctions that exist between male and female, heterosexual and homosexual, and so on, presumably leading to a systemwide binary meltdown. According to the principles of subversivism, drag is inherently "subversive," as it reveals that our society's binary notions of maleness and femaleness are not natural, but rather are actively "constructed" and "performed" by all of us. Another way that one can be "transgressively gendered" is by identifying as genderqueer or genderfluid—i.e., refusing to identify fully as either woman or man.

The notion that certain gender identities and expressions are inherently "subversive" or "transgressive" can be seen throughout the queer/trans community, where drag and gender-bending are routinely celebrated, where binary-confounding identities such as "boy-identified-dyke" and "pansexual trannyfag" have become rather commonplace. On the surface, subversivism gives the appearance of accommodating a seemingly infinite array of genders and sexualities, but this is not quite the case. Subversivism does have very specific boundaries; it has an "other." By glorifying identities and expressions that appear to subvert or blur gender binaries, subversivism automatically creates a reciprocal category of people whose gender and sexual identities and expressions are by default inherently conservative, even "hegemonic," because they are seen as reinforcing or naturalizing the binary gender system. Not surprisingly, this often-unspoken category of bad, conservative genders is predominantly made up of feminine women and masculine men who are attracted to the "opposite" sex.

One routinely sees this "dark side" of subversivism rear its head in the queer/trans community, where it is not uncommon to hear individuals critique or call into question other queers or trans folks because their gender presentation, behaviors, or sexual preferences are not deemed "subversive" enough. Indeed, if one fails to sufficiently distinguish oneself from heterosexual feminine women and masculine men, one runs the risk of being accused of "reinforcing the gender binary," an indictment that is tantamount to being called a sexist. One of the most common targets of such critiques are transsexuals, and particularly those who are heterosexual and gender-normative post-transition. Indeed, because such transsexuals (in the eyes of others) transition from a seemingly "transgressive" queer identity to a "conservative" straight one, subversivists may even claim that they have transitioned in order to purposefully "assimilate" themselves into straight culture. While these days, such accusations are often couched in the rhetoric of current queer theory, they rely on many of the same mistaken assumptions that plagued the work of cissexist feminists like Janice Raymond and sociologists like Thomas Kando decades ago.[2]

The practice of subversivism also negatively impacts trans people on the MTF spectrum. After all, in our culture, the meanings of "bold," "rebellious," and "dangerous"—adjectives that often come to mind when considering subversiveness—are practically built into our understanding of masculinity. In contrast, femininity conjures up antonyms like "timid," "conventional," and "safe," which seem entirely incompatible with subversion. Therefore, despite the fact that the mainstream public tends to be more concerned and disturbed by MTF spectrum trans people than their FTM spectrum counterparts, subversivism creates the impression that trans masculinities are inherently "subversive" and "transgressive," while their trans feminine counterparts are "lame" and "conservative" in comparison. Subversivism's privileging of trans masculinities over trans femininities helps to explain why cissexual queer women and FTM spectrum folks tend to dominate the queer/trans community: Their exceptional gender expressions and identities are routinely empowered and encouraged in such settings. In contrast, there is generally a dearth of MTF spectrum folks who regularly inhabit queer/trans spaces.[3]

To me, the most surreal part of this whole transgressing-versus-reinforcing-gender-norms dialogue in the queer/trans community (and in many gender studies classrooms and books) is the unacknowledged hypocrisy of it all. It is sadly ironic that people who claim to be gender-fucking in the name of "shattering the gender binary," and who criticize people whose identities fail to adequately challenge our societal notions of femaleness and maleness, cannot see that they have just created a new gender binary, one in which subversive genders are "good" and conservative genders are "bad." In a sense, this new gender binary isn't even all that new. It is merely the original oppositional sexist binary flipped upside down. So now, gender-nonconforming folks are on top and gender-normative people are on the bottom—how revolutionary! Now, I understand the temptation for a marginalized group to turn the hierarchy that has oppressed them upside down, as it can feel very empowering to finally be atop the pecking order, but it's absurd to claim that such approaches in any way undermine that binary. If anything, they only serve to reinforce it further.

Subversivism's binary flip is very reminiscent of another binary flip that was forwarded by cultural feminists in the mid-1970s. While subversivism reverses oppositional sexism, cultural feminism sought to reverse traditional sexism by claiming that women were naturally creative and cooperative and therefore superior to men, who were seen as inherently destructive and oppressive. While it is always difficult to draw comparisons between different social/political movements for fear of oversimplifying them, there are other striking parallels between subversivism and cultural feminism that are worth bearing out. As historian Alice Echols describes in her book *Daring to Be Bad: Radical Feminism in America, 1967–1975*, cultural feminism evolved from its more outwardly focused predecessor, radical feminism.[4] While radical feminism—which asserted that neither sex was inherently superior to the other—actively engaged the mainstream public (and men in particular) to challenge and change their sexist ways, cultural feminism was a more insular movement, focusing on creating women-run organizations and women-only spaces rather than organizing public demonstrations. And unlike radical feminism, which attempted to accommodate a variety of different female perspectives (in fact, issues over "difference" in class and sexuality consumed much of the movement's energy), cultural feminists forwarded the idea of "sameness" and "oneness"—that all women were part of a universal sisterhood, united by their female biology.

This concept of female "oneness" was perhaps most responsible for cultural feminism's exclusionist, even separatist, tendencies. After all, if one believes in a female "oneness" that is distinct from, and superior to, maleness, then anyone who brings that distinction into question automatically becomes threatening. Indeed, that's exactly what happened throughout much of the 1970s and 1980s. Those women who disagreed with cultural feminist dogma—or who engaged in certain gender expressions and sexual practices that were associated with men—were derided as promoting masculine values and being "antifeminist," and were accordingly excluded from the movement. Further, as Echols points out, while cultural feminists "used the language of sisterhood, they often assumed a patronizing stance toward those 'unliberated' women who were still living in 'The Man's' world."[5] This exclusionary shift from a movement that sought to benefit *all* women (i.e., radical feminism) to one that only sought to benefit a select group of women was made possible by cultural feminism's binary flip and its sense of "oneness."

The queer and transgender movements came into their own in the early 1990s in response to this sort of exclusionary "oneness" that was promoted by cultural feminists and many mainstream gay rights activists. The words "transgender" and "queer" came into vogue during this time as umbrella terms: "Queer" attempted to accommodate lesbians and gays as well as the growing bisexual and transgender movements; and "transgender" was used to promote a coalition of distinct groups (including crossdressers, transsexuals, butch women, femme men, drag performers, intersex people, etc.) that previously believed they had little in common with one another. These alliances were not based on a presumed shared biology or set of beliefs, but on the fact that these different groups faced similar forms of discrimination. In fact, the notion that transgender people "transgress binary gender norms" came about to create a cause for its varied constituents to unite behind, not as a litmus test or a criteria for them to meet. At that time, the idea of "shattering the gender binary" was outward-focused; if we could push our culture to move beyond the idea that female and male are rigid, mutually exclusive "opposite sexes," that would make the lives of all transgender constituent subgroups far easier.

Just as cultural feminism's binary flip fostered that movement's inward focus on women-only culture and spaces, I believe that the recent rise of subversivism may be an early sign that the more outward-looking, changing-the-world-focused transgender and queer movements of the 1990s are shifting into a more insular and exclusionary queer/trans community, one that favors only a select group of queers and trans folks, rather than all people who fall under those umbrella terms. Indeed, unlike our predecessors in the groups Queer Nation (who held public "kiss-ins" in suburban malls) and Transexual Menace (who staged protests in small Midwestern towns where trans people were murdered), many in the queer/trans community these days often seem more content celebrating our fabulous queer selves or enjoying the safety of our own organizations and events.[6] While there is nothing inherently wrong with creating our own queer/trans spaces and culture, what troubles me is that we are clearly sacrificing diversity in the process. For example, in queer/trans spaces, one rarely sees MTF crossdressers (despite the fact that they make up a large portion of the transgender population) and there are very few trans women. Some might suggest that these groups are choosing not to attend of their own accord, but that only leads to the next question: *Why* are they choosing not to come? Often when trans women ask me when I'm performing next, and I tell them that it's a queer/trans event, they will tell me that they'd rather not go because they do not feel comfortable or safe in those spaces, that they have been dismissed or belittled at such events before. Even trans women who are dyke- or bisexual-identified often don't feel welcome or relevant in queer/trans spaces. And whenever a trans woman or ally points out aspects about the queer/trans community that contribute to these feelings of irrelevancy and disrespect—such as the way our community coddles those who support trans-woman-exclusionist events or who make trans-misogynistic comments—we are described as being "divisive." This use of the word "divisive" is particularly telling, as it implies that "queer/trans" represents a uniform movement or community—a "oneness"—rather than an alliance where all voices are respected.

Perhaps the only thing more ironic than the fact that the transgender movement's "shatter the gender binary" slogan is now being used to enforce a new subversive/conservative gender binary is the fact that the queer/trans community's growing sense of "oneness" evolved out of a well-meaning attempt to prevent exclusivity. From the outset, many early transgender activists feared that one particular transgender subgroup might come to dominate the transgender community, that they would begin to police the movement's borders and enforce their own sense of "oneness." Because the exclusivity of cultural feminism and the mainstream "gay rights" movement seemed to center on disputes over identity—who counts as a "woman" or who is legitimately "gay"—many activists advocated the idea that the transgender coalition should be borderless, one where there was no set criteria for an individual to join. Many also worked to play down or blur the distinctiveness of individual transgender subgroups in order to prevent any kind of hierarchy from developing. The transgender movement, in effect, became an anti-identity movement.

In retrospect, I would say that the assumption that distinct identities would automatically lead to exclusivity was entirely misplaced. After all, an identity is merely a label, a descriptive noun to express one particular facet of a person's experiences. And if we look beyond gender and sexual identity politics, we can find many examples of flexible and fluid identities. For example, if I were to identify myself as a "cat person," nobody would be outraged or confused if I said I also loved dogs. Further, when I tell people that I'm a "musician," no one makes unwarranted assumptions about what instruments I play or what styles of music I prefer. Nonpoliticized identities like "musician" and "cat person" allow us to see that the recurring problems in gender and sexual identity politics arise not from identity per se, but rather from opposite-think (e.g., that a cat person cannot be a dog person, and vice versa) and from a sense of "oneness" (e.g., the assumption that all musicians are or should be punk rock guitarists.)

I believe that if the transgender movement had simply continued to view itself as an alliance of disparate groups working toward a shared goal (like making the world safer for gender-variant folks), it may have avoided such exclusivity while respecting the distinct differences and specific concerns of its various constituents. Instead, by promoting the idea that we must move beyond the supposedly outdated concept of "identity," the transgender movement has created its own sense of "oneness." Rather than viewing ourselves as a fragile political coalition of distinct subgroups, some activists instead encourage us to see ourselves as one big homogeneous group of individuals who blur gender boundaries. Rather than learning to respect the very different perspectives and experiences that each transgender subgroup brings to the table, the transgender community has instead become a sort of gender free-for-all, where identities are regularly co-opted by others within the community. These days, many transsexuals assume that they have the right to appropriate the language of, or speak on behalf of, intersex people; similarly, many cissexual genderqueers feel they have the right to do the same for transsexuals. This needlessly erases each group's unique issues, obstacles, and perspectives.

This sort of "gender anarchy"—where individuals are free to adopt or appropriate any identity as they please—might seem very limitless and freeing on the surface, but in practice it resembles gender-libertarianism, where those who are most marginalized become even more vulnerable to the whims of those who are more established. In this case, it leaves those of us who are cross-gender-identified susceptible to negation at the hands of the greater cissexual queer community. Indeed, it has become increasingly common for people who are primarily queer because of their sexual orientation to claim a space for themselves within the transgender movement.[7] This is particularly true in the queer women's community, which has become increasingly involved in transgender politics and discourses due to the recent sharp increase in the number of (1) previously lesbian-identified people transitioning to male, (2) dykes who now take on genderqueer or other FTM spectrum identities, and (3) non-trans queer women who seek a voice in the transgender community because they are partnered to FTM spectrum individuals.

Because of our history, the fact that cissexual queers now dominate transgender and queer/trans communities and discourses is highly problematic for those of us who are transsexual. During the 1970s, transsexuals and other cross-gender-identified queers were banished from the "gay rights" movement as it began to focus solely on sexual orientation. This was a calculated maneuver: By jettisoning cross-gender queers (who were typically seen as the "most deviant" by a reluctant mainstream public), sexuality-queers could make the case that they were just like "normal people" except for their sexual orientation. And from the perspective of a lesbian or gay person, this strategy was highly effective. Sexuality-queers, while still marginalized to a certain degree, have made tremendous legal gains with regard to domestic partnership, including reversing "sodomy laws" and gaining protection against discrimination. They now have their own social and political organizations, cable channels, university departments, and even their own Olympics. There are out lesbian and gay politicians and celebrities, and popular TV shows that revolve around lesbian and gay characters. Gay-themed jokes in the media are now more likely to make fun of someone for being homophobic than for being homosexual. Perhaps most significant of all, it has become generally accepted among most Americans—even among those who are stern opponents of "gay rights"—that there is natural variation in human sexual orientation. (Or, as the popular saying goes: "Some people are just born that way.")

As a direct result of the exclusion of cross-gender-identified trans people from the "gay rights" movement, public awareness and acceptance of our identities and issues are about twenty years behind those of lesbians and gays, because the transgender movement didn't gain momentum until the 1990s. Because of this exclusion, our cross-gender identities and perspectives are not acknowledged to nearly the same extent as lesbian and gay identities and perspectives. For example, when I come out to people as a transsexual, I am often barraged with highly personal questions about my motives, my physical body, and my male past. In contrast, I have never once been interrogated by someone upon coming out to them as a lesbian; that aspect of my person is generally accepted at face value. In other words, I am allowed to exist without question as a lesbian in ways that I am not allowed as a transsexual. In a climate where same-sex attraction has become a given while cross-gender identification has most certainly not, the merging of "sexuality-queers" and "gender-queers" (as seen in the queer/trans community) essentially subsumes transsexuals within the more well-established cissexual queer community. The more inclusive the word "transgender" becomes, the more thoroughly the voices of transsexuals and other cross-gender/cross-living individuals are drowned out by those who do not share our perspectives and experiences.

This "cissexualization" of transgenderism has taken a devastating toll on the ability of transsexuals to articulate our own perspectives and visions for gender activism. Rather than being listened to and appreciated on our own terms, we are instead forced to adhere to lesbian/gay rhetoric and values in order to have a voice within our own community. One can see this in the way that lesbian/gay-specific definitions of "passing" (as a synonym for "hiding") are inappropriately applied to our decisions to physically transition and live in our identified sex, or in the way that our descriptions of subconscious sex, gender dissonance, and physical transitioning are patronizingly dismissed by cissexual queers who favor social constructionist views of gender. It is evident in the way that queer theorists, ignorant of their own cissexual privilege, nonconsensually ungender us (or blur the distinctions between us and other queers) in order to artificialize gender; claim that "all gender is drag" without recognizing how dismissive that is to the transsexual experience; and ignorantly apply the "gay rights" tactic of calling for the all-out demedicalization of transgenderism without considering the effects this would have on transsexuals' ability to access and afford hormones and sex reassignment procedures. Finally, as Viviane Namaste has pointed out in her books, the "cissexualization" of the transgender movement ensures that discourses about transsexuals inevitably revolve around the cissexual queer obsession over "identity" (who counts as a woman or man, who is legitimately queer), rather than examining the very real institutional obstacles and biases we face for being transsexual.[8]

I worry that the dominance of cissexual voices in the queer/trans community, and the exclusionary practice of subversivism, are together fostering a sense of queer/trans "oneness" that excludes trans women such as myself. My fears stem not so much from my own concern about being excluded, or for the many other subgroups not mentioned here who also feel increasingly left out of this community. Rather, I fear that this inward, homogenizing trend represents a lost opportunity to learn from one another and to change the minds of the public at large. If we hope to correct this insular, exclusionary trend, then we must begin to (once again) think in terms of alliances rather than monolithic communities. Alliance-based activism begins with the recognition that we are all individuals, each with a limited history and experiencing a largely unique set of privileges, expectations, assumptions, and restrictions. Thus, none of us have "superior knowledge" when it comes to sexuality and gender. By calling ourselves an alliance, we explicitly acknowledge that we are working toward a common goal (how about "making the world safe and just for people of all genders and sexualities"?), while simultaneously recognizing and respecting our many differences. There can be no legitimate accusations of "divisiveness" in an alliance, as differences of opinion would be expected from the start. Thinking in terms of alliances can encourage us to move beyond the single goal of creating safe queer/trans spaces, to recognize that, in reality, there is no such thing as a "safe space." After all, the very notion of safety is often predicated on a presumed and exclusionary sense of "sameness" and "oneness." And unlike subversivism, which fosters a grim and belittling view of the heterosexual, gender-normative majority, alliance-based gender activism recognizes that the only way we will change society is by engaging the mainstream public and working with, rather than against, our straight allies.

If we hope to build alliances that are respectful of all queer and transgender perspectives, then we must stop talking about *the* gender binary system, as if there is only one. As a trans woman, I deal with lots of gender binaries: male/female, heterosexual/homosexual, cissexual/transsexual, cisgender/transgender, and so on. As someone who is marginalized in queer/trans spaces for not being "subversive" or "transgressive" enough, I find that calls to "shatter the (male/female) gender binary" sound hollow. And when cissexual queers try to frame all forms of gender/sexual discrimination in terms of "heterosexist gender norms," they deny the fact that, as a transsexual woman, I experience way more cissexist and trans-misogynistic animosity and condescension from members of my own lesbian community than I ever have from my straight friends and acquaintances. The truth is that whenever we enter a different space, or speak with a different person, we are forced to deal with a somewhat different set of binaries and assumptions. Indeed, my experience living in the San Francisco Bay Area—where most straight people I know are very comfortable with queerness, yet many queer people I know harbor subversivist attitudes toward straightness—makes it clear that there needs to be a more general strategy to challenge *all* forms of sexism, not just the typical or obvious ones.

Rather than focusing on "shattering the gender binary," I believe we should turn our attention instead to challenging all forms of *gender entitlement,* the privileging of one's own perceptions, interpretations, and evaluations of other people's genders over the way those people understand themselves. After all, whenever we assign values to other people's genders and sexualities—whether we call them subversive or conservative, cool or uncool, normal or abnormal, natural or unnatural—we are automatically creating or reaffirming some kind of hierarchy. In other words, when we critique any gender as being "good" or "bad," we are by definition being sexist. After all, isn't what drives many of us into feminism and queer activism in the first place our frustration that other people often place rather arbitrary meanings and values onto our sexed bodies, gender expressions, and sexualities? Is there really any difference between the schoolyard bullies who teased us for being too feminine or masculine when we were little, the arrogant employer who assumes that we aren't cut out for the job because we're female, the gay men who claim that we are holding back the gay rights movement because we are not straight-acting enough, and the people—whether lesbian-feminists of the 1970s and 1980s, or subversivists in the 2000s—who decry us for not being androgynous enough to be "true gender radicals"?

Some might argue that it's simply human nature for us to assign different values to different genders and sexualities. For example, if we tend to prefer the company of men over women, or if we find androgynous people more attractive than feminine or masculine ones, isn't that assigning them a different worth? Not necessarily. There is a big difference between rightly recognizing these preferences in terms of our personal predilections ("I find androgynous people attractive") and entitled claims that imply that there are no other legitimate opinions ("Masculine and feminine people are not sexy, period"). Similarly, there's a big difference between calling yourself a woman or a genderqueer because you feel that word best captures your gendered experience and using that identity to make claims or presumptions about other people's genders (e.g., assuming that "men" or "gender-conforming people" are your "opposites").

Some might also argue that there is such a thing as "bad" gender—for instance, a woman who feels coerced into living up to stereotypically feminine ideals. As someone who was closeted for many years, I can understand why someone might be tempted to describe genders that are enforced by others (e.g., stereotypical femininity or masculinity) as being "bad." The problem is that there is no way for us to know whether any given person's gender identity or expression is sincere or coerced. While we experience our own genders and sexualities firsthand, and thus are capable of separating our own intrinsic inclinations from the extrinsic expectations that others place on us, we are unable to do so on behalf of other people. We can only ever make assumptions and educated guesses about the authenticity of someone else's sexuality or gender—and that's always dangerous.

The thing that always impresses me about human beings is our diversity. Even when we are brought up in similar environments, we still somehow gravitate toward very different careers, hobbies, politics, manners of speaking and acting, aesthetic preferences, and so forth. Maybe this diversity is due to genetic variation. Or maybe, being naturally curious and adaptive creatures, we invariably tend to scatter all over the place, exploiting every niche we can possibly find. Either way, it's fairly obvious that we also end up all over the map when it comes to gender and sexuality. That being the case, if we take the subversivist route and focus our energies on deriding stereotypically feminine and masculine genders, we will inevitably disparage some (perhaps many) people for whom those genders simply feel right and natural. Furthermore, by critiquing those gender expressions in an entitled way, we actively create new gender expectations that others may feel obliged to meet (which is exactly what's now starting to happen in the queer/trans community). That is why I suggest that we turn our energies and attention away from the way that individuals "do" or "perform" their own genders and instead focus on the expectations and assumptions that those individuals project onto everybody else. By focusing on gender entitlement rather than gender performance, we may finally take the next step toward a world where all people can choose their genders and sexualities at will, rather than feeling coerced by others.

Notes

Preface

1 As of August 2015, *Whipping Girl* has been cited or discussed in numerous mainstream publications, including *Alternet, The Atlantic, BuzzFeed, The Chicago Reader, The Daily Beast, The Guardian, Huffington Post, Marie Claire, Ms. Magazine, NBC News, New York Magazine, The New Yorker, New Republic, New Statesman, NPR, Playboy, Rolling Stone, Salon, The San Francisco Chronicle, Slate, The Telegraph, Time, Variety, Vice, Vogue,* and *Washington Post.*

2 Trans people's involvement in both the gay liberation and queer movements is detailed in Susan Stryker, *Transgender History* (Berkeley: Seal Press, 2008), 59-89, 121-153. For demographics regarding trans people and sexual orientation, see Jaime M. Grant, Lisa A. Mottet, Justin Tanis, Jack Harrison, Jody L. Herman, and Mara Keisling, *Injustice at Every Turn: A Report of the National Transgender Discrimination Survey* (Washington: National Center for Transgender Equality and National Gay and Lesbian Task Force, 2011), 28.

3 I wrote about my 2003 Camp Trans experience in Julia Serano, *Excluded: Making Feminist and Queer Movements More Inclusive* (Berkeley, CA: Seal Press, 2013), 22-36.

4 Julia Serano, *On the Outside Looking In: a trans woman's perspective on feminism and the exclusion of trans women from lesbian and women-only spaces* (Oakland, CA: Hot Tranny Action, 2005).

5 Serano, *Excluded,* 138-168.

6 I discuss how these slogans undermine transsexual perspectives and experiences in Serano, *Excluded,* 105-108. Many people misattribute these slogans to gender theorist Judith Butler, and thereby misinterpret my writings as a direct critique of her work, which is not actually the case as

I explain in Julia Serano, "Julia Serano on Judith Butler," (http://juliaserano.blogspot.com/2015/09/julia-serano-on-judith-butler.html).

7 Specifically, I detail how double standards work in Serano, *Excluded,* 169-199, and expand on *gender entitlement* (a concept that I introduce here in *Whipping Girl* to describe how projecting assumptions and meanings onto other people plays a central role in sexism) in Serano, *Excluded,* 239-256.

8 I have since written multiple follow up essays about the origins and uses of cis terminology—they are compiled in Julia Serano, "Julia Serano's compendium on cisgender, cissexual, cissexism, cisgenderism, cis privilege, and the cis/trans distinction" (http://juliaserano.blogspot.com/2014/12/julia-seranos-compendium-on-cisgender.html).

9 Erica Schwiegershausen, "Wait, *Cisgender* Wasn't in the Oxford English Dictionary Already?" *New York Magazine*, June 25, 2015 (http://nymag.com/thecut/2015/06/wait-cisgender-wasnt-in-the-oed-already.html); Anna Diamond, "Why the Oxford English Dictionary's Addition of *Cisgender* Matters," *Slate*, June 29, 2015 (http://www.slate.com/blogs/outward/2015/06/29/cisgender_oxford_english_dictionary_addition.html).

10 Specifically, in my essays "Reclaiming Femininity" (Serano, *Excluded,* 48-69) and Julia Serano, "Empowering Femininity," *Ms.*, July 28, 2014 (http://msmagazine.com/blog/2014/07/28/empowering-femininity).

11 Serano, *Excluded*, 70-98.

12 Trudy Ring, "This Year's Michigan Womyn's Music Festival Will Be the Last," *The Advocate*, April 21, 2015 (http://www.advocate.com/michfest/2015/04/21/years-michigan-womyns-music-festival-will-be-last).

13 Specifically in "Part 3: Pathological Science Revisited," in Julia Serano, *Outspoken: A Decade of Transgender Activism and Trans Feminism* (Oakland: Switch Hitter Press, 2016). In brief, gender dysphoria is a slight improvement over gender identity disorder, although they share many of the same problems—e.g., biased wording of the diagnosis seems to encourage gender-reparative therapies over transitioning, and renders happy and healthy post-transition trans people as "forever diagnosable" with gender dysphoria. Transvestic disorder is a greatly expanded version of transvestic fetishism, as it can now potentially be applied to transgender people of any gender or sexual orientation, as well as to those who have experienced it in the past but not the present.

14 Julia Serano, "The Case Against Autogynephilia," *International Journal of Transgenderism* 12, no. 3 (2010), 176-187; Julia Serano, "Reconceptualizing 'Autogynephilia' as Female/Feminine Embodiment Fantasies (FEFs)," May 26, 2015 (http://juliaserano.blogspot.com/2015/05/reconceptualizing-autogynephilia-as_26.html); Julia Serano, "Psychology, Sexualization and Trans-Invalidations" (keynote lecture presented at the 8th Annual Philadelphia Trans-Health Conference), June

12, 2009 (http://www.juliaserano.com/av/Serano-TransInvalidations.pdf). A brief list of recent research and reviews disproving autogynephilia theory, and examples of how the theory has been misused to undermine trans women, can be found in Julia Serano, "The real 'autogynephilia deniers'," July 13, 2015 (http://juliaserano.blogspot.com/2015/07/the-real-autogynephilia-deniers.html).

15 Over the last couple years, there has been a growing chorus of activists calling for trans characters to only be portrayed by trans actors. I sympathize with this sentiment, not because I believe that cis actors are incapable of portraying trans people in a realistic and respectful manner (they sometimes do, despite the many who have failed), but rather because trans actors are (at this point in time) systematically denied any opportunities to play cis characters. Personally, I'd rather see the focus of this debate shift to championing trans actors being cast to play cis roles—this would provide trans actors with far more opportunities while simultaneously challenging societal cissexism (i.e., the notion that our genders are inherently inferior or inauthentic). Also, I'd like to see calls for increased trans representation throughout all levels in Hollywood and the media, rather than only raising the issue on those rare occasions where a film or TV show is casting an actor to play a trans character.

16 Julia Serano, "Rethinking Sexism: How Trans Women Challenge Feminism," *AlterNet*, August 4, 2008 (http://www.alternet.org/story/93826/rethinking_sexism%3A_how_trans_women_challenge_feminism).

17 Riki Wilchins and Taneika Taylor, *70 under 30: Masculinity and the War on America's Youth* (Washington, DC: Gender Public Advocacy Coalition, 2008); Grant et al., *Injustice at Every Turn;* National Coalition of Anti-Violence Programs, "Lesbian, Gay, Bisexual, Transgender, Queer, and HIV-Affected Hate Violence in 2013 (2014 Release Edition)" (http://equalitymi.org/files/2013-ncavp-hv.pdf).

18 Julia Serano, "Cissexism and Cis Privilege Revisited—Part 1: Who Exactly Does 'Cis' Refer To?" (http://juliaserano.blogspot.com/2014/10/cissexism-and-cis-privilege-revisited.html); Julia Serano, "Cissexism and Cis Privilege Revisited—Part 2: Reconciling Disparate Uses of the Cis/Trans Distinction" (http://juliaserano.blogspot.com/2014/10/cissexism-and-cis-privilege-revisited.html).

19 I introduce and explain the concept of the Activist Language Merry-Go-Round in Julia Serano, "A Personal History of the 'T-word' (and some more general reflections on language and activism)" (http://juliaserano.blogspot.com/2014/04/a-personal-history-of-t-word-and-some.html), and discuss the idea further in Julia Serano, "On the 'activist language merry-go-round,' Stephen Pinker's 'euphemism treadmill,' and 'political correctness' more generally" (http://juliaserano.blogspot.com/2014/06/

on-activist-language-merry-go-round.html) and Julia Serano, "Regarding Trans* and Transgenderism" (http://juliaserano.blogspot.com/2015/08/regarding-trans-and-transgenderism.html).

20 Most trans-related terms that I use in this book are defined in Chapter 1, "Coming to Terms with Transgenderism and Transsexuality"; see also Julia Serano, "There is No Perfect Word: a Transgender Glossary of Sorts" (http://www.juliaserano.com/terminology.html). In Serano, "A Personal History of the 'T-word'," I not only address the increasingly controversial word "tranny" (which only appears a handful of times in this book), but also discuss the ever (de)evolving nature of trans-related language (see the final section of that essay: "Words don't kill people, people kill words . . ."). Potential concerns about cis terminology are addressed in Serano, "Julia Serano's compendium on cisgender, cissexual, cissexism, cisgenderism, cis privilege, and the cis/trans distinction." Other relevant transgender terminology-themed essays include: Julia Serano, "*Whipping Girl* FAQ: on the words transsexual, transgender and queer" (http://juliaserano.blogspot.com/2011/08/whipping-girl-faq-on-words-transsexual.html); Julia Serano, "Bisexuality and Binaries Revisited" (http://juliaserano.blogspot.com/2012/11/bisexuality-and-binaries-revisited.html); Serano, "Regarding Trans* and Transgenderism." Finally, many disputes about specific terms hinge on whether people conceptualize and use the word in an essentialist manner, as an identity label, and/or as an umbrella term—I discuss these varying usages in Serano, *Excluded*, 11-14.

Trans Woman Manifesto

1 Viviane K. Namaste, *Invisible Lives: The Erasure of Transsexual and Transgendered People* (Chicago: University of Chicago Press, 2000), 145, 215–216; Viviane Namaste, *Sex Change, Social Change: Reflections on Identity, Institutions, and Imperialism* (Toronto: Women's Press, 2005), 92–93.

2 American Psychiatric Association, *Diagnostic and Statistical Manual of Mental Disorders, Fourth Edition, Text Revision (DSM-IV-TR)* (Washington, D.C.: American Psychiatric Association, 2000), 574–575.

3 Jacob Anderson-Minshall, "Michigan or Bust: Camp Trans Flourishes for Another Year," *San Francisco Bay Times*, August 3, 2006, and my open letter in response to that article (www.juliaserano.com/frustration.html). For more on how lesbian attitudes toward trans women tend to be far more negative than toward trans men, see Michelle Tea, "Transmissions from Camp Trans," *The Believer*, November 2003; Julia Serano, "On the Outside Looking In," *On the Outside Looking In: A Trans Woman's Perspective on Feminism and the Exclusion of Trans Women from Lesbian and Women-Only Spaces* (Oakland: Hot Tranny Action Press,

2005); Zachary I. Nataf, "Lesbians Talk Transgender," *The Transgender Reader*, Susan Stryker and Stephen Whittle, eds. (New York: Routledge, 2006), 439–448.

4 For an overview of feminist anti-trans-woman sentiment, see Pat Califia, *Sex Changes: The Politics of Transgenderism* (San Francisco: Cleis Press, 1997), 86–119; Joanne Meyerowitz, *How Sex Changed: A History of Transsexuality in the United States* (Cambridge: Harvard University Press, 2002), 258–262; Kay Brown, "20th Century Transgender History and Experience" (www.jenellerose.com/htmlpostings/20th_century_transgender.htm); and Deborah Rudacille, *The Riddle of Gender: Science, Activism, and Transgender Rights* (New York: Pantheon Books, 2005), 151–174. For pertinent examples of trans-misogynistic feminist writings, see Mary Daly, *Gyn/Ecology: The Metaethics of Radical Feminism* (Boston: Beacon Press, 1990), 67–72; Andrea Dworkin, *Woman Hating* (New York: E. P. Dutton, 1974), 185–187; Margrit Eichler, *The Double Standard: A Feminist Critique of Feminist Social Science* (London: Croom Helm, 1980), 72–90; Germaine Greer, *The Madwoman's Underclothes: Essays and Occasional Writings* (New York: Atlantic Monthly Press, 1987), 189–191; Germaine Greer, *The Whole Woman* (New York: Alfred A. Knopf, 1999), 70–80; Sheila Jeffreys, *Beauty and Misogyny: Harmful Cultural Practices in the West* (New York: Routledge, 2005), 46–66; Robin Morgan, *Going Too Far* (New York: Random House, 1977), 170–188; Janice G. Raymond, *The Transsexual Empire: The Making of the She-Male* (Boston: Beacon Press, 1979); Gloria Steinem, "If the Shoe Doesn't Fit, Change the Foot," *Ms.*, February 1977, 76–86.

1

Coming to Terms with Transgenderism and Transsexuality

1 Intersex Society of North America website: www.isna.org/faq/transgender.

2 The term "transgender" was initially popularized by Virginia Price to dissociate trans people such as herself, who lived full-time as a member of her identified sex without ever undergoing sex reassignment surgery, from transsexuals, whom she reportedly disdained; see Brown, "20th Century Transgender History and Experience," and Leslie Feinberg, *Transgender Warriors: Making History from Joan of Arc to Dennis Rodman* (Boston: Beacon Press, 1996), x. For more on transsexuals who find organizing under the term "transgender" problematic, see Namaste, *Sex Change, Social Change*, 12–33, 51–57, 86–126; Max Wolf Valerio, "'Now That You're a White Man': Changing Sex in a Postmodern World—Being,

Becoming, and Borders," *This Bridge We Call Home: Radical Visions for Transformation,* Gloria Anzaldúa and Analouise Keating, eds. (New York: Routledge, 2002), 239–254.

3 I was inspired to begin using the term "cissexual" after reading one of Emi Koyama's Interchange entries (www.eminism.org/interchange/2002/20020607-wmstl.html). Apparently, the related term "cisgender" was first coined in 1995 by a transsexual man named Carl Buijs.

2

Skirt Chasers: Why the Media Depicts the Trans Revolution in Lipstick and Heels

1 Steve Rogers, "Lawsuit Settled, 'Crying Game'–Like 'There's Something About Miriam' Premieres in UK," RealityTVWorld.com, February 23, 2004; Debi Enker, "Reality Reaches New Low," *The Age,* May 20, 2004; Emily Smith, "Miriam's Secret," *The Sun Online* (www.thesun.co.uk).

2 Nazila Fathi, "As Repression Eases, More Iranians Change Their Sex," *New York Times,* August 2, 2004.

3 Shawna Virago, in correspondence with author, April 12, 2004.

4 Nancy Nangeroni and Gordene O. MacKenzie, in conversation on *GenderTalk,* program 538, November 26, 2005 (www.gendertalk.com/real/500/gt538.shtml).

5 Meyerowitz, *How Sex Changed,* 9, 148, 276–277; Califia, *Sex Changes,* 61.

6 As quoted in Califia, *Sex Changes,* 239.

7 Ibid., 178. It should be noted that Pat Califia and Patrick Califia are the same person; he is a trans man, and I refer to him as Patrick Califia, the name he currently uses, throughout the text. In the notes section, I use whichever name appears on the book that I am citing.

8 Raymond, *The Transsexual Empire,* 79.

9 Ibid., 99.

10 Ibid., 100.

11 Ibid., 99.

12 Ibid., xix.

13 Lisa Vogel, "Michigan Womyn's Music Festival Sets the Record 'Straight,'" press release issued by Lisa Vogel, August 22, 2006.

14 Anderson-Minshall, "Michigan Or Bust"; Sarah Liss, "Politics of Pussy: Bitch and Animal on a Revolutionary Gender-Bender," *Now* (Toronto), July 25, 2002.

3

Before and After: Class and Body Transformations

1 American Society of Plastic Surgeons, "9.2 Million Cosmetic Plastic Surgery Procedures in 2004—Up 5% Growth Paces U.S. Economy Despite Reality TV Fad," press release, March 16, 2005; Nancy Hellmich, "Gastric Bypass Surgery Seeing Big Increase," *USA Today,* December 19, 2005.

2 Suzanne J. Kessler and Wendy McKenna, *Gender: An Ethnomethodological Approach* (Chicago: University of Chicago Press, 1978), 142–153.

4

Boygasms and Girlgasms: A Frank Discussion About Hormones and Gender Differences

1 For trans male accounts of hormones, see Patrick Califia, *Speaking Sex to Power: The Politics of Queer Sex* (San Francisco: Cleis Press, 2002), 393–401; Jamison Green, *Becoming a Visible Man* (Nashville: Vanderbilt University Press, 2004), 98–102, 151–152; Henry Rubin, *Self-Made Men: Identity and Embodiment Among Transsexual Men* (Nashville: Vanderbilt University Press, 2003), 152–163; and Max Wolf Valerio, *The Testosterone Files: My Hormonal and Social Transformation from Female to Male* (Emeryville, CA: Seal Press, 2006).

2 Summarized in Joan Roughgarden, *Evolution's Rainbow: Diversity, Gender, and Sexuality in Nature and People* (Berkeley: University of California Press, 2004), 220–221; see also sources cited in the previous note.

5

Blind Spots: On Subconscious Sex and Gender Entitlement

1 Carina Dennis, "The Most Important Sexual Organ," *Nature* 427, no. 6973 (2004), 390–392; Arthur P. Arnold, "Sex Chromosomes and Brain Gender," *Nature Reviews: Neuroscience* 5 (2004), 1–8; Anne Vitale, "Notes on Gender Role Transition: Rethinking the Gender Identity Disorder Terminology in the *Diagnostic and Statistical Manual of Mental Disorders IV,*" from a paper presented at the 2005 HBIGDA Conference, April 7, 2005 (a fully referenced version of the paper can be found at www.avitale.com/hbigdatalkplus2005.htm).

2 John Colapinto, *As Nature Made Him: The Boy Who Was Raised as a Girl* (New York: HarperCollins, 2000); William G. Reiner and John P. Gearhart, "Discordant Sexual Identity in Some Genetic Males with

Cloacal Exstrophy Assigned to Female Sex at Birth," *New England Journal of Medicine* 350, no. 4 (2004), 333–341.

3 Jiang-Ning Zhou, Michel A. Hofman, Louis J. G. Gooren, and Dick F. Swaab, "A Sex Difference in the Human Brain and Its Relation to Transsexuality," *Nature* 378 (1995), 68–70; Frank P. M. Kruijver, Jiang-Ning Zhou, Chris W. Pool, Michel A. Hofman, Louis J. G. Gooren, and Dick F. Swaab, "Male-to-Female Transsexuals Have Female Neuron Numbers in a Limbic Nucleus," *Journal of Clinical Endocrinology and Metabolism* 85, no. 5 (2005), 2034–2041.

6

Intrinsic Inclinations: Explaining Gender and Sexual Diversity

1 For simplicity's sake, in this chapter and throughout much of this book, I will refer to "gender expression" in singular form. Unfortunately, some may misinterpret this to mean that femininity and masculinity are singular, monolithic programs or entities—this is not my intention. I believe that gender expression is best thought of as a collection of heterogeneous traits, each having potentially different biological and/or sociological origins. For a more nuanced discussion on this subject, see chapter 19, "Putting the Feminine Back into Feminism."

2 Roughgarden, *Evolution's Rainbow,* 280–288.

3 Bruce Bagemihl, *Biological Exuberance: Animal Homosexuality and Natural Diversity* (New York, St. Martin's Press, 1999); Roughgarden, *Evolution's Rainbow.*

4 Richard A. Lippa, *Gender, Nature, and Nurture,* 2nd ed. (Mahwah, New Jersey: Lawrence Erlbaum Associates, Inc., 2005), 4–9.

5 Melanie Blackless, Anthony Charuvastra, Amanda Derryck, Anne Fausto-Sterling, Karl Lauzanne, and Ellen Lee, "How Sexually Dimorphic Are We? Review and Synthesis," *American Journal of Human Biology* 12 (2000), 151–166.

6 For an overview of these different groups, see Serena Nanda, *Gender Diversity: Crosscultural Variations* (Prospect Heights: Waveland Press, 2000), and references therein. Also, there are many examples of FTM spectrum transgender people in other cultures, although they tend to receive less attention than their MTF spectrum counterparts. While "berdache" is the term most often found in Western literature on the subject, contemporary Native Americans increasingly use "two-spirit" as an umbrella term to describe indigenous North American gender-variant identities.

7
Pathological Science: Debunking Sexological and Sociological Models of Transgenderism

1 Meyerowitz, *How Sex Changed,* 255–256. The HBIGDA has very recently changed its name to the World Professional Association for Transgender Health (www.wpath.org).

2 Harry Benjamin International Gender Dysphoria Association, *The HBIGDA Standards of Care,* 4th ed., 1990.

3 For discussions on the efficacy of modern sex reassignment procedures, see A. Michel, M. Ansseau, J. J. Legros, W. Pitchot, and C. Mormont, "The Transsexual: What About the Future?" *European Psychiatry* 17 (2002), 353–362; P. T. Cohen-Kettenis and L. J. G. Gooren, "Transsexualism: A Review of Etiology, Diagnosis, and Treatment," *Journal of Psychosomatic Research* 46, no. 4 (1999), 315–333; Meyerowitz, *How Sex Changed,* 124; and Arlene Istar Lev, *Transgender Emergence: Therapeutic Guidelines for Working with Gender-Variant People and Their Families* (Binghamton: Haworth Clinical Practice Press, 2004), 41.

4 Vern L. Bullough and Bonnie Bullough, *Cross Dressing: Sex and Gender* (Philadelphia: University of Pennsylvania Press, 1993); Califia, *Sex Changes*, 120–162; Gilbert Herdt, ed., *Third Sex, Third Gender: Beyond Sexual Dimorphism in Culture and History* (New York: Zone Books, 1994); Feinberg, *Transgender Warriors;* Lev, *Transgender Emergence,* 55–77; Nanda, *Gender Diversity*; Roughgarden, *Evolution's Rainbow,* 329–386. For an even more exhaustive collection of sources on this point, see note 1 (pages 185–186) in Dallas Denny, "Transgender Communities of the United States in the Late Twentieth Century," *Transgender Rights,* Paisley Currah, Richard M. Juang, Shannon Price Minter, eds. (Minneapolis: University of Minnesota Press, 2006), 171–191.

5 Harry Benjamin, introduction to *Transsexualism and Sex Reassignment,* Richard Green and John Money, eds. (Baltimore: Johns Hopkins Press, 1969), 1–10.

6 Ibid., 4; Harry Benjamin, *The Transsexual Phenomenon* (New York: Julian Press Publishers, 1966), currently accessible in electronic format at www.symposion.com/ijt/benjamin.

7 Benjamin, *The Transsexual Phenomenon;* Meyerowitz, *How Sex Changed*, 102.

8 Meyerowitz, *How Sex Changed,* 220; Richard Green, "Attitudes Toward Transsexualism and Sex-Reassignment Procedures," in Green and Money, *Transsexualism and Sex Reassignment,* 235–242.

9 Meyerowitz, *How Sex Changed,* 222–226; Green and Money, *Transsexualism and Sex Reassignment.*

10 Meyerowitz, *How Sex Changed,* 255–256; Green, *Becoming a Visible Man,* 194–196.

11 Meyerowitz, *How Sex Changed,* 142, 221–222. For other accounts of gender identity clinics and other gatekeepers (past and present) treating few patients and providing delayed and/or inadequate care, see Claudine Griggs, *S/he: Changing Sex and Changing Clothes* (Oxford: Berg, 1998), 31; Namaste, *Invisible Lives,* 190–234; Meyerowitz, *How Sex Changed,* 156–158; Gordene Olga MacKenzie, *Transgender Nation* (Bowling Green, OH: Bowling Green University Popular Press, 1994), 77; Maxine E. Petersen and Robert Dickey, "Surgical Sex Reassignment: A Comparative Survey of International Centers," *Archives of Sexual Behavior* 24, no. 2 (1995), 135–156.

12 Just, "Origins of the Real-Life Test," *Trans-Health.com* (www.trans-health.com); Namaste, *Invisible Lives,* 198–201, 216; Lev, *Transgender Emergence,* 45.

13 Meyerowitz, *How Sex Changed,* 225; Anne Bolin, *In Search of Eve: Transsexual Rites of Passage* (South Hadley, MA: Bergin and Harvey, 1988), 121; Frank Lewins, *Transsexualism in Society: A Sociology of Male-to-Female Transsexuals* (South Melbourne: Macmillan Education Australia, 1995), 103.

14 The *DSM (Diagnostic and Statistical Manual of Mental Disorders)* is published by the American Psychiatric Association and is the world's most widely used reference for diagnosing mental illnesses. The homosexuality diagnosis was removed from the *DSM* in 1973, to be replaced by "ego-dystonic homosexuality" in 1980. This latter diagnosis—which only applied to those who experienced persistent distress over their own homosexuality—was removed in 1986. During the late 1980s, it was still commonplace for gatekeepers to require trans people to be heterosexual and stereotypically feminine (or masculine)—in fact, Anne Bolin, whose book *In Search of Eve* was published in 1988, spends a great many pages debunking earlier gatekeepers' assumptions about transsexual orientations (see Bolin, *In Search of Eve,* 61–68, 106–120).

15 Jon K. Meyer and Donna J. Reter, "Sex Reassignment," *Archives of General Psychiatry* 36 (1979), 1010–1015; Michael Fleming, Carol Steinman, and Gene Bocknek, "Methodological Problems in Assessing Sex-Reassignment Surgery: A Reply to Meyer and Reter," *International Journal of Transgenderism* 2, no. 2 (1998), (www.symposion.com); Lev, *Transgender Emergence,* 42.

16 Norman Knorr, Sanford Wolf, and Eugene Meyer, "Psychiatric Evaluation of Male Transsexuals for Surgery," in *Transsexualism and Sex Reassignment,* 279; John Randell, "Preoperative and Postoperative

Status of Male and Female Transsexuals," *Transsexualism and Sex Reassignment,* 355–367; Meyerowitz, *How Sex Changed,* 164.

17 Knorr et al., "Psychiatric Evaluation," 274; Meyerowitz, *How Sex Changed,* 161–162.

18 Robert Veit Sherwin, "Legal Aspects of Male Transsexualism," in *Transsexualism and Sex Reassignment,* 417–430; Meyerowitz, *How Sex Changed,* 166.

19 Ira B. Pauly, "Adult Manifestations of Male Transsexualism," in *Transsexualism and Sex Reassignment,* 45; Meyerowitz, *How Sex Changed,* 197, 225.

20 Sherwin, "Legal Aspects of Male Transsexualism," 423.

21 Richard Green, "Psychiatric Management of Special Problems in Transsexualism," in *Transsexualism and Sex Reassignment,* 287.

22 Pauly, "Adult Manifestations of Male Transsexualism," 45–46.

23 Lev, *Transgender Emergence,* 9–11, 47; Katherine K. Wilson, "The Disparate Classification of Gender and Sexual Orientation in American Psychiatry," 1998 Annual Meeting of the American Psychiatric Association, Workshop IW57: Transgender Issues, Toronto, Ontario, Canada, June 1998 (http://gidreform.org/kwapa98.html).

24 Lev, *Transgender Emergence,* 38; Meyerowitz, *How Sex Changed,* 9.

25 Meyerowitz, *How Sex Changed,* 149; Lev, *Transgender Emergence,* 34, 143.

26 *DSM-IV-TR,* 566, 574–575; Katherine K. Wilson, "The Disparate Classification of Gender."

27 Katherine K. Wilson, GID Reform Advocates website (http://gidreform.org/tf3023.html).

28 Ibid (http://gidreform.org/gid3026.html).

29 Phyllis Burke, *Gender Shock: Exploding the Myths of Male and Female* (New York: Anchor Books, 1996), 3–136.

30 Ibid., 32–33, 60–65. Along with Richard Green, *The "Sissy Boy Syndrome" and the Development of Homosexuality* (New Haven: Yale University Press, 1987), another classic example of effemimaniacal research is Robert Stoller, *Presentations of Gender* (New Haven: Yale University Press, 1985). For other references regarding feminine boys receiving the lion's share of psychological/psychiatric interest and attention, see MacKenzie, *Transgender Nation,* 22–23, 90–93; Stephen J. Ducat, *The Wimp Factor: Gender Gaps, Holy Wars, and the Politics of Anxious Masculinity* (Boston: Beacon Press, 2004), 25–29; and Lev, *Transgender Emergence,* 176.

31 Stoller, *Presentations of Gender,* 28–33; Lev, *Transgender Emergence,* 120–124.

32 MacKenzie, *Transgender Nation,* 92; Benjamin, *The Transsexual Phenomenon;* Richard Green and E. B. Keverne, "The Disparate Maternal Aunt-Uncle Ratio in Male Transsexuals: An Explanation Invoking Genomic Imprinting," *Journal of Theoretical Biology* 202 (2000), 55–63; Sven Bocklandt, Steve Horvath, Eric Vilain, and Dean H. Hamer, "Extreme Skewing of X Chromosome Inactivation in Mothers of Homosexual Men," *Human Genetics* 118, no. 6 (2006), 691–694.

33 Ethel S. Person and Lionel Ovesey, "The Transsexual Syndrome in Males: Primary Transsexualism," and "The Transsexual Syndrome in Males: Secondary Transsexualism," in Ethel S. Person, *The Sexual Century* (New Haven: Yale University Press, 1999), 110–145.

34 J. Michael Bailey, *The Man Who Would Be Queen: The Science of Gender-Bending and Transsexualism* (Washington, D.C.: Joseph Henry Press, 2003).

35 *DSM-IV-TR,* 578.

36 "The Ups and Downs of J. Michael Bailey," *Transgender Tapestry,* no. 104, Winter 2004, 53 (www.ifge.org).

37 Burke, *Gender Shock,* 53.

38 Eve Kosofsky Sedgwick, "How to Bring Your Kids Up Gay: The War on Effeminate Boys," *The Columbia Reader on Lesbians & Gay Men in Media, Society, and Politics,* Larry Gross and James D. Woods, eds. (New York: Columbia University Press, 1999), 201–206.

39 Lev, *Transgender Emergence,* 142.

40 Robert J. Stoller, *Sex and Gender* (New York: Science House, 1968), 195–205; MacKenzie, *Transgender Nation,* 52–53, 87–89; Lev, *Transgender Emergence,* 141–143.

41 Kessler and McKenna, *Gender: An Ethnomethodological Approach,* 118. Some have also claimed that Harry Benjamin only worked with trans women who he thought were attractive (Rudacille, *The Riddle of Gender,* 88).

42 Randell, "Preoperative and Postoperative Status," 378.

43 Bailey, *The Man Who Would Be Queen,* 180. Other recent evidence of trans women being sexualized by male gatekeepers can be found in Namaste, *Invisible Lives,* 202–205.

44 Bolin, *In Search of Eve,* 107.

45 Ibid., 108.

46 Namaste, *Invisible Lives,* 163–164.

47 John Money and Clay Primrose, "Sexual Dimorphism and Dissociation in the Psychology of Male Transsexuals," in *Transsexualism and Sex Reassignment,* 115–131; John Money and John G. Brennan, "Sexual Dimorphism in the Psychology of Female Transsexuals," in *Transsexualism and Sex Reassignment,* 137–152.

48 Bolin, *In Search of Eve,* 63, 106–120.

49 http://en.wikipedia.org/wiki/Pathological_science.

50 Dwight B. Billings and Thomas Urban, "The Socio-Medical Construction of Transsexualism: An Interpretation and Critique," *Social Problems* 29, no. 3 (1982), 266–282.

51 Ibid., 276.

52 Raymond, *The Transsexual Empire,* xvi, 2.

53 Ibid., 180, 183.

54 Ibid., xiii–xiv; Billings and Urban, "The Socio-Medical Construction," 266; evidence to the contrary can be found in Currah, Juang, and Minter, *Transgender Rights.*

55 Knorr et al., "Psychiatric Evaluation," 273–274, 279; Meyerowitz, *How Sex Changed,* 131–132, 164.

56 Reviewed in Bullough and Bullough, *Crossdressing;* Califia, *Sex Changes,* 120–162; Herdt, *Third Sex, Third Gender;* Feinberg, *Transgender Warriors;* Lev, *Transgender Emergence,* 55–77; Nanda, *Gender Diversity;* and Roughgarden, *Evolution's Rainbow,* 329–386. For more sources on this point, see note 1 (pages 185–186) in Denny, "Transgender Communities of the United States," *Transgender Rights.*

57 Harry Benjamin, introduction to *Transsexualism and Sex Reassignment,* 1–2; Rudacille, *The Riddle of Gender,* 74–78; Harold Garfinkel, *Studies in Ethnomethodology* (Englewood Cliffs, New Jersey: Prentice-Hall, 1967), 285–288. For other examples of transsexuality, sex reassignment, and trans people petitioning doctors to help them change their sex prior to the widespread public awareness of sex reassignment (i.e., pre-Jorgensen), see F. Abraham, "Genital Reassignment on Two Male Transvestites," *International Journal of Transgenderism* 2, no. 1 (1998) (www.symposion.com/ijt/ijtc0302.htm); Benjamin, *The Transsexual Phenomenon;* Meyerowitz, *How Sex Changed,* 14–50. Joanne Meyerowitz, "Sex Research at the Borders of Gender: Transvestites, Transsexuals, and Alfred C. Kinsey," *Bulletin of the History of Medicine* 75, no. 1 (2001), 72–90; Vern L. Bullough, "Transsexualism in History," *Archives of Sexual Behavior* 4, no. 5 (1975), 561–571; Jay Prosser, *Second Skins: The Body Narratives of Transsexuality* (New York: Columbia University Press, 1998), 135–169; and Rudacille, *The Riddle of Gender,* 44–48, 52–56.

58 Bernice L. Hausman, *Changing Sex: Transsexualism, Technology, and the Idea of Gender* (Durham: Duke University Press, 1995), 2–3, 195.

59 Ibid., 3.

60 Ibid.

61 Nanda, *Gender Diversity,* 96.

62 Ibid., 96–97.

63 Ibid., 97–98.

64 Ibid., 94.

65 Will Roscoe, *Changing Ones: Third and Fourth Genders in Native North America* (New York: St. Martin's Press, 1998), 129.

66 Ibid.

67 Will Roscoe, "How to Become a Berdache: Toward a Unified Analysis of Gender Diversity," in Herdt, *Third Sex, Third Gender,* 360–362.

68 Ibid., 362, 365.

69 For examples, see Roughgarden, *Evolution's Rainbow,* 343–346; and Califia, *Sex Changes,* 147–149.

70 Lewins, *Transsexualism in Society,* 144.

71 David E. Grimm, "Toward a Theory of Gender: Transsexualism, Gender, Sexuality, and Relationships," *American Behavioral Scientist* 31, no. 1 (1987), 70.

72 Eichler, *The Double Standard,* 75.

73 Greer, *The Whole Woman,* 71.

74 Judith Shapiro, "Transsexualism: Reflections on the Persistence of Gender and the Mutability of Sex," in *Body Guards: The Cultural Politics of Gender Ambiguity,* Julia Epstein and Kristina Straub, eds. (New York: Routledge, 1991), 253.

75 Thomas Kando, "Males, Females, and Transsexuals: A Comparative Study of Sexual Conservatism," *Journal of Homosexuality* 1, no. 1 (1974), 63–44.

76 Bolin, *In Search of Eve,* 107; Namaste, *Invisible Lives,* 191–234.

77 Bolin, *In Search of Eve,* 41.

78 Ibid., 118.

79 For a general review of how transsexuals are rarely accepted socially and legally in the United States, see Currah, Juang, and Minter, *Transgender Rights*—this book also contains Kylar W. Broadus's account of how much worse he was treated by coworkers as a trans man than when he was perceived as a butch dyke (page 94)

80 Mildred L. Brown and Chloe Ann Rounsley, *True Selves: Understanding Transsexualism—For Families, Friends, Coworkers, and Helping Professionals* (San Francisco: Jossey-Bass Publishers, 1996), 105–107.

81 For example, see Tom Waddell Health Center, "Protocols for Hormonal Reassignment of Gender," July 24, 2001 (downloadable at www.dph.sf.ca.us/chn/HlthCtrs/transgender.htm).

82 Lev, *Transgender Emergence.*

83 Ibid., 180–181; Rudacille, *The Riddle of Gender,* 18.

8

Dismantling Cissexual Privilege

1 Greer, *The Whole Woman,* 74.

2 Califia, *Sex Changes,* 116.

3 During the 1996 Olympics in Atlanta, eight of 3,387 female athletes screened for Y chromosomal material tested positive; the Olympics has since discontinued its genetic sex testing (Myron Genel, "Gender Verification No More?" *Medscape Women's Health* 5, no. 3 [2000], www.medscape.com/viewarticle/408918). Infertility clinics have found that up to 11 percent of azoospermic males (i.e., males who have no sperm in their semen) have a XXY karyotype (Hiroshi Okada, Hitoshi Fujioka, Noboru Tatsumi, Masanori Kanzaki, Yoshihiro Okuda, Masato Fujisawa, Minoru Hazama, Osamu Matsumoto, Kazuo Gohji, Soichi Arakawa, and Sadao Kamidono, "Klinefelter's Syndrome in the Male Infertility Clinic," *Human Reproduction* 14, no. 4 [1999], 946–952).

4 Tarynn M. Witten, Esben Esther Pirelli Benestad, Ilana Berger, R. J. M. Ekins, Randi Ettner, Katsuki Harima, Dave King, Mikael Landén, Nuno Nodin, Volodymyr P'yatokha, and Andrew N. Sharpe, "Transgender and Transsexuality," *The Encyclopedia of Sex and Gender: Men and Women in the World's Cultures,* C. R. Ember and M. Ember, eds. (New York: Kluwer/Plenum, 2003), 216–229; Lynn Conway, "How Frequently Does Transsexualism Occur?" LynnConway.com (2001–2002; http://ai.eecs.umich.edu/people/conway/TS/TSprevalence.html).

5 The notion of "doing" gender is often attributed to Candace West and Don H. Zimmerman's article, "Doing Gender," *Gender and Society* 1, no. 2 (1987), 125–151, and can also be found in Kessler and McKenna, *Gender: An Ethnomethodological Approach,* 155–159. The idea that gender is "performed" is typically attributed to Judith Butler, although she has refuted this interpretation of her work; this is explained in full in chapter 19, "Putting the Feminine Back into Feminism."

9

Ungendering in Art and Academia

1 Kate Bornstein, quoted in Mattilda, a.k.a. Matt Bernstein Sycamore, "Suicide Notes: Gender Outlaw Kate Bornstein's *Hello Cruel World* Offers Alternatives to Offing Yourself," *San Francisco Bay Guardian,* May 30, 2006.

2 Thea Hillman, "*Middlesex* and the Limitations of Myth," *ISNA News,* Spring 2003 (www.mindfully.org/Reform/2003/Middlesex-Limitations-MythMar03.htm).

3 Interview with Jane Anderson on HBO.com (www.hbo.com/films/normal/interviews/jane_anderson.html).

4 Ibid.

5 Ibid.

6 Ibid.

7 Interview with Tom Wilkinson on HBO.com (www.hbo.com/films/normal/interviews/tom_wilkinson.html).

8 Dave Weich, "Jeffrey Eugenides Has It Both Ways," book review on Powells.com, www.powells.com/authors/eugenides.html. For an intersex perspective on the word "hermaphrodite," see www.isna.org/faq/hermaphrodite.

9 From an interview with Jeffrey Eugenides in *3:AM Magazine* (www.3ammagazine.com/litarchives/2003/sep/interview_jeffrey_eugenides.html).

10 Ibid.

11 Jeffrey Eugenides, *Middlesex* (New York: Farrar, Straus and Giroux, 2002), 401–496.

12 Diane DiMassa, *The Complete Hothead Paisan: Homicidal Lesbian Terrorist* (San Francisco: Cleis Press, 1999), 312.

13 Ibid., 380.

14 Keely Savoie, "Lady Die," *Bitch,* no. 25 (2004), 35–41.

15 Ibid., 39.

16 Garfinkel, *Studies in Ethnomethodology,* 185.

17 Ibid., 285–288.

18 Ibid., 119.

19 *Herculine Barbin,* Michel Foucault, ed. (New York: Pantheon Books, 1980), xii.

20 Ibid., xi.

21 Ibid., 119–151, 155–199.

22 Kessler and McKenna, *Gender: An Ethnomethodological Approach,* 112–141.

23 Hausman, *Changing Sex,* vii.

24 Ibid.

25 Namaste, *Invisible Lives,* 52, 9–70.

26 Ibid., 16.

27 Prosser, *Second Skins.*

12
Bending Over Backwards: Traditional Sexism and Trans-Woman-Exclusion Policies

1 Califia, *Sex Changes,* 115.

2 For an overview of feminist anti-trans woman sentiment, see Califia, *Sex Changes,* 86–119; Meyerowitz, *How Sex Changed,* 258–262; Brown, "20th Century Transgender History and Experience"; and Rudacille, *The Riddle of Gender,* 151–174. For pertinent examples of transmisogynistic feminist writings, see Daly, *Gyn/Ecology,* 67–72; Dworkin, *Woman Hating,* 185–187; Eichler, *The Double Standard,* 72–90; Greer, *The Madwoman's Underclothes,* 189–191; Greer, *The Whole Woman,* 70–80; Jeffreys, *Beauty and Misogyny,* 46–66; Morgan, *Going Too Far,* 170–188; Raymond, *The Transsexual Empire;* and Steinem, "If the Shoe Doesn't Fit, Change the Foot." According to Dallas Denny ("Transgender in the United States: A Brief Discussion," *SIECUS Report,* Oct/Nov 1999), in 1980 Janice Raymond prepared a paper for the National Center for Health Care Technology titled "The Social and Ethical Aspects of Transsexual Surgery." Pertinent information about Sandy Stone and Beth Elliott can be found in the above references. For more on Nancy Burkholder and the Michigan Womyn's Music Festival's trans-woman-exclusion policy, see Tea, "Transmissions from Camp Trans," and Emi Koyama, *A Handbook on Michigan Womyn's Music Festival for Trans Activists and Allies* (Portland: Confluere Publications, 2002; www.confluere.com/store/pdf-zn/mich-handbook.pdf).

3 For more information on Michigan's policy basing festival entry on whether one was "born and raised a girl," see Vogel, "Michigan Womyn's Music Festival Sets the Record 'Straight.'" Musicians Lynnee Breedlove and Animal have both performed at Michigan on multiple occasions despite identifying as trans and answering to male pronouns (Anderson-Minshall, "Michigan or Bust"; Sarah Liss, "Politics of Pussy"). For more on the lesbian community's privileging of trans men over trans women, see Serano, "On the Outside Looking In"; Tea, "Transmissions from Camp Trans," and Nataf, "Lesbians Talk Transgender."

4 Kessler and McKenna, *Gender: An Ethnomethodological Approach,* 145–155.

5 Ibid., 153.

6 Ilene Lelchuk, "When Is It OK for Boys to Be Girls, and Girls to Be Boys?" *San Francisco Chronicle,* August 27, 2006; Zak Szymanski, "TG Specialists, Parents Ask: When Is Young Too Young?" *Bay Area Reporter,* March 16, 2006.

7 Tali Woodward, "Transjobless," *San Francisco Bay Guardian,* March 15, 2006.

8 During the late 1960s and early 1970s, lesbians were excluded from liberal feminist organizations such as NOW, and it was not uncommon for heterosexual feminists to characterize lesbian-feminists as hypersexual, oppressively male, out to exploit other women, and reinforcing the sex class system—see Alice Echols, *Daring to Be Bad: Radical Feminism in America, 1967–1975* (Minneapolis: University of Minnesota Press, 1989), 210–228.

9 Examples include Charlotte Croson, "Sex, Lies and Feminism," *Off Our Backs,* June 2001; "A Fest in Distress" (a roundtable on the politics of the Michigan Womyn's Music Festival's entrance policy with Robin Finkelstein, Emi Koyama, and Grover Wehman, moderated by Lisa Miya-Jervis), *Bitch,* Summer 2002, no. 17; Bitch & Animal, "Michigan Womyn's Music Festival," *Velvetpark Magazine,* no. 6; and "Generations of Gender" (a conversation between Boo Price and Lynn Breedlove), *Girlfriends,* August 2004.

10 According to TransgenderLaw.org, as of January 2007, nine states and eighty-six cities and counties in the United States have extended their nondiscrimination laws to explicitly include transgender people (www.transgenderlaw.org/ndlaws/index.htm#jurisdictions).

13
Self-Deception

1 National Transgender Advocacy Coalition, "Araujo Murder Trial Scheduled to Begin April 5," press release, March 2004 (http://portland.indymedia.org/en/2004/03/284303.shtml); Kelly St. John, "Defense in Araujo Trial Gives Final Argument: Slaying Wasn't Premeditated, Lawyers Say, Fighting for Manslaughter Verdict for Clients," *San Francisco Chronicle,* June 3, 2004; Michelle Locke, "Prosecution Star Witness Testifies in Transgender Killing Case," Associated Press, June 7, 2005. In a retrial, two of Gwen's killers were charged with second-degree murder, and the other two took plea bargains to voluntary manslaughter (www.transgenderlawcenter.org/gwen/index.html#update).

2 Raymond, *The Transsexual Empire,* 104.

3 Roughgarden, *Evolution's Rainbow,* 93–99.

4 Jay Leno questioned Hugh Grant after Grant had allegedly solicited a prostitute who was rumored to be transgender; reported in Nadine Brozan, "Chronicle," *New York Times,* July 11, 1995.

5 Patrick Califia, "Sex with an Imperfect Stranger," *Good Vibes Magazine,* December 9, 2002 (www.passionpress.com).

14

Trans-Sexualization

1 Lori B. Girshick, *Woman-to-Woman Sexual Violence: Does She Call It Rape?* (Boston: Northeastern University Press, 2002); Lorraine Gamman and Merja Makinen, *Female Fetishism* (New York: New York University Press, 1995); Ruth Papazian, "Women and Boys—Sexual Assault or Initiation? The Law Says Rape, but Americans Are Ambivalent," *APBNews.com*, March 30, 2000 (http://members.iquest.net/~dkoons/news.html).

2 Michael Musto, "La Dolce Musto," *Village Voice,* February 13, 2006 (www.villagevoice.com/nyclife/0607,musto,72165,15.html).

3 Based on movies that I have personally seen, combined with those that I found during a brief Internet search for movies that supposedly depict trans women as prostitutes or strippers, I have compiled the following list of films that reportedly include MTF spectrum sex workers: *40 Year Old Virgin, All About My Mother, American Heart, Angel, Anger Management, Boys from Brazil, Breath of Life (Sopla de Vida), Bridget Jones: Edge of Reason, Change My Life (Change Moi Ma Vie), Cop Target, Cruising, Dude Where's My Car?, Fleshpot on 42nd Street, Gangs of New York, Got Papers, Heaven, Hollywood Chainsaw Hookers, Hollywood Homicide, Love in Concrete (Amor en Concreto), Mercy, Never Again, Night on Earth, The Night Stalker, The Pharmacist (Le Pharmacien de Garde), Place Without Limits, Q & A, Risky Business, Saint Jack, Surrender, The Way You Want Me (Come Mi Vuoi), Wild Side, Yup Yup Man.* Not only is this list not comprehensive, but it does not include any of the TV dramas or daytime talk shows that depict trans female sex workers.

4 Woodward, "Transjobless."

5 Gamman and Makinen, *Female Fetishism,* 51–84.

6 For examples, see Ray Blanchard, "The Classification and Labeling of Nonhomosexual Gender Dysphorias," *Archives of Sexual Behavior* 18, no. 4 (1989), 315–334; and Stoller, *Presentations of Gender.* This tendency is also reviewed in Lev, *Transgender Emergence,* 133–143.

7 *DSM-IV-TR,* 574–575; Wilson, "The Disparate Classification of Gender."

8 Lev, *Transgender Emergence,* 133–139; Helen Boyd, *My Husband Betty: Love, Sex, and Life with a Crossdresser* (New York: Thunder's Mouth Press, 2003), 115–148.

9 Ray Blanchard, "The Concept of Autogynephilia and the Typology of Male Gender Dysphoria," *Journal of Nervous and Mental Disease* 177, no. 10 (1989), 616–623; Blanchard, "The Classification and Labeling of Nonhomosexual Gender Dysphorias."

10 Bailey, *The Man Who Would Be Queen; DSM-IV-TR,* 578. For scientific and psychological critiques of autogynephilia, see Joan Roughgarden, "The Bailey Affair: Psychology Perverted," February 11, 2004 (http://ai.eecs.umich.edu/people/conway/TS/Reviews/Psychology/); Katherine K. Wilson, "Autogynephilia: New Medical Thinking or Old Stereotype?" *Transgender Forum Magazine,* April 16, 2000; Madeline H. Wyndzen, "Everything You Never Wanted to Know About Autogynephilia (But Were Afraid You Had to Ask)," *Psychology of Gender Identity and Transgenderism,* www.genderpsychology.org/autogynephilia (2004).

11 Blanchard, "The Concept of Autogynephilia," 617.

12 Bailey, *The Man Who Would Be Queen,* 146.

13 Blanchard, "The Concept of Autogynephilia," 616.

14 Ibid., 621–622.

15 Ibid., 616–617.

16 Bolin, *In Search of Eve,* 75–76; Lev, *Transgender Emergence,* 133–139; Boyd, *My Husband Betty,* 132–140.

17 Blanchard, "The Concept of Autogynephilia"; Ray Blanchard, "Varieties of Autogynephilia and Their Relationship to Gender Dysphoria," *Archives of Sexual Behavior* 22, no. 3 (1993), 241–251. For more on this, see Wyndzen, "Everything You Never Wanted to Know," and Anne A. Lawrence, "Sexuality and Transsexuality: A New Introduction to Autogynephilia," *Transsexual Women's Resources,* www.annelawrence.com/newintroagp.html.

15
Submissive Streak

1 In role-playing, "safe words" are previously agreed-upon words that may be uttered by any player if they wish to halt the "scene" for any reason. Safe words are particularly important in scenarios where one party "dominates" or "tops" another, as they provide a means for the bottom to say "no" if they feel uncomfortable with what is happening, thus ensuring that all play is consensual.

17
Crossdressing: Demystifying Femininity and Rethinking "Male Privilege"

1 Emily Kane, "'No Way My Boys Are Going to Be Like That!' Parents' Responses to Children's Gender Nonconformity," *Gender and Society* 20, no. 2 (2006), 149–176.

2 Ducat, *The Wimp Factor,* 24–59. See also Burke, *Gender Shock,* 60–65, 123–125.

3 Ducat, *The Wimp Factor,* 26–27.

4 http://en.wikipedia.org/wiki/Marginalization.

5 bell hooks, preface to *Feminist Theory: From Margin to Center* (Boston: South End Press, 1984).

6 Ducat, *The Wimp Factor,* 24–59.

7 Ibid., 30–31; "Gender Constancy," *Enotes.com Encyclopedia of Children's Health* (http://health.enotes.com/childrens-health-encyclopedia/gender-constancy); Lev, *Transgender Emergence,* 124.

8 For other interesting trans perspectives on "male privilege," see Valerio, "'Now That You're a White Man,'" and Diana Courvant, "Speaking of Privilege," *This Bridge We Call Home,* 239–254 and, 458–463 respectively.

9 Green, *Becoming a Visible Man,* 35–37; Rubin, *Self-Made Men,* 165–168; Valerio, "'Now That You're a White Man,'"; Valerio, *The Testosterone Files.*

10 Norah Vincent, *Self-Made Man: One Woman's Journey into Manhood and Back Again* (New York: Viking, 2006).

19

Putting the Feminine Back into Feminism

1 Reviewed in Joanne Hollows, *Feminism, Femininity and Popular Culture* (Manchester: Manchester University Press, 2000), 1–18; Linda M. Scott, *Fresh Lipstick: Redressing Fashion and Feminism* (New York: Palgrave Macmillan, 2005), 1–22.

2 Majorie Garber, *Vested Interests: Cross-Dressing and Cultural Anxiety* (New York: HarperPerenial, 1993), 1.

3 Betty Friedan, *The Feminine Mystique: Twentieth Anniversary Edition* (New York: W. W. Norton and Company, 1983). Pertinent critiques of *The Feminine Mystique* can be found in hooks, *Feminist Theory,* 1–15; Hollows, *Feminism, Femininity and Popular Culture,* 9–13; and Scott, *Fresh Lipstick,* 223–250.

4 The sex/gender distinction is generally attributed to Robert Stoller (*Sex and Gender*). For two varying feminist critiques of the sex/gender distinction, see Judith Butler, *Bodies That Matter: On the Discursive Limits of "Sex"* (New York: Routledge, 1993), and Moira Gatens, *Imaginary Bodies: Ethics, Power and Corporeality* (London: Routledge, 1996), 3–20.

5 Hollows, *Feminism, Femininity and Popular Culture,* 9–18.

6 Ibid., 15–17; Daly, *Gyn/Ecology,* 287. I use the term "cultural feminists" according to Echols, *Daring to Be Bad.*

7 For discussions on class, culture, and femininity, see Hollows, *Feminism, Femininity and Popular Culture,* and Scott, *Fresh Lipstick.*

8 Hollows, *Feminism, Femininity and Popular Culture,* 10; Radicalesbians, "The Woman Identified Woman," *Radical Feminism,* Anne Koedt, Ellen Levine, and Anita Rapone, eds. (New York: Quadrangle/New York Times Book Co., 1980), 245; N. Y. Radical Feminists, "Politics of the Ego: A Manifesto for N. Y. Radical Feminists," *Radical Feminism,* 382.

9 Radicalesbians, "The Woman Identified Woman," 244; Daly, *Gyn/Ecology,* 26–27; Betsy Belote, "Masochistic Syndrome, Hysterical Personality, and the Illusion of a Healthy Woman," *Female Psychology: The Emerging Self,* Sue Cox, ed. (New York: St. Martin's Press, 1981), 320–333; Dee L. R. Graham, with Edna I. Rawlings and Roberta K. Rigsby, *Loving to Survive: Sexual Terror, Men's Violence, and Women's Lives* (New York: New York University Press, 1994), xiv.

10 Scott, *Fresh Lipstick*, 5; Hollows, *Feminism, Femininity and Popular Culture,* 13; Vicki Coppock, Deena Haydon, and Ingrid Richter, *The Illusions of 'Post-Feminism': New Women, Old Myths* (London: Taylor and Francis, 1995), 24; Alice Embree, "Media Images I: Madison Avenue Brainwashing—The Facts," *Sisterhood Is Powerful: An Anthology of Writings from the Women's Liberation Movement,* Robin Morgan, ed. (New York: Random House, 1970), 191.

11 Daly, *Gyn/Ecology,* 67–72, 334–335.

12 Hollows, *Feminism, Femininity and Popular Culture,* 14; Greer, *The Madwoman's Underclothes,* 189–191; Greer, *The Whole Woman,* 70–80.

13 Jeffreys, *Beauty and Misogyny,* 24, 50–53.

14 Judith Butler, *Gender Trouble: Feminism and the Subversion of Identity* (New York: Routledge, 1999). The specific example of a person being "girled" is from Butler, *Bodies That Matter,* 7–8.

15 For an example of gender as "performance," see Judith Halberstam, "F2M: The Making of Female Masculinity," *The Lesbian Postmodern,* Laura Doan, ed. (New York: Columbia University Press, 1994), 210–228. The example of the drag queen was first put forward by Butler (*Gender Trouble,* 174–176), but she has on multiple occasions refuted the popular, literal interpretation of this passage to mean that gender *is* a performance (see *Gender Trouble,* xxii–xxiv; *Bodies that Matter,* 125–126; "Gender as Performance: An Interview with Judith Butler," *Radical Philosophy* 67, Summer 1994, 32–39; and Sara Salih, *Judith Butler* [London: Routledge, 2002], 62–71).

16 Reviewed in Prosser, *Second Skins,* 1–60.

17 Echols, *Daring to Be Bad,* 232.

18 For more on the way that feminine lesbians and gay men have historically been marginalized by their respective communities, see Joan Nestle, "The Femme Question," *The Persistent Desire: A Butch Femme Reader,* Joan Nestle, ed. (Boston: Alyson Publications, 1992), 138–146; Laura Harris and Elizabeth Crocker, eds., *Femme: Feminists, Lesbians, and Bad Girls* (New York: Routledge, 1997); Tim Bergling, *Sissyphobia: Gay Men and Effeminate Behavior* (Binghamton: Harrington Park Press, 2001).

19 Ducat, *The Wimp Factor.*

20 Virginia Valian, *Why So Slow? The Advancement of Women* (Cambridge: MIT Press, 1997).

21 Ibid., 111–112. See also earlier references in Burke, *Gender Shock;* Ducat, *The Wimp Factor;* and MacKenzie, *Transgender Nation.*

20

The Future of Queer/Trans Activism

1 I do not have any problems with describing a gender as "transgressive" per se—I recognize how the notion that transgender people "transgress gender norms" has tremendously aided activists in articulating the discrimination that many of us face due to oppositional sexism. Neither do I have any issues with any specific gender identity or expression *in and of itself.* Things become problematic, however, when we move beyond simply claiming that "transgressive" genders are just as legitimate as any other gender, and into the realm of arguing that "transgressive" genders are *better* than "non-transgressive" genders. In other words, it is the value judgements often placed on "transgressive" gender identities and expressions (rather than those specific identities and expressions) that I critique with this piece. I should also mention that, throughout this book, I have placed the word "transgressive" in quotes. My reason for doing so is similar to the argument I have made regarding the word "pass." By talking about whether trans people "pass" or "transgress gender norms," we place undue focus on what a trans person "does" while ignoring the gendering and judgments of others. I would argue that a trans person doesn't "transgress" gender norms per se, but rather a gender-entitled public judges them as being either "transgressive" or "nontransgressive."

2 Hand-wringing by cissexuals over whether transsexuals either "reinforce" or "challenge" gender norms has dominated academic discourses on transsexuality for over thirty years now. Examples include Butler, *Bodies That Matter,* 121–140; Greer, *The Whole Woman,* 71; Jeffreys, *Beauty and Misogyny,* 65–66; Kando, "Males, Females, and Transsexuals," Kessler and McKenna, *Gender: An Ethnomethodological Approach,* 112–141; Judith Lorber, *Paradoxes of Gender* (New Haven: Yale University Press, 1994), 18–22; Nanda, *Gender Diversity,* 94–98; Lewins, *Transsexualism in Society,* 153–160; and Raymond, *The Transsexual*

Empire. The issue is so pervasive that sociologist Henry Rubin has proposed "a ban on the question of whether transsexualism and transsexuals are unequivocally subversive or hegemonic," because he believes that this "sort of scholarship fetishizes transsexuals." (Rubin, *Self-Made Men,* 163–164) For transsexual critiques of this myopic and cissexist practice, see Carol Riddell, "Divided Sisterhood: A Critical Review of Janice Raymond's *The Transsexual Empire,*" in *The Transgender Studies Reader,* Susan Stryker and Stephen Whittle, eds. (New York: Routledge, 2006), 144–158; Namaste, *Invisible Lives,* 9–70; Namaste, *Sex Change, Social Change,* 6–11; Prosser, *Second Skins,* 1–60; and Valerio, "'Now That You're a White Man.'"

3 Serano, "On the Outside Looking In"; Tea, "Transmissions from Camp Trans."

4 Echols, *Daring to Be Bad.*

5 Ibid., 281.

6 Queer Nation and Transexual Menace were activist organizations that regularly staged public demonstrations during the early 1990s to protest injustices and to increase queer and trans visibility, respectively.

7 Currah, Juang, and Minter, *Transgender Rights,* 154; Harris and Crocker, *Femme,* 219–220; Namaste, *Invisible Lives,* 60–65; Namaste, *Sex Change, Social Change,* 51–57, 89–90; Valerio, "'Now That You're a White Man.'"

8 Namaste, *Sex Change, Social Change,* 17–26, 60–81.

Credits

Excerpts from *Sex Changes: The Politics of Transgenderism* by Patrick Califia reprinted by permission of Cleis Press.

Excerpts from Bram van Moorhem's interview with Jeffrey Eugenides appear courtesy of 3AM magazine, www.3ammagazine.com.

Excerpts from Ray Blanchard, "The Concept of Autogynephilia and the Typology of Male Gender Dysphoria," *The Journal of Nervous and Mental Disease* (1989) Vol. 177, No. 10, 616-623 appear courtesy of Lippincott Williams & Wilkins.

Excerpts from Viviane Namaste, *Invisible Lives: The Erasure of Transsexual and Transgendered People* appear courtesy of the University of Chicago Press.

Excerpts from Janice G. Raymond's *The Transsexual Empire: The Making of the She-Male* appear courtesy of the author.

Excerpts from Bernice Hausman's *Changing Sex: Transsexualism, Technology, and the Idea of Gender* appear courtesy of Duke University Press.

Excerpts from www.gidreform.org appear courtesy of Kelley Winters (formerly under pen-name Katherine Wilson).

Anne Bolin, *In Search of Eve: Exploding the Myths of Male and Female*. Copyright © 1988. Reproduced with permission of Greenwood Publishing Group, Inc., Westport, CT.

Acknowledgments

BEFORE I BEGIN THANKING all of the people who have helped me in this endeavor, I figured that—since this is the acknowledgments section, after all—I should acknowledge the privileges that have enabled me to write this particular book. There are a number of them, but the one privilege that I believe has most influenced this project is one of time and place. I had the invaluable experience of transitioning in the early 2000s in the San Francisco Bay Area, one of the trans-friendliest places on the planet. While I certainly wouldn't describe my transition as a "cakewalk," I was able to change my lived sex without losing my job, my housing, my wife, my family and friends, and so on. Nearly everybody in my life gave me the benefit of the doubt, the space to grow, the opportunity to change my physical sex without feeling like I had to revamp my entire personality or start from scratch in a brand-new life someplace else. While I thank my family, friends, and coworkers for the support and understanding they've given me, I also realize that my experience—my relatively nontraumatic transition, that is—is a relatively recent phenomenon, one that did not generally exist even a decade or two ago. My experience was only made possible due to the countless transsexuals who have gone before me, who took on the hard work of clearing the path that many of us now follow. It was also made possible through the work of many gender activists (transsexual, transgender, queer, and feminist) who have helped to create a little cultural wiggle room, gender-wise, for all of us over the years. While I spend a good deal of this book critiquing the views put forward by past feminists and transgender and queer activists, it's not because I don't appreciate the work these previous generations have carried out. It's simply that I believe that this new and very different time and place requires very different strategies of gender activism. Having said that, most of the ideas that I put forward in this book were developed on the foundation that these earlier writers and activists have built, and for that I am grateful.

A second privilege that I would like to acknowledge, as it has greatly shaped the ideas in this book, is what many in the trans community call "passing privilege." This privilege (one that most cissexual people take for granted) allows me to be accepted in my identified gender, to move through the world without constantly having to correct people's use of pronouns, deflect their unwanted stares, or have them harass me because of my gender difference. For me, this privilege mostly stems from my size—it is the flip side of the same coin that made my life as male so difficult to manage, as I grappled with gender difference both in regard to being trans and because I was inevitably the smallest guy in any room that I entered. While my small stature made me the target of other people's anxiety and ridicule, particularly during my school years, it turned out to be a blessing in disguise. Once I began taking female hormones, my small size allowed me to be gendered by others as female without having to alter my appearance or behaviors, which gave me unique insight into the processes of gendering and cissexual privilege that I describe in this book. Needless to say, if I did not "pass" on a regular basis, I probably would have written a much different book.

For better or for worse, I have found that the fact that people tend to experience me as female before they learn that I'm transsexual helps make it easier for me to defuse or debunk their misconceptions about transsexuality and gender. It forces them to consider (often for the first time in their lives) how their own expectations and assumptions greatly shape they way they perceive gender in other people. While I often exploit the fact that I "pass" in order to bring into question the way that people project gender stereotypes onto other people's behaviors and bodies, I am also aware that this can be a double-edged sword, one that could inadvertently lead to the perspectives of trans people who "pass" trumping or drowning out the views of those who do not. Similarly, the fact that other privileges that I experience (e.g., that I am white, middle-class, able-bodied, etc.) remain largely unmarked in this book could lead others to mistakenly assume that my rather specific perspective is somehow representative of the entire trans community. That would be a grave error. All trans people have different insights into gender, insights that arise out of the unique combination of privileges and life histories that we each bring to the table. Each of us has a somewhat different take on being trans, and all of our voices need to be heard before we can even begin to develop any kind of overarching understanding of what it means to be transsexual. Therefore, I hope that people who read this book will see it not as the "definitive statement" on transsexuality or trans womanhood, but rather as simply one piece of a much larger project that involves many other people.

I want to thank everyone in the San Francisco Bay Area spoken word and queer/trans performance communities, who offered me much love, support, and the opportunity to read and perform my work when I first began writing. I also want to thank everyone I met at Camp Trans when I attended in 2003 and upon becoming more involved in the organization in 2004. It was during those experiences that I first began to give some thought to the ways that trans women are viewed and treated very differently (both in straight and queer culture) from our FTM spectrum counterparts; that recognition was the germ that eventually grew into this project. I also want to thank *Bitch* magazine for publishing "Skirt Chasers: Why the Media Depicts the Trans Revolution in Lipstick and Heels"—the essay that in many ways became the starting point for this book—in their Fall 2004 issue (no. 26). Special thanks to Rachel Fudge, my editor on that piece, and to Lisa Jervis and Andi Zeisler, for later including the piece in their *BITCHfest* anthology.

Other pieces included in this collection have also previously appeared elsewhere. The essays "Bending Over Backwards" and "Trans Woman Manifesto" (originally entitled "Hot Tranny Action Manifesto") first appeared in my chapbook *On the Outside Looking In* (2005). "Barrette Manifesto" originally appeared in my chapbook *Either/Or* (2002) and in *Cubby Missalette 13: The Girly Mag* (2003). And "Deconstructive Surgery," "Self-Deception," and "Submissive Steak" all originally appeared in my chapbook *Draw Blood* (2004). Special thanks to the organizers of the 2004 UC Berkeley production of *The Vagina Monologues,* who offered me the opportunity to write and perform "Deconstructive Surgery" for that event. Other snippets and sentences in this book may have been lifted from previous pieces that I have written, most of which are contained within the three aforementioned self-published chapbooks, or on the following websites: www.juliaserano.com, www.hottrannyaction.org, and www.switchhitter.net.

While many of the perspectives and concepts put forward in this book have originated with me, others are simply my interpretations of ideas that have been kicking around in the trans community for a while, or that have been previously expressed by others. In particular, I would like to thank the following writers, artists, and activists who—through their work and/or in conversations we have shared—have influenced and inspired many of the thoughts and arguments in this book: Carolyn Connelly, Sadie Crabtree, Sean Dorsey, Thea Hillman, Rocco Kayiatos, Emi Koyama, Viviane Namaste, Jay Prosser, Lauren Steely, Michelle Tea, Max Wolf Valerio, and Shawna Virago. Extra-special thanks to my wife, Dani Eurynome, for being a vital sounding board for me, for providing invaluable insight and focus to my work, and for indulging my incessant need to talk about the book when it was a work in progress.

Finally, I'd like to thank my editor, Brooke Warner, and everybody else at Seal Press for giving me the opportunity to share my ideas with the rest of the world, and for being perhaps the only woman-focused publishing house with the courage to release a book that claims a place for trans women within the feminist movement, and that critiques many taken-for-granted feminist assumptions about trans women, femininity, and sexism. This book would not be possible without their hard work and the wonderful support they have provided me.

About the Author

JULIA SERANO is an Oakland, California–based writer, performer, activist, and biologist. She is the author of two other books, *Excluded: Making Feminist and Queer Movements More Inclusive* (which was a finalist for the 2013 Judy Grahn Award for Lesbian Nonfiction), and *Outspoken: A Decade of Transgender Activism and Trans Feminism*. Julia's other writings have appeared in over a dozen anthologies, in magazines and news outlets such as *The Guardian, The Advocate, The Daily Beast, Bitch, AlterNet, Out,* and *Ms.*, and have been used as teaching materials in queer and gender studies, sociology, psychology, and human sexuality courses across North America. As a scientist, Julia has a PhD in Biochemistry from Columbia University, and spent seventeen years as a researcher at the University of California, Berkeley, in the fields of genetics and evolutionary-developmental biology. *juliaserano.com.*